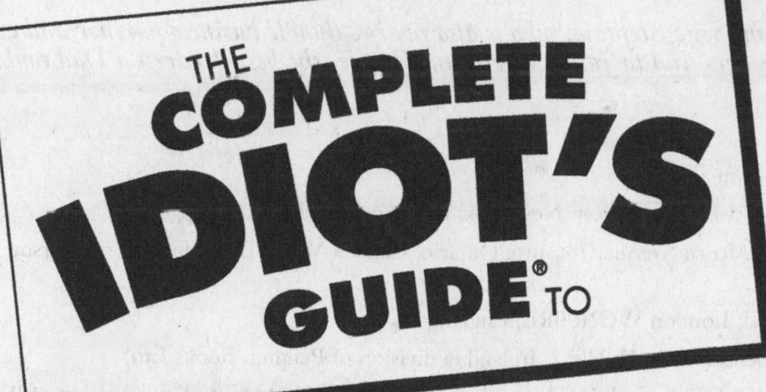

Starting and Running a Retail Store

by *James E. Dion*

A member of Penguin Group (USA) Inc.

This book is dedicated to my wife Stefania, who is also my invaluable business partner and every day gives me a new reason to love her. And to Julie, Marie, and Jamie, the best children a Dad could ever want.

ALPHA BOOKS

Published by the Penguin Group

Penguin Group (USA) Inc., 375 Hudson Street, New York, New York 10014, U.S.A.

Penguin Group (Canada), 10 Alcorn Avenue, Toronto, Ontario, Canada M4V 3B2 (a division of Pearson Penguin Canada Inc.)

Penguin Books Ltd, 80 Strand, London WC2R 0RL, England

Penguin Ireland, 25 St Stephen's Green, Dublin 2, Ireland (a division of Penguin Books Ltd)

Penguin Group (Australia), 250 Camberwell Road, Camberwell, Victoria 3124, Australia (a division of Pearson Australia Group Pty Ltd)

Penguin Books India Pvt Ltd, 11 Community Centre, Panchsheel Park, New Delhi—110 017, India

Penguin Group (NZ), cnr Airborne and Rosedale Roads, Albany, Auckland 1310, New Zealand (a division of Pearson New Zealand Ltd)

Penguin Books (South Africa) (Pty) Ltd, 24 Sturdee Avenue, Rosebank, Johannesburg 2196, South Africa

Penguin Books Ltd, Registered Offices: 80 Strand, London WC2R 0RL, England

International Standard Book Number: 978-1-59257-726-2
Library of Congress Catalog Card Number: 2007939743

12 13 14 20 19 18 17 16 15

Interpretation of the printing code: The rightmost number of the first series of numbers is the year of the book's printing; the rightmost number of the second series of numbers is the number of the book's printing. For example, a printing code of 08-1 shows that the first printing occurred in 2008.

Printed in the United States of America

Publisher: *Marie Butler-Knight*
Editorial Director: *Mike Sanders*
Senior Managing Editor: *Billy Fields*
Senior Acquisitions Editor: *Paul Dinas*
Development Editor: *Ginny Munroe*
Production Editor: *Kayla Dugger*
Copy Editor: *Jennifer Connolly*
Cartoonist: *Richard King*
Cover Designer: *Bill Thomas*
Book Designer: *Trina Wurst*
Indexer: *Heather McNeill*
Layout: *Ayanna Lacey*
Proofreader: *Aaron Black*

Contents at a Glance

Contents

Introduction

Retail in the United States is a trillion-dollar industry, and over 90 percent of all retail outlets are independent retailers. While a significant number of independent retailers don't make it beyond the first year, many of them do.

You'll find there's a lot of opportunity to go around, and you'll find those opportunities in just about any category of retail that you might consider. The key to success is developing a unique concept and going that extra mile to get and keep loyal customers.

In this book, I give you the basics for doing just that. Yes, it's a lot of hard work, but the rewards of owning and running your own retail business are tremendous.

How to Use This Book

You'll start your trip in the world of retail, taking a quick look back in time to how retail got started, where it is today, and where it is going. Then be ready for a whirlwind tour of the basics, from researching your customers and competition to running a store on a day-to-day basis.

We've organized the book into six parts:

Part 1, "When I Grow Up, I Want to Be a Retailer," looks at what retail used to be, where it is today, and where it's going in the future. You'll then explore what it takes to become a retail legend, focusing on the courage, talent, hard work, perseverance, and luck needed to be a successful retailer.

Part 2, "Sizing Up Your Options and Your Competition," helps you evaluate your idea, research your competition, and get to know the industry you plan to work in.

Part 3, "What You Can Imagine, You Can Achieve," helps you define your vision and develop the strategy for your store. Once you define that strategy, you'll find tools for developing a business plan and ideas for raising capital.

Part 4, "Running the Store, or Wearing Many Hats," starts with how to set up store operations, review the crucial things you need to know about location, and sort out how you buy the right merchandise at the right price. Once you have all that in place, you'll find information on managing your inventory, designing your store, and displaying your products.

Part 5, "Nuts and Bolts of Opening and Running the Store," focuses on how to market your store, find the right people to staff your store, and train and motivate those people to serve your customers and exceed their expectations every day. You'll also explore how to pick the right technology and make use of the Internet. Then you'll discover how to track your store's results. Finally, you'll review key negotiation styles and how to deal with each type of negotiator you may face, including vendors, the bank, the landlord, and your staff.

Part 6, "On the Right Track," takes you through the key measures you can use to track your performance during the first year and beyond. You'll learn techniques that will help you avoid losing your customers. Finally, you'll learn how to mine the data of the customers you have and use that information to personalize your service and stand out from the competition.

Extras

I've developed a few helpers you'll find in little boxes throughout the book:

Better Not!

These are warnings about things you need to avoid.

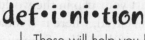

def•i•ni•tion

These will help you learn the language of retail.

Selling Points

These give you ideas for how to set up your retail store and how to find the resources you need.

Savvy Retailer

These help you explore additional information about key retail topics.

Acknowledgments

To all those incredible retailers I have worked for and with over the past 45 years, who taught me that this is the best industry in the world—thank you.

Trademarks

Part 1

When I Grow Up, I Want to Be a Retailer

Have you ever heard a child say: "When I grow up, I want to be a retailer"? Probably not! Yet, the world is full of retailers large and small who are very successful and love what they do. So how does someone decide to become a retailer? What does it take to make it in retail? What will it take you?

In this part, I introduce you to how retail evolved over the years and how it's expected to change in the future. You will also explore the qualities and traits of a good retailer and assess if you have them.

"I don't want to be a carrier pigeon at all. I want to sell bathing suits."

Chapter 1

So You Want to Be a Retailer

In This Chapter

- Learning from the past
- Exploring today's marketplace
- Reading retail's future

Deciding whether starting and running a retail store is what you really want to do requires that you learn what retailers do. You also need to know how today's retail has been shaped by the way it used to be and how it will change in the future.

Retailers must do a little bit of everything today. They need to wear many different hats—a business strategist, a store designer, a marketer, a merchandiser, a buyer, a financial wiz, a personnel officer, a coach, a trainer, and anything else that comes about when you run your own business.

It's impossible for you to know if retail is for you without knowing what it used to be, what it is today, and the prospects for retail in the future. In this chapter, we take a walk through time and then gaze into the future.

From the 1950s to Today

In the 1950s and 1960s, customers were almost like buses—if you missed one there was another coming along in a few minutes. You didn't worry about customer service because you knew that if a customer didn't like your service or product, someone else would walk into the store soon afterward who would be okay with it.

That's why many retailers got into the business in the 1950s, 1960s, and 1970s, because it was very easy. They believed the line from the movie *Field of Dreams*—"If you build it, [they] will come."

You could count on a 20 to 30 percent sales increase every year in the 1950s and 1960s. As a matter of fact, if you opened your store in the 1970s or the 1980s and weren't getting 20 to 25 percent sales increases every year, something was wrong.

Well, those days are over. Customers don't come that easily any more. Retailers have to earn their customers' business every day. And today, we are in the single digits of sales increases and retailers have to work very hard to get even that level of sales increase.

What's different? Competition and consumers' expectations that if they can't find what they want, how they want it, where and when they want it in your store, they have plenty of other options. There wasn't a lot of competition until about 1985, but times have changed a lot in the past 20 years. Today competition is everywhere. It's unrelenting and cannot be ignored even for a minute.

Today's Retail

Becoming a retailer today is a challenging and complex choice. Technology, for example, is changing the way we must do business. The Internet continues to have a tremendous and ever-changing impact on retail, including challenging retailers to always look for new and more exciting ways to sell their products in their stores and give a reason to customers to shop brick and mortar (in the store) instead of from the comfort of home (online). Also, shoppers have been trained over the years to look for discounts—the bigger the better. If 10 percent off used to be a big deal a few years ago, today, unless it's 50 percent off and sometimes even 70 percent off, shoppers don't even look.

Internet Shoppers

When the Internet first came on the scene, it was mainly used by young technologically savvy people. They were the ones buying from CD NOW, Amazon.com, and all of the other virtual retail stores.

Today, the fastest-growing segment on the Internet is senior citizens. The second fastest-growing segment is middle-aged Americans with average incomes in the six digit range. These new web customers are not buying only from virtual retailers. They are shopping at stores where they can purchase items in person, online, by telephone, or from a catalog. This new world of retail is called multichannel retail, and the winners are the retailers who give their customers the ability to shop 24 hours a day, 7 days a week—when it's most convenient for them.

As an independent retailer, today and even more so in the future, you too need to structure your business so that you can do business with your customers any way your customers want to do business with you. So if customers don't want to come into your store and want to call you, you had better be at the other end of that phone. If customers want to shop from a catalog, you had better be prepared to offer that as well as a website they can buy from at 2 A.M.

Selling Points

Fewer and fewer Americans are going to shopping malls. According to the International Council of Shopping Centers (ICSC), in 1980, the average American family went to the mall 3.1 times in a month; by the year 2000, these visits had dropped down to 1.6. In 1980, they spent about ten hours in a mall per month. By the year 2000 that had dropped to three-and-a-half hours. That is very frightening news for most retailers—especially if they chose to open their store in a mall!

Discount Shoppers

Eighty-four percent of households with incomes over $70,000 shop at discount stores regularly. What does this tell us? Even high-income shoppers are looking for bargains. That high-income shopper is no longer blindly loyal to high-end specialty stores.

Savvy Retailer

We're also seeing a tremendous consolidation of retail companies. In 1986, the top three department stores had a 39 percent share of the entire department store market. By the year 2005, they had almost 80 percent. So the big are getting bigger. It's even more dramatic in discount stores—the top three went from 61 percent to over 88 percent in recent years.

Wal-Mart, over the years, has become the absolute juggernaut of the world. It's not just the world's largest retailer—it's the world's largest company—bigger than ExxonMobil, General Motors, and General Electric. Wal-Mart sold $344.9 billion worth of goods in 2006. In its category of general merchandise and groceries, Wal-Mart no longer has any real rivals. It does more business than Target, Sears, Kmart, JCPenney, Safeway, and Kroger combined. Wal-Mart wields its power for just one purpose—to bring the lowest possible prices to its customers—and the customers love it.

Having a low-price strategy and trying to compete with the Wal-Marts of the world would be foolish for an independent retailer. Where you can win is with customer service and everything you do in store design, product selection, product presentation, staff training, etc., that make you stand out from the low price-only marketers. Even price-conscious customers reach a point when service trumps price, and you need to be there to fill that gap for them. In this book, you learn how you can build better relationships with your customers, how you can create a store environment that will excite them, and how you can deliver to them a shopping experience that no other store will ever be able to match. So you can join the ranks of the truly great retailers.

What's in the Future for Small Retailers?

Small retailers will clearly have to change the way they do business to thrive in the future. They have to go back to the good old days of being local merchants, who knew their customers personally and knew what their customers needed. But they also need to keep up with the technology of the future and master the basics of multichannel marketing.

They will have to become much more customer centric, more environmentally sensitive, and better at serving their target customers be they women, minorities, seniors, teens, or whatever group retailers choose to focus on. And that focus will be the key to their success. In the past, it was said that great retailers are students of their customers, and this is truer today than ever before.

Customers have ever-increasing expectations about service, price, brands, companies, time, and many other components of our retail stores. You need to know how customers feel when they do business with you. You need to understand the kind of experience you are providing for them. The future is about emotions and excitement.

Multichannel Retailing

Small retailers will need to become masters of *multichannel retailing*—dealing with a customer any way the customer wants to deal with you. That means you'll need to be able to serve your customers in person, by phone, on the web, and even on their cell phones.

While e-consumers may seem like a nuisance to you—they have ever-increasing expectations about service—their numbers are growing and the average transactions on the Internet reportedly are higher than the average transactions in retail stores. As customers become more time poor, they are also more inclined to use the web for its efficiency, that's why e-consumers are often called efficient consumers. For example, they want to know two minutes after they placed an order if the order was received and when it's going to be shipped. They want it shipped the next day. They want to be able to return it easily. And you need to meet all these ever-increasing expectations if you are to succeed. I discuss the basics of setting up a website in Chapter 20.

def•i•ni•tion

Multichannel retailing means serving a customer by whatever means the customer wants to deal with you—via telephone, e-mail, cell phone, in person at your store, through a catalog, or on your website.

In the world of brick and mortar, if your competitor is five miles away, your customers aren't likely to take the time to drive those five miles to save a few dollars. But on the Internet, the competition is a mouse click away. That's a big difference. So these customers are not afraid to switch if they're just shopping price and convenience. Loyalty is not a factor for them. Often they are much more fragmented than customers who come to your store, because they come from all over the country and not just your local area.

Selling Points

The Internet is having, and will continue to have, a profound impact on retail over the next 10 years. "Bricks and clicks," stores with websites, are the most successful retailers today. Companies that are only selling on the web are not growing as quickly. You have a greater chance of success today if you have both a retail store and a website.

In the future, multichannel marketing will become one channel. Kids growing up today will see no difference between using a computer or using a telephone. Multichannel communication will be part of their lifestyle. And they won't find any difference between ordering something on their cell phones, on their computers, or by walking into a store. It's going to all be one shopping experience to them.

The problem with this is that a large percentage of multichannel retailers remain unable to track customer's behavior across those channels today. So they don't even know when they have a multichannel customer. Some of the most successful multichannel retailers in the United States can not track the same customer who shops both in their retail stores and on their websites. What we have to do is use our technology to see each of them as one customer not as two separate customers. I talk more about using your customer database strategically in Chapter 26.

Urban Revival

We're seeing an urban revival in the United States. Inner cities are being reborn. Baby boomers—people born between 1946 and 1964—who ran out to the suburbs back in the 1960s and 1970s are now leaving the suburbs and coming back downtown. Residential building is booming in downtowns across the country. People are moving back into the cities. Walking to shop will replace driving. This can have a real impact on where you may choose to locate your store. I talk more about picking the right location for your store in Chapter 10.

Women

Women are driving real changes in retailing. More and more women are in or will soon be in the workforce. These women won't waste their time with inefficient stores—they just don't have the time. It is also estimated that almost 80 percent of all purchases in retail stores are made or directly influenced by women. The opportunities for growth are tremendous if you design your store and merchandise it with products in a way that will appeal to the female shopper. I talk about designing a store to meet your customers' needs in Chapter 13 and about filling that store with the right products in Chapter 11.

Boomers

Boomers are redefining aging. This baby boom generation is experiencing at least a $10,000 increase in discretionary income when their kids leave the house. After the kids leave, these boomers have money to spend, and they spend it on the most amazing things. Every minute from now until 2014, seven boomers in the United States will turn 50. So we have a huge population going into not quite middle age. Middle age used to be 40 but today it is closer to 60. Remember, no matter what age you are as you read this, you are at least 10 years younger than your parents were at the same age. The boomers represent an incredible market for at least the next 30 years. And remember, they are the wealthiest generation in the history of this country.

Reward Loyalty

Not all customers are created equal. We talk about customer loyalty, but loyalty is a two-way street. We expect customers to be loyal to us, but they will not be unless we are loyal to them. And by being loyal to them, I mean that we reward and do something for customers who shop in our store on a regular basis. These loyal customers cost us less to maintain. They produce high margins and we make more money from them.

Smart retailers are learning that they have to get rid of customers who do not meet their financial contribution threshold. Learn to recognize customers who don't produce profits for you.

For example, I would argue that to succeed in retail today, a store should be able to produce a list, by name and address, of their 100 most profitable customers. That's still a major challenge for most retailers, but it will be a necessity in the future. Once you've compiled this list, focus on those customers. They are the ones upon whom you can build the future of your store. Go back to the good old days of personal service and get to know these customers who believe in you.

Sophisticated consumers, consumers with three out of four of these characteristics—high education, work experience, high income, and/or access to technology—are changing the way we have to practice retail. They are very demanding. Think of this as an opportunity for growth by satisfying their demands in a way no one else can—going that extra mile (see Chapter 18).

This book discusses how you can build your retail store to respond to these trends and satisfy the customer of the future. It gives you the tools you need to build a successful retail business with your top-100 loyal customers and move the next 500 into the same group.

The Least You Need to Know

- In the past, retailers could count on profit increases year-to-year of 20 to 30 percent; today you can only count on profit increases in the single digits.
- You can't win on price. Large retailers have control there, so you must find other means to get your customers and to keep them.
- Learn to serve your customers through multiple channels and find ways to track your customers across those channels.

Chapter 2

Retail Legends—Can You Be One?

In This Chapter

- Benefits and trade-offs of owning a store
- The retailer's job
- What successful retailers have in common
- Determining if you have what it takes
- Learning what to do if you don't

Owning and opening a new store is very appealing. The idea of building something from scratch and turning it into a successful business, the lure of total freedom and being one's own boss, the prospect of endless opportunities and good money are just a few of the many reasons why many of us dream of doing it one day. However, opening and running a successful store takes more than just a dream. It takes courage, talent, hard work, perseverance, and yes, luck, too.

In this chapter, you first learn about the opportunities, challenges, and responsibilities of managing your own store and what separates successful retailers from those who fail. Then you can assess your skills and personal characteristics and find out if you have what it takes to become a retail legend. If you find you don't have all the skills, I discuss how you can develop them or how you can hire people who do have them to help you.

Explore Your Reasons

Before opening your first store, you must ask yourself: "Why do I really want to open a store?" For most people, the common answers include financial independence, freedom from the 9-to-5 daily routine, being your own boss, making more money, or using personal skills better and more fully, just to name a few. In addition, of course, you have a store concept or a product in mind for which you feel that there's a need.

While all of these reasons are valid, they don't tell you the whole story. You must take the time to investigate the implications of owning your own store, or you run the risk of making the wrong decision. Or you could make what appears to be the right decision but for the wrong reasons.

You may find that if you own a store and the store is successful, you can make a lot of money, but it can also be true that this might not happen right away or at all. In fact, it's more likely that for months and even years you will be making a lot less than you made before you opened the store.

Your workday will be much longer, too. While it is true that, if you own a store, you are no longer stuck with a 9-to-5 work routine, it is also true that your new schedule is not likely to be less demanding. On the contrary, it's more likely to be 12 to 16 hours a day, for 6 or 7 days a week. You're also likely to work on holidays. This is something you should seriously consider when determining if you are really cut out for retail.

Knowing the reasons why you want to open a store means understanding the benefits as well as the trade-offs of owning a store.

The Opportunities

When you own a store, you are in charge. You decide and define your success and the success of your business. You choose what you want to sell, how you want to sell it, and whom you want to sell it to. You choose the name of your store, who is going to work there, and so on. When you own a store, you can control your future if you do it right; if not, it will own you.

The feeling of accomplishment if and when you succeed can be exhilarating. You feel a great sense of accomplishment knowing that "you did it," you were able to take an idea, a vision that you had, and turn it into a successful business reality.

Add to this the potential of making a lot more money than if you worked for somebody else, of having better job security because nobody can fire you, of doing something you really like and enjoy, and you will understand why so many people get into the retail business every day.

The Challenges

As a business owner, your challenges are the risks you need to take. The risk of failure is probably the biggest one. There is no guarantee of success in business in general and particularly in retail. Even when you spend time learning the job, planning for it, and do everything right, the risk of failure is always there.

External economic, political, or social conditions can affect your business directly or indirectly. Think of what happened to a lot of businesses after September 11, 2001. Airlines, travel agencies, retailers of all sizes suffered tremendously after those terrible events because customers would not travel and therefore shop at their establishments anymore. Opening a store in a hurricane-prone area or another weather-risk area should also give you pause.

> **Savvy Retailer**
>
> External disasters over which you have no control can quickly turn a successful business into a failure. The devastation of buildings in the World Trade Center area of New York on September 11, 2001, destroyed a half million square feet of retail space. Think about the number of retail business owners that were out of business in a matter of hours. A tornado or hurricane can shut down a business just as quickly.

Or you could fail because of internal reasons. For example, your idea wasn't good enough or it was not executed properly.

You may liken it to walking on a high wire without a safety net. And with no net, if you fall, there's usually nothing or nobody to catch you and save you from getting hurt. As Willy Loman put it in *Death of a Salesman*, "You are out there on a wing and a prayer." While some people might find the risk aspect of owning a business tremendously exhilarating and a real reason for doing it, to others this can be a frightening feeling.

Even before you succeed, another big challenge of starting your own store is the risk of losing money. To open your first store, you will most likely need to use a small, or a not so small, portion of your personal savings. Your income, for the first few months or more, might not be the same that you had before you opened the store. Before you can pay yourself, you need to make sure you have enough money to pay the bank, your vendors, your lawyer, your accountant, and before all these are paid, your employees, who are always paid first.

Your time might not be yours anymore (or your family's). Working 10 or more hours a day for 6 or 7 days a week is likely to be the standard, at least for a while.

Retail is detail, and there are millions of details that you will need to attend to every single day. Some of them might be boring, like crunching numbers; some might be drudgery, like washing the front door window for the tenth time in one day; and some might be unpleasant, like firing an employee you trusted.

The Responsibilities

As a store owner, you are first and foremost responsible for the cash that you put into your business. In most cases, the cash is either your life's savings or comes from the second mortgage you took on your home. Or you may borrow money from family or friends or both. Your job and responsibility is to preserve the money and make it work hard for the business.

Often you have a family and a spouse, and so you may have a responsibility to them, too. It's their future that you are putting on the line, not just yours.

Since you are most likely going to bring employees into your business, you also have responsibilities to them. You need to make sure that the people that you are asking to join your dream will have food on their tables and will be guaranteed jobs with you for some time.

As a retail owner, your responsibilities are also the many hats that you will wear, or in other words, you will be responsible for performing a lot of different roles that relate to running a store. This is true whether you assign people to do a particular task for you or not. Your employees will always need direction from you because you are the leader.

Strategic and Business Planner

As the store owner, you are the president, the chief executive officer, and the administrator of your company. You are in charge of devising and developing the strategy and the vision for your business. You are also responsible for setting the goals that will need to be achieved, and you will need to define the tactics that will be deployed to meet those goals. You will need to be able to communicate to your employees, the bank, your landlord, and others your goals and how you are planning to achieve them and make money in the process.

You are also responsible for planning for your store's long-term growth after the first year and beyond. We talk about this in Chapter 24.

Real Estate Agent

While a commercial real estate agent will help find the right location for your store, you are responsible for providing directions to your agent on what you need based on your business model—what you sell and to whom—and your goals. You are also in charge of making the final decision and selecting from the various options presented to you, negotiating the best deal, and making sure that your location is in compliance with legal requirements.

Store Designer

Even when you hire a construction company or a retail store design firm to help you pick the best design for your store, you are responsible for deciding on the right look and feel based on what you sell and whom you plan to sell it to. Because you know your target customer, you are better equipped to decide on the right image and presentation to ensure maximum impact, sales, and repeat business.

Buyer and Merchandiser

As the store owner, you are responsible for sourcing product to sell in your store, for negotiating the best prices and terms, planning for the right assortment of colors/sizes/models/etc., and the best quantities for maximum sales and profit. Being your own buyer and merchandiser will require some traveling, a lot of analysis and study of both market and consumer trends, and some good mathematical skills to analyze and plan your inventory levels (although you might be able to hire someone to help with the numbers if that's not your forte!).

Marketing and Sales Manager

As your company's marketing and sales manager, you are responsible for budgeting, designing, and executing marketing and sales plans. Your campaigns must attract customers, generate excitement, satisfy customers' needs, and give them a reason to come back.

You are also responsible for creating and maintaining a customer database, making sure that you capture relevant data to help better define and target your customers' product and service needs and expectations. And, most important, you are in charge of training your staff in how to sell and provide exceptional customer service all the time.

Financial and Accounting Manager

From raising the capital you need to open your store, to developing a financial plan for your business, to counting the money and balancing the books, your financial and accounting skills are important to your success in this new career. You are most likely going to hire an accountant to help you with these important tasks but, again, you are ultimately responsible for making your store profitable. You need to know how to monitor your finances very closely.

Selling Points

An excellent book that shows you how to set up and maintain an accounting system for a small business is *The Complete Idiot's Guide to Accounting* by Lita Epstein. She takes the reader through the process of initially setting up the books, then covers the day-to-day maintenance of those books, and finally shows you how to develop financial statements.

Manager and Boss

As the owner of your store, you are responsible for hiring the staff that will help you run it. You will need to know how to find qualified candidates, how to interview them, and how to select the right candidates for your store. You will then be responsible for training, developing, compensating, and rewarding them.

Once they are on board, you will then need to keep them motivated, enthusiastic, and knowledgeable about the process of selling and the product that they are selling. And if they don't meet your performance expectations, you will need to learn how to discipline and eventually fire them legally if necessary.

Store Operations Manager

As the store owner, you are responsible for operating the store. You need to open the store, receive merchandise, count it, stock it, ticket it, price it, and put it out on the shelves in the store. If you sell online, you need to set up and coordinate all shipping and delivery operations. You need to count the money and deposit it in the bank at the end of every day and make sure that you pay your staff, bank loans, vendors and suppliers, landlord, and any other creditors in an accurate and timely fashion. You are responsible for coordinating promotional activities and events, such as sales, new product launches, and so on.

Technology Expert

As the technology expert, you are responsible for selecting the right technology for your store. This includes at a minimum your point-of-sale/service (POS) technology—what used to be called cash registers—your credit card processor, and your inventory, financial, and sales and payroll management software.

You are also responsible for maintaining the technology and making sure that all your data gets backed up regularly with no loss or corruption of data.

E-Commerce Expert

Even if you are not planning on selling online, you still must have a presence on the web. You can contract or hire webmasters and graphic designers to help you develop a website for your store. However, you will need to decide what your website is going to look like and communicate to your customers in order for it to promote your image and boost sales.

Legal Expert

To open a store, you will need to hire a lawyer to help you wind your way through the maze of business ownership laws. Your lawyer will help you with employment law, finance law, lease-agreement law, any law that may regulate the sale of the products you sell, the local regulations and store permits required, as well as any licenses and registrations that may be needed. Your legal advisor will not always be there with you to make sure that you do not violate any laws in conducting your business, though. That's why, as the owner of your store, you will need to have a general understanding of the legal aspects of owning a business.

This list of responsibilities, although daunting, is meant to help you understand the complexities of being a retail store owner and help you to realistically assess whether this is something that you can and want to do.

While there is plenty of help for you in this book in the form of step-by-step guidelines as well as tips and recommendations, you will still need to play the most important role of getting it done the right way.

Traits of Successful Retailers

According to various studies, only about 30 percent of businesses in the United States survive past their fifth year. The two most common reasons for failure are bad management (the owner doesn't have the necessary skills) and lack of money (the owner doesn't have enough capital to support the business long enough for it to be successful).

Success in retail is not a guarantee. Success depends for the most part on your planning, preparation, and insight. Part of this preparation is assessing your strengths and weaknesses as a prospective retailer.

One of the best ways to assess your potential for success as a retailer is to evaluate your skills and personal characteristics against those of retailers who were and are successful. Don't get discouraged if you find out that you don't have all of the characteristics. Even the best retailers often don't have each and every one. What's important is that you become aware of what you can contribute—your strengths—and what you need to learn—your weaknesses—and that you hire people who have what you may be lacking.

Savvy Retailer

The saying that entrepreneurs are born, not made, is a myth. The truth is that good planning, preparation, and study can make you a very successful entrepreneur.

High Energy

Running a store can be very exciting, but it can also wear you down physically and emotionally. Some store owners burn out quickly from having to carry all the responsibilities for the success of their store on their shoulders. Others aren't able to deal with the 12-to-16-hour days for 6 days a week and maybe even the Sunday and holiday schedules. Or they can't deal with the pressure to be more available to their families as the store takes them away so often. Competition can also wear you out because it is always there, you cannot take your eyes off of it for a minute. And last, customers can be challenging; unless you really know how to amaze them, it can be very hard to deal with their ever-increasing and ever-changing expectations and demands.

Successful retailers understand the demands of their job and are able to cope with the very difficult balance between work and family and between success and very hard work. These are people who are constantly seeking new challenges to further grow and welcome any competitor or other kind of pressure as an opportunity to improve.

> **Savvy Retailer**
>
> Gordon Segal, founder of Crate & Barrel, and Sam Walton, founder of Wal-Mart, as well as thousands of successful independent retailers that I have met during my career, all had incredible energy and drive. Sam Walton was working seven days a week almost to the day he died. Gordon Segal can still be found in the office on a Saturday morning 45 years after he first opened his store.

Passion

Successful retailers have an absolute passion for what they do, whether it is their product, their customer, their people, or, in many cases, all three. They believe in their hearts, minds, and souls in what they are doing, what they are selling, and what they are bringing to their customers. They truly eat, sleep, and breathe their store every minute of every day.

This is a quality that is very important in retail. I have seen so many retail businesses fail because there was no passion for what the owner was doing. Remember, retail is very demanding, and your time does not belong to you anymore. Customers also can be challenging at times and drain energy from you if you are not careful. Banks, the government, and vendors can be difficult to deal with, and you really must love what you are doing to balance all of these sometimes conflicting demands of your job.

Desire to Learn

Successful retailers are insatiable learners and students of both their customers and their competition. Their goal is to always learn something new or different that they can use in their businesses. They look for better ways to sell their products or more effective ways to communicate with their customers. They seek more exciting ways to display their products or better ways to treat employees. They are always looking for new opportunities to do better themselves and continue to grow.

Ideas and Creativity

One of the things that I think is true of very successful retailers is that their joy is in creating, not maintaining. Great retailers are driven to do something new and different every day. These retailers tend to be very inquisitive, curious, adaptable, and challenge oriented, and are always looking for new ideas.

Through lots of reading, observing, talking to experts, and spending time trying different ways of improving things, you can help enhance your creative abilities. Brainstorming, the process of sharing ideas or solutions to a problem with a group of employees, can also help develop your creative skills.

Another very effective way to help you develop your ability to generate new ideas is simply to observe and listen. A customer's complaint, a change in customer demographics, or a new competitor down the street, are all opportunities and reasons for rethinking what you are doing and creating new opportunities for your business.

Positive Attitude

As a store owner, it is important that you maintain a positive mindset in the face of adversity.

There may be financial difficulties until the store becomes profitable, which could take months or years to happen. This may require that you lower your standard of living until your business is fully established. Even when your store is up and running and doing well, there are still going to be months (maybe years) when business may be slow. Or you might get hit by a lawsuit or other hard-to-predict difficulty.

Successful store owners don't let these events discourage them. They deal with them, they learn from them, and they come out of them more aggressive and resolute to make their stores even better.

Organization

Poor planning can lead to failure in every kind of business enterprise. Planning is everything in retail. Retail owners plan their finances, their inventory, their staffing levels and schedules, their store promotions, their advertising campaigns, their sales, and so on. Very little should ever come as a surprise.

Organization grows out of planning and allows a coordinated and logical implementation of every plan. It is about setting priorities, assigning tasks, establishing deadlines, tracking results, and recording procedures and outcomes. Great store owners love organizing tasks and they are fanatics about creating procedures and then documenting every step of the process. They understand that a store can only function if there are written and well-documented policies, procedures, and practices that then become the standard for everyone to follow.

They also understand that a store with no documented procedures is very hard to sell when it comes time—and someday it will. Buyers don't buy businesses that have no documented procedures and instructions of how things are done in the businesses. Great retailers can sell their stores at a moment's notice because the stores can run themselves. Imagine even buying a TV today without an instruction manual: you could probably turn it on, but you would not know how to adjust the picture or likely make it work with your home theater system. Good companies like good products have instruction manuals.

Other Characteristics

Passion, drive, organization, and all the skills that we just talked about may earn you a spot amongst the legends of retail. However, there are other traits and skills that are also important for your business that you will need to develop if you don't already have them. Successful retailers are:

- **Great leaders.** They are able to make sound decisions constantly—often quickly, independently, and under pressure. They are role models capable of inspiring their employees and providing them with guidance and direction.
- **Self-starters.** They develop their own projects, organize their own time, and follow through on details.
- **Great at building strong working relationships.** When you own your own store, you often don't get to choose whom you are dealing with. Some people you will enjoy; others you may not. Regardless of how you feel about people, you will need to build strong relationships and consensus with everyone including bankers, lawyers, accountants, government officials, employees, and yes, even customers.
- **Focused on helping people.** Most people don't buy products because they need them. They buy them because those products make them happy. As a retailer, your job is not to sell products. Your job is to make a difference in your customers' lives by helping them make the right choices. Successful retailers care about their staff, too. They love helping them succeed and grow because successful retailers know that, if their staff is happy, the staff will make customers happy and happy customers come back again and again.

- **Excellent salespeople.** Retail owners are generally most concerned with operating their businesses and making them profitable. However, great retailers are incredible salespeople who make it a rule to spend some time on the floor working with customers. That's how they develop their strategies to improve service and, as a result, sales.

Persistent, demanding, competitive, committed, with a high degree of tolerance for ambiguity—nothing is straightforward in retail—and tolerance for failure, as well as a high level of integrity and reliability can also be added to our list of success factors in retail management. And, of course, one last factor: luck!

Do You Have What It Takes?

If it is true that there are some good reasons not to start a business, it is also true that for the right person, the advantages of owning your own store far outweigh the risks. Are you that kind of person?

Personal Conditions

Personal conditions refer to the demands of your new career. Are you prepared to work 7 days a week, 10 to 12 hours a day or more? When answering this question, you will need to think about your personal situation. It's quite different if you have a 2-year-old child than if you have an 18 or 21 year old, or no children. It is also different if your spouse is employed and can help you with the store and with home commitments.

Will you have access to the capital that will be required to turn your vision into reality? Will you be able and willing to make the lifestyle changes that will be required by your new business, changes that, most likely, will affect your personal relationships, too?

Personal Traits

Do you have the passion, the vision, the discipline, and the stamina to execute your plan and make it work? Are you creative, competitive, goal oriented, and a very hard worker willing to do it every day? Do you love helping people and making them happy? These and many more are the questions that you will need to ask yourself.

Learning New Skills

As I said earlier, it is not likely that you have all the skills right now that are required to effectively run a store. However, you can learn them.

While learning new skills by trial and error could be a solution—you develop the skills over time by learning from your mistakes—I don't personally recommend this approach. Let's say you have never done a window display before and don't know how to do it. If you do it the way you guess it should be done, you run the risk of having a window that does not look very good and maybe even causes customers to pass you by. The chances of them coming back after that first bad impression can be slim.

You should also subscribe to newspapers and business magazines and learn to focus your attention on articles and topics related to the world of business and more specifically consumer behaviors, market trends, selling trends, and retail development. There's a lot of information available and useful ideas and tips can be found in many publications and stories which can enhance your business savvy and, as a result, your chances of success.

> **Selling Points**
>
> Trial and error can work for small projects and new ideas. The key is to keep the project or the idea real simple; start small (a pilot or sample); and try, try, and try again. Remember, you never want to look like you are "playing store." You are a professional, look like one.

Hiring Help

In many cases, while you could learn how to perform certain tasks, it is a lot more productive and cost-effective for you to hire expert help. So, for instance, you could search for a proper location for your store yourself, or you could hire a commercial real estate agent to find one for you. While you are still responsible for making the final selection based on your understanding of the market and your goals, what your real estate agent brings to the table is years of experience and expertise finding the right options for you to choose among.

At a minimum, you need to hire:

- A lawyer to advise you on all the legal requirements of your business—business structure, labor law, insurance, industry regulations, permits and registrations, loan agreements, lease agreements, and more.

- An accountant to help you with bookkeeping, balancing the books, taxes, and financial planning.
- A store designer or construction company to help you source and select the right materials and fixtures for your store and help build your space.
- A webmaster to help you design and develop your website, including your e-commerce pages if you sell online.
- A graphic designer to help you define and design your brand and create a template for your signage, logo, shopping bags, posters, promotional flyers, business cards, and everything else that can help communicate your identity.
- A sales associate(s) to help you on the floor. Your store may be open an average of 10 to 12 hours a day, 6 to 7 days a week. You can't possibly run it on your own and expect to provide good, quality service. The number of associates that you will need to hire will vary depending on the size of your store and the hours that you are open.
- An assistant manager to help you open, run, and close the store. This will depend on the size of your store and on how reliable your sales associates are. If you have a very small store, you might not need an assistant.

Finding a Partner

If there are skills on your list that you do not have or do not enjoy and do not want to hire someone else to do, such as managing people, your best bet may be to partner up with someone whose skill set will complement yours.

Finding a good partner might not be easy, though. Most people tend to consider family or friends—in other words, people they can trust, who share the same values and goals and who they know have the required skills and temperament. A business association, such as a chamber of commerce, a retail networking group, or a buying group could also be a source to consider when looking for a partner.

When choosing a partner, be aware that a partner can be both an asset and a liability. If you are incredibly passionate, driven, and have the vision but you don't feel comfortable with the day-to-day running of a business—hiring people, managing them, managing inventory and operations—a good fit for a partner would be someone who absolutely loves organizing and managing but is not motivated by strategizing. Taking on a partner in this particular case would not be a bad idea. However, in some cases it might not work and, if your partner happens to be a friend or family member, this could end up damaging the personal relationship as well as the professional one—and it could be difficult to end the partnership.

Again, and I can't say it often enough, retail is in the details. If you don't enjoy sweating the details, opening a retail business may not be right for you.

The Least You Need to Know

- The decision to open a retail store should not be taken lightly; it is a life-changing endeavor that requires dedication and commitment.
- The two most common reasons for failure in a retail business are lack of money and lack of management skills.
- There are many skills required to be a successful retailer. You have to understand accounting, legal, marketing, financial, human resources, real estate, and operations just to name a few. You do not have to be an expert at all of them, just have a good understanding of what is required.
- Successful retailers share many characteristics; the two most important are a vision of what they want to be and a passion to achieve it.

Part 2

Sizing Up Your Options and Your Competition

Whenever you start a new business, you have a lot to learn. Your success is directly proportional to the amount of time you spend developing an in-depth understanding of your customer, your competitors, and your industry. The more you know about your customers' likes and dislikes; your competitors' strengths and weaknesses; and your industry's trends, opportunities, and constraints, the greater your chances of success.

In this part, I give you the tools to learn and research what you need.

"So do you sell any bathing suits for birds?"

Chapter 3

Evaluate Your Idea

In This Chapter

- Analyzing the market
- Finding a market opportunity
- Matching your idea to an opportunity
- Making sure your idea is profitable

After you've decided that retail is right for you and you are right for retail, before you pump your savings into a new store, you need to determine if your idea will work.

You do this with strategic planning. While most independent retailers think that strategic planning is something meant only for big retailers, don't believe this. Strategic planning is equally applicable to small businesses. With this type of planning, you seek to match your idea of a store to available market opportunities.

In this chapter, we'll explore how to assess the market and identify what unmet needs you can focus on for a profitable store. You will learn to evaluate the strengths and weakness of your idea and determine if your store has a chance to succeed.

What Is Your Idea?

If you are like most retailers, you already have an idea of the kind of store that you want to open and the product that you want to sell. It could be a store concept or a product that you like or know very well. For example, if you like wine and know a lot about it, you might think of opening a wine store. In this case, you are essentially matching your skills, passion, and experience to a retail store concept that requires those skills. Your idea of a product to sell or a store to open could also be something that is not offered yet or not offered in the best way. You think you could be the first to sell it, or you could sell it better than others.

Or you can be like the rest of retailers out there: you know that you want to open a store but you don't know exactly what kind of store and what kind of product you are going to sell, and you need to find those things out.

Study the Market

Whether you know what you are going to sell or you don't know, you need to determine if your idea is feasible before you start.

To do so, you need to study the market to examine your idea with respect to …

- **Market potential.** Will there be enough customers who will want to buy your products and be interested in your services?
- **Competition.** Who else is offering similar products or services, and are they meeting customer's needs today?
- **Product industry.** Is your chosen product industry healthy, and are regulations not too restrictive?

You will also need to assess resources required to enter the market, consumer/buyer demand, and of course, uniqueness of your idea.

Affordable Market Research Techniques

Market study or research is something that most small retailers don't do either because they don't know how to do it themselves or they can't afford it. Primary market research, which is specific to a store or company, can be quite expensive; however, secondary market research, which uses readily available data, can be very low cost.

Secondary market research allows you to gather information on your market and find out about opportunities for your store. You can buy or access secondary market studies and data for your product industry on the Internet or at your local library. These research studies have already been compiled, and from them you can learn basic information on your particular product industry, including consumer profiles, competition, and growth predictions.

You can also find valuable market information in newspapers and popular magazines, such as *The New York Times*, *The Wall Street Journal*, *USA Today*, *Time*, *U.S. News & World Report*, *Newsweek*, *The Economist*, and even *People* magazine on occasion. You may find articles on market trends in business magazines like *Fortune*, *Forbes*, *Business Week*, or any of the other business periodicals to which you may have access. All of these resources provide you with up-to-date and thorough information on economic, business, and market trends that can help you learn about the market and opportunities that are available.

Selling Points

You can find useable secondary market research for free by just doing a little research on the Internet. One good website you can start with is KnowThis.com (www.knowthis.com/studies/focus-on-market-research/reports.htm). There you can find free market research on many industries. In addition, www.ask.com is a great place to look for retail-specific information.

Talk to your friends, relatives, business associates, and other small retail owners about ideas they may have or needs in the market they don't believe are being met. You can often find helpful ideas.

And, last but not least, don't forget the most overlooked resource—yourself. You're a consumer. If you have wished that a particular product or service were available, chances are that others have, too.

Savvy Retailer

Healthy Back's founder, Anthony Mazlish, a former investor turned entrepreneur, decided to open the first store in his chain of stores after searching for ergonomically designed products to help relieve his own back problems. He opened his first store after becoming frustrated at the lack of options on the market.

Trends to Spot

When reading articles or market studies in newspapers, the web, or business periodicals, your goal is to learn about social, economic, and business trends. Look for opportunities to profit from these trends by selling your products or services.

Trends that are happening today and that are going to shape the future of the market for many years to come include demographic changes, the disappearance of the middle class, and the rush to save the environment to name a few.

Demographic Changes

Three key demographic trends that offer tremendous market opportunities for retailers both old and new include the aging of baby boomers, the growth in buying power of the Gen Xers and Yers, and the growth of the Hispanic population.

Baby boomers, people born between 1946 and 1964, are just starting to enter their 60s. This group has the largest amount of disposable income in history. They're driving growth in many areas, including services, recreation, and, of course, retailing. Here are some key statistics from the U.S. Census Bureau about this age group:

- Thirty percent of the 78 million boomers in the United States are or are about to be empty nesters this year.
- This is the wealthiest generation in the history of the world and will be for the next 30 years.
- Baby boomers have ever-increasing expectations about service and brands.
- By 2030, one in five Americans will be over 65 and most will live another 25 years or more.

> **Savvy Retailer**
>
> David Walker once said that "Demographics are destiny," and what he meant was that knowing demographic facts can profoundly influence trends.

Some key points to remember when targeting this age group include:

- Offer reasonably priced goods. As baby boomers age and begin thinking about living on fixed incomes, they will look for good buys, which we can already see in the growth of discount and dollar stores.
- Sell experience, not age. Notice that advertisements targeting this group use words like "mature" or "prime" rather than "older" or "senior." An ad that indicates your products are designed for older people probably won't attract baby boomers. They are not going into their senior years gently!
- Baby boomers don't want to buy into the old stereotypes. They want to live actively and don't want to be reminded of the challenges they may face with growing older. In your ads, use healthy, active, age-appropriate models to attract them as customers.

- Make sure your signs, packaging, marketing materials, and nametags are easy for baby boomers to read. Think large type sizes and a good use of "white space."
- Keep the store well lit, adequately heated, and with background music that is not too loud. Also, place chairs in strategic locations so customers can sit down and rest.

The second group includes both Generations X and Y. Although there is much disagreement about the exact definition of these generations, those generally pegged as Generation Xers were born between 1965 and 1985 and are independent and skeptical. Generation Yers, who were born between 1986 and 2006, are generally idealistic, optimistic, and patriotic but do not believe in traditional advertising, relying only on word-of-mouth advertising. Both groups have a lot in common. They grew up during recessions and many lived in single-parent households. Some key things to remember about marketing to these age groups include:

- They are media savvy with constant access to cable television, the Internet, and other technology toys as they were growing up. It is likely you won't reach them through traditional marketing channels.
- Direct mail and online marketing have proven to be the most effective for reaching these demographic groups.
- When reaching out to Gen Xers, who are normally skeptical, promote the benefits of your product as well as some form of guarantee.
- Both generations are used to getting information at high speed, so they look for more varied and faster-changing trends. Don't expect brand loyalty from this group. They'll switch their loyalty in an instant to a store that will get them ahead of the style curve. If you want to target this group, you need to keep ahead of the trends and be ready to have the latest and greatest on hand.

The third demographic group to target is the Hispanic market, which is the fastest-growing consumer segment in the United States. If the Hispanic population has grown in your area, don't forget to consider ways to reach this population. You will need to have bilingual sales people to serve this market. Your best way to reach this market segment is through Spanish radio and cable television marketing. Internet advertising can also be an effective way to target this market segment.

Better Not!

When targeting the Hispanic market, most businesses think of the Mexican market only. Yet, the Hispanic market is really 20 markets at least, including Chilean, Puerto Rican, Cuban, Bolivian, and other groups from other Spanish-speaking countries. For example, a costly Cinco de Mayo (a Mexican holiday) promotion ended up in a big disappointment for a large company when they decided to have it in Miami, not realizing that the Hispanic population in Miami is mainly Cuban.

Some key statistics from the census bureau you need to remember when targeting the Hispanic market include:

- Twenty five million current U.S. residents (10 percent) were not born in the United States.
- The Hispanic population will increase from 37 million today to 55 million by 2020 (a 49 percent increase).
- By 2020, the median age of Hispanics will be 28.8 versus 37.6 for the total population.

Another demographic change is the gay market, which is "going mainstream" and exploding. While in the past many gay couples were afraid to go public with their relationships, in many communities this lifestyle is now more acceptable. In communities where a gay lifestyle is acceptable, you can market directly to these couples. Many companies are targeting this demographic because it is often a two income household that has significant disposable income and a significant appreciation of good design and quality products.

The Rich Are Getting Richer

The disparity between rich and poor is growing and, as a result, the middle class is shrinking. You will need to make a choice regarding whether you want to target the rich and develop your retail store catering to their luxury purchases or target the dwindling middle class and lower classes. But remember, to sell high-end products, you'll need to create a store environment for your upscale customer where service, image, and product match your customer's expectations and lifestyle. Price is not a concern to them. What matters to them is that the experience that they have in your store is the "best of the best."

De-Massification

De-massification, or the marketing of products to niche markets, is not an oxymoron but a response to global homogeneity. Consider what that means for opportunities in stores that provide products or services individually tailored to each customer.

By selling something that is unique and tailored to a specific niche, a retailer manages to stand out from the pack. This is more effective when your product and target market are high-end. Consumers of luxury goods value status more than anything else and one of the ways to achieve it is by owning something unique that no one else has. As John Galliano, famous Italian fashion designer, said very eloquently in an ad which appeared in the *Financial Times*, "One desire that is getting stronger than all other demands remains the desire to be unique."

In addition, as consumers are exposed to more choices, loyalty has become less important than it once was. Customers will bolt to a competitor for a slightly better deal. You can also lose customers if you experience a temporary shortage of stock.

Green Options

Environmentalism made it into the spotlight with the success of former vice president Al Gore's documentary on global warming, *An Inconvenient Truth*. You can develop a sustainable retail business focusing on green options or environmentally friendly products provided you can prove the benefits to your customers. To succeed, you must sell a product that is not only environmentally friendly, but one that also works effectively and is priced competitively. While most consumers say that they would choose a green product over less environmentally friendly options, they would only do it if the price difference is not significant.

Lifestyle Changes

Peoples' lives are busier than ever, and you won't find many customers who go out and only shop for the entire day. Most people don't have the time to leisurely look through the aisles of your store. They usually want to find whatever it is they are looking for fast. Your store design, product displays, service, checkout operations, and deliveries all must reflect this change of pace in the consumer's life. Retailers will compete more and more on speed as consumers are raising their expectations for instant gratification (I want it now) and efficiency (I want it fast).

Find Your Niche

A market in its entirety is too broad in scope for any but the largest retailers to tackle successfully. The best strategy for a smaller retailer is to divide demand into manageable market niches. Small operations can then offer specialized goods and services attractive to a specific group of prospective buyers.

To find your market niche, you need to look at market trends, competitors, and your prospective market base. When analyzing them, you are looking for gaps or, in other words, an unmet need or a need that has not been met completely and that you can help fill.

Market Trends

You can find business opportunities by looking at trends in the market or the economy. The question you are going to ask yourself is: "Are there any trends out there that will generate a strong demand for certain products or services?"

Let's have a look at the trends that I talked about earlier, for a moment. Do you see any market opportunities as a result of changes in demographics? Maybe a spike in demand of travel, recreation, vacations, entertainment products and services, as well as food and clothing to meet the need of baby boomers as they age.

What kind of demand can de-massification create? How about stores that provide products or services individually tailored to each customer?

What does the growth of the upper class mean for the sale of cars, entertainment, luxury products, and exclusive and personalized products and services?

This is the kind of analysis that you need to conduct to identify a need and an opportunity for you to service that need.

Competitor Analysis

You found a niche or, in other words, a need that you can fulfill. Now, you need to ask yourself if there's anybody else offering similar products or services.

Let's assume that you believe that selling affordable designer furniture is the way to go. Do you know who else is doing it? If there are other stores that sell designer furniture at reasonable prices, are there any competitive advantages that you possess that other stores can't offer customers even if they wanted to? Or is there anything that you could improve on?

When looking for a niche, it is important to think in terms of products and services. Most businesses involve a mixture of both, but this dichotomy can help narrow the focus. Suppose you wanted to open a light store, but there are a lot of specialty lighting stores in your area. You may choose to differentiate yourself through a service that is not offered by other stores. For example, you could choose to offer private consultation to customers who require a new lighting system for their home but are not interested in hiring an interior decorator, or offer installation of the lighting fixtures.

Selling Points

To find your niche, look for areas that are weak or absent to identify possible market opportunities. Finding these will help you define your niche either as a new product that you can offer that is currently not offered, or, as an improvement of an existing product or service that is already being provided. This could be in the form of better service, wider selection, lower prices, or through providing an incredible experience.

The uniqueness of your idea or concept is not so much the product you will sell, but the service that you are able to provide that others don't. Remember, you can charge substantially higher prices for the service you are offering, as long as you are located where there's a market for what you are offering.

Customer Analysis

Once you have a handle on your competitors, you need to focus on your prospective customers. Conducting surveys is the best way to find out your prospective customers' needs, buying preferences, and spending habits. Surveys can help you identify who will make a good customer base for your store.

Marketing research firms are best equipped to conduct these types of Primary Research studies. Although this might be a costly proposition, they are able to provide you with a wealth of data that can save you money down the road. If you know your target market well, you can make informative choices about your business that are more likely to be the right ones.

Nonexpensive ways to collect data about your target customer base can be the web, newsgroups, and forums. You could also contact noncompeting companies that share your prospective target market.

Your customer survey should include questions that obtain information on the following aspects of your potential customers.

- **Demographic information.** Includes age, sex, ethnicity, etc. You want to know this key demographic information so you know how to target your advertising and bring these customers into the store, as well as know how many of them actually live in your trade area.
- **Psychographic information.** Includes lifestyle data like hobbies, interests, opinions, etc.
- **Geographic information.** Includes information about where customers live and where they purchase products and services. This can be as broad as the country or state in which they live, or as narrow as the county, city, and neighborhood.
- **Behavioral information.** Includes information about how the customer uses products or services. This can help you find out if your target customer is already using similar products or services.
- **Benefit information.** Includes information about the perceived benefits the subject receives from products and services.

Profitability Review

You have studied the market and spotted a fabulous trend that allowed you to identify a niche in which you feel you can succeed. You have determined that your competition is not currently meeting the customers' demand for the products that you are planning to sell or the service you want to offer. You have analyzed your prospective customer base and concluded that there are customers who will be interested in buying your products. You have analyzed your product industry and learned that it's booming and is not governed by too many regulations. Now, the real test is: can you do it and do it profitably?

More specifically, here are some of the questions that you will need to ask yourself:

- Will my products (or services) serve an existing market in which demand exceeds supply?
- Is my idea practical and how much income can I expect to derive from it?
- Can I create a demand for my product or service?
- How can I learn more about my chosen industry and about the resources that are available to help me?

The answers to these questions will not only allow you to assess the strengths and weaknesses of your idea and decide if it's the right idea, they will become part of your strategy and business plan for how you are going to succeed.

Tips to Help You Choose the Right Niche

How do you pick the right niche? We have compiled this list of practical suggestions to help you choose the right niche for your store. It is based on market conditions as well as personal considerations.

Look for Repeat Business

You should try to look for businesses where you will have a lot of repeat customers or where people will need to keep buying supplies from you. A good example of this concept is Soda-Club, a seller of soda makers to make soda or seltzer at home. You purchase the soda maker, and then you continue to purchase cartridges from them to make your water.

Another common strategy used by convenience stores is to sell a cup of coffee in a store brand cup and offer refills at a considerably reduced price if you bring back the cup. This gets the customer back into the store for the refill and hopefully other purchases as well. Think about ideas that will keep your customer coming back again and again.

Seasonal Stores Are, Well, Seasonal

Try to stay away from seasonal businesses. If, however, you're willing and able to ride out the slow months, these businesses—such as beachwear shops, ski shops, farm produce, Christmas-related stores and services, and anything to do with schools and colleges—can provide you with a lot of time off. They can be the perfect business if you've retired and want to operate a retail business part of the year and travel the rest of it.

Discount Stores Are for the Big Guys

Avoid choosing a low-price store concept. Competing with discounters or with well-established businesses is a no-win strategy, because it will be just about impossible to compete with their prices. Instead, you'll have to compete in service and unique offerings.

Avoid Direct Competition

Try to find the right configuration of products, services, quality, and price that will ensure the least direct competition. Unfortunately, there is no universally effective way to make these comparisons. Your best bet is to shop the stores you believe will be your key competitors on a regular basis and think about what you can do to differentiate your store.

Don't ever design your store with the idea of just beating the competition on price. You need to offer more than just price competition to build customer loyalty. A price war by the competition will quickly draw a price-conscious customer away from your store.

A Store That You Enjoy

Whatever you decide to do, it is very important that when you look at your list of market opportunities—niches—you consider eliminating any of the stores or products that you don't believe you'll really enjoy owning. As a small store owner, you'll be living, sleeping, and breathing your business—if you don't enjoy what you are doing, your chances for success will be very low.

Better Improve Than Start from Scratch

Also more effective and less risky than starting a new concept from scratch is to look for ways that you can perform a service or provide a product that is similar to, but not quite the same as, a service or product already being provided. You must be honest about the real difference you provide and be sure customers understand your unique service and be willing to switch to you.

The Least You Need to Know

- Identify the type of store you want to open, and carefully research your market before spending too much money on opening your store.
- Know the trends for the market and customers you want to target, and follow these trends daily both before and after you open your store.
- Know your customers, their interests, and how to market to them.
- Find your niche by surveying your potential customers, as well as assessing your competitors. Be sure you can offer something your competitors are not selling.

Chapter 4

Know Thy Competition

In This Chapter

- Head-on competition
- Competing indirectly
- Observing your competitors
- Analysis using SWOT

When you open a new store, you want to create something unique and different. That's why it is important that you learn about your competition and identify ways to stand out. The question you need to ask yourself is "Why will they shop with me?" or, in other words, "What do I have to offer that is so unique and special?"

You must know your competition in order to answer this question. In this chapter, I discuss both direct and indirect competitors and give you tools you can use to study your competition.

Direct Competition

You're probably wondering how you can tell if a store is a *direct competitor*. Ask yourself this question, "If customers do not buy a given item from my store, will they be able to buy the same item from the other store instead?" If the answer is yes, the other store is a direct competitor.

def•i•ni•tion

A **direct competitor** is any store which sells the same or similar products to those you sell in your store, and customers have a choice to buy from them or from you.

When checking your direct competitors, you want to find out what type of products they offer, what type of services they provide, what promotions they run, and, of course, you want to carefully check out their pricing structure and compare it to yours. I include a worksheet later in this chapter that you can use to evaluate and compare your direct competitors.

Indirect Competition

You may think your store is quite different or even unique and doesn't have any direct competitors. In this case, you should evaluate the existing stores that you perceive as *indirect competitors*. These are stores in a different business that serve the same customers as you—which means that you may need to take business away from them in order to grow profitably. So even if your product is different, will the customer choose to spend his money with you or the competitor?

def•i•ni•tion

An **indirect competitor** is any other store that serves the same customers as you, even though it does not offer the same products as you.

In addition to evaluating the existing stores that you perceive as direct or indirect competitors, you should also evaluate the existing stores that your customers perceive as alternatives to your business. You may need to speak with some of your target customers to get this information, but it will be worth the effort.

Finding Your Competition

While you may be aware of a few stores that you consider your competition, don't depend solely on places you've seen. Make a detailed list of all possible competitors, even stores you've never been near. A good place to start is the Yellow Pages in your local telephone book. Any serious competitors should have a listing there.

Your next place to check is the local chamber of commerce. They will likely have information about your key competitors, and you may even be able to find a competitive analysis for the industries you plan to serve.

Retail Study Tour

After you've identified your direct and indirect competitors, it's time to plan a field trip to visit them. By visiting what you perceive to be your direct or indirect competitors, as well as stores your potential customers perceive as alternatives to your business, you will develop a good understanding of the diversity that exists in the retail market place in your area today. You will also come back with lots of ideas that will help you clarify your vision for your business.

How to Shop the Competition

After you complete your initial visits with all your types of competitors—direct, indirect, and alternatives—identify your three most important competitors and examine those businesses in greater detail. Get to know their strengths and weaknesses, so you will be able to design your business in a way that avoids their strengths and either attacks or simply fills in around their weaknesses.

Use the following worksheet to compare key points about the direct competitors you decide to investigate further. As you jot down key strengths or weaknesses on this worksheet, keep in mind what you as a customer see when you shop in each store. Appendix C provides a worksheet complete with a notes section to provide more detail.

Competitor Worksheet

	Competitor 1	Competitor 2	Competitor 3
Exterior and exterior sign			
Window displays			
New experience or "same old"			
General atmosphere			
Overall visual appeal			
General organization			
Color and texture			
Mood set by lighting			
Everything visible from the front door			
Spotlights highlight merchandise			

continues

Competitor Worksheet (continued)

	Competitor 1	Competitor 2	Competitor 3
Front-and-forward displays			
Displays with props, related merchandise			
Brand names in evidence			
Merchandise in departments			
Presentation tells a story			
Printed product information			
Price tickets and signs			
Consistency of interior signs			
Sign holders			
Number of sales associates			
Staff appearance and identification			
Level of in-store service			
Level of product knowledge			
Type of shopping experience			
Price range			
Price competitiveness			
Value			
Merchandise quality			
Merchandise "romance"			
Special sales			
Speed at checkout			
Payment methods			
Delivery service			
Returns policy			
Music			
Neat and clean			
Other—add other items you think are important.			

Customers Shop Horizontally

Keep in mind as you do your competitive analysis that customers will often compare your store to any other store, institution, or business that they visit or interact with in a day, week, or month.

What this means is that even if you are opening a small shoe store, you are going to be compared to every other store that your customer shopped in, every restaurant that they ate at, theater that they went to, airline that they flew with, online retailer that they bought from, etc., over the past few weeks. This could include stores like Old Navy, Gap, and Victoria's Secret; grocery stores like Giant Eagle; or restaurants like Ruth's Chris. When shopping with you, they expect your store to match and even exceed the best experience that they had with these businesses or other stores (including online stores). So, for example, if next day deliveries are what most businesses are offering and your customers are getting, maybe you should think about offering the same, because that's what your customers have been accustomed to expect and you are not competitive unless you offer it, too.

Selling Points

The way a product is displayed in the store and presented to the customer during a sale that shows that you care and are passionate about it is called "merchandising romance." The way you hold a product with both hands or the way you place it neatly in the shopping bag at checkout so that it doesn't get damaged are very good examples of romancing merchandise.

Doing a SWOT Analysis

After you've collected all this information, you are ready to do a SWOT analysis. SWOT stands for Strengths, Weaknesses, Opportunities, and Threats. By analyzing your competition from these four perspectives, you can use the information to develop your marketing plan.

With a SWOT analysis, you assess your competitors' strengths (what your competitors do well) and your competitors' weaknesses (what your competitors do poorly). In addition, you look for opportunities for making inroads against your competitors as well as threats, which are things your competitors do extremely well that can make it difficult for you to succeed. Your SWOT analysis can be a crucial step for designing your store and developing your marketing plan.

Identifying Strengths and Weaknesses

As you identify strengths and weaknesses remember to stay in the mind-set of the customer to gain maximum benefit from your efforts. You should always think about how the strengths or weaknesses you identify will impact the customer and her needs.

Some key questions you should ask as part of this analysis include:

- What do your competitors do extremely well?
- What are your competitors' key marketing strategies?
- Who do your competitors target as customers?
- What do your competitors do poorly?
- What products or services could be improved?
- What do your competitors do that should be avoided?

Finding Opportunities or Threats

When looking for opportunities or threats, you can identify some by evaluating what your competitors do well or do poorly, but you also must think about the economic, political, legal, technological, and cultural environments outside your small universe of identified competitors. Some key areas to consider include:

- **Changes in competitive environment.** One of the biggest threats to small, independently owned businesses in the country today are retail giants that gobble up small mom-and-pop stores. A national reputation can be difficult to compete against. You won't be able to compete with pricing, so you will need to find your niche through service, convenience, and by providing an extraordinary in-store experience.
- **Changes in cultural environments.** Look for changes in attitudes, beliefs, norms, customs, and lifestyles. If you can stay ahead of these changes, your store will be ready to lead the competition.
- **Changes in political/legal environment.** Keep your eye on any regulatory actions by local, state, or the federal government that could impact the way you operate your store by reading newspapers or getting updates from your local chamber of commerce. For example, the Americans with Disabilities Act dictates how you must design certain parts of your store.

Savvy Retailer

ABT Electronics, the largest single-store electronics and appliance dealer in the United States, located just outside Chicago, is owned by Bob Abt, who is often referred to as the "king" of independent retailing. ABT manages to best its competition (Best Buy, Fry's, Circuit City) by leveraging one strength: being small. Small means that service must be at the highest level. For example, while everyone else is outsourcing their delivery and installation service, ABT does it itself to ensure professional quality. While everyone else says no to a price deal, ABT's motto is "The answer is Yes to any reasonable request" and its associates are authorized to make the decision themselves about whether to honor a request or not. While many stores pay the minimum for staff, ABT offers higher pay to ensure that its associates stay and go the extra mile with every customer.

Using SWOT Strategically

After you've collected all your SWOT information, you're ready to develop your strategic plans for designing your store and your marketing. Review your competitors' strengths and decide how you can avoid direct competition in those areas. Analyze your competitors' weaknesses and design your store and marketing to capitalize on selling against these weaknesses. That's how you will draw customers away from your competition.

Make a list of all the opportunities you identified and develop plans for taking advantage of these opportunities to grow your business. Also, list any threats you identify and develop strategic plans for how you will deal with these threats.

Taking the time to investigate your competitors—their strengths and their weaknesses—will help develop a much more valuable strategic plan. You'll be ready to hit the competition head-on from the day you open your store.

The Least You Need to Know

- You must get to know your competition. Take the time to visit any store you consider a direct or indirect competitor.
- Pick your top-three competitors and prepare a worksheet comparing their strengths and weaknesses.
- Develop a SWOT analysis to help you formulate your store's design and marketing plans.

Chapter 5

Know Thy Industry

In This Chapter

- Think legally
- Buying groups
- Retail associations

After you've selected the industry in which you want to open your store, take the time to learn more about it and the laws that regulate it. Get to know what the analysts are saying about future trends for that specific industry.

Join groups and entities that support your industry, as well as your business. Education, better negotiating power with vendors, networking, and marketing opportunities are just a few of the many benefits you can get by learning about these entities and joining them.

In this chapter, I help you learn how to research your industry and find the groups that can help you improve your business skills, as well as build effective networks.

Laws and Regulations

Numerous laws regulate the way retailers can do business and sell to their customers. Most laws you'll have to worry about are state based, so you'll need to contact your local clerk's office or local enforcement agency for details. For example, if you sell wines and spirits, you need to know what you can and cannot do and protect your business against liabilities that can put you out of business.

If you plan to hire people, another key body of laws that you'll need to worry about are labor laws. These impact the amount of wages you must pay, when you must pay overtime, health and safe standards, rules on benefits you offer your employees, and so on.

Selling Points

A good online source for searching these laws and regulations is the U.S. Department of Labor website's Employment law guide at www.dol.gov/compliance/guide/index.htm.

Sales of tobacco products are heavily regulated in many states. If you do plan to sell tobacco products, be sure to research the laws for your state. To give you an example of one state's rules, take a look at what retailers must do in the state of California (www.rivcoph.org/healthed/law_explain.pdf).

As you can see from the example, you have a lot of research to do about laws and regulations that might impact the way you do business. Two good places to start are your local chamber of commerce and the *National Retail Federation* (www.nrf.com).

def•i•ni•tion

The **National Retail Federation,** the world's largest retail trade association, represents members from all retail formats—department, specialty, discount, catalog, Internet, and independent stores, as well as chain restaurants, drug stores, and grocery stores. The Federation conducts industry research, develops education and workforce development programs, and promotes retailing as a career choice.

Future Directions

In addition to getting to know the laws and regulations that impact your business, you need to know more about the industry you chose and its future trends. While you may be bombarded with news every day, does that news focus on items crucial to the running of your business? Probably not!

You need to develop a list of sources that can help you gather information specific to your store's industry. Here are some tasks that can help you get started in developing the information base you need:

- Research trade publications for the industry in which you plan to work and subscribe to those publications. For example, if you plan to open a golf store, the Association of Golf Merchandisers (www.agmgolf.org) provides extensive information on its website, as well as industry reports you can purchase. Also, if you are a member of the National Retail Federation, you receive e-mail updates and its *Stores* magazine regularly, which are incredible sources of information on trends in retail and consumer behavior.
- Join local networking groups to learn more about local business trends. I talk more about this later in this chapter.
- Buy your local business weekly newspaper or magazine, if one is published in your community. One good internet source for researching news through local business weeklies is BizJournals (www.bizjournals.com).
- Talk to customers and vendors and listen to their responses. Find out their concerns about your store, as well as similar vendors, and think about how you can respond to their needs or complaints. You'll probably get lots of good business ideas for new items you could sell in your store or for new ways you can provide customer service to beat out your competition.
- Attend regional and national conferences sponsored by the trade associations you join. If you find the speaker particularly helpful, talk with him after the speech to thank him for the ideas. Also get contact information so you can call or e-mail the speaker at a later time. Be sure to share information about your area that you think might be relevant to his area of interest. You could build a longtime source for your network. Whenever I speak at a conference, I always have retailers approaching me after the speech, and I have kept in touch with many of them and provided them with feedback on problems and opportunities that they have.
- Check out your local library, as well as the library at a nearby college or university. Find out what resources are available for you to research your industry and its trends.
- Don't hesitate to hire a consultant when you realize that you need help to understand a crucial issue or implement a specific plan. You can never know everything and sometimes a specialist can help you get it done faster and better.

Buying Groups

One of the best types of groups you can join is a buying group. Retailers organize as a group to buy from manufacturers. Why is this an advantage? By banding together, retailers can order in larger volume and take advantage of volume discounts.

In addition to benefiting financially, many buying groups …

- Share information, problems, and solutions regarding sales, expenses, profit, and losses.
- Trade overstocked merchandise, which frees up funds for purchasing needed merchandise.
- Meet periodically (usually quarterly) and bring in speakers of interest to the group.
- Arrange special rates for the group with retail consultants.
- Develop marketing campaigns that can be used by any member of the group. Each retailer uses its own logo when using the advertisements, brochures, or mailers.
- Assist customers by finding them an item that is out of stock in your store, but available at a store owned by a member of the buying group.

Selling Points

To form a successful buying group, you must set ground rules about what topics can be discussed. All members of the group must be willing to discuss those topics. Your group should include only business owners. If the group includes both owners and buyers, the owners likely will be reluctant to share key financial information or problems if nonowners are present.

Businesses who sell the same types of merchandise but not in the same market area can get extensive benefits by joining a buying group. You shouldn't form a buying group with one of your key competitors because you won't want to reveal key financial data, which takes away some of the advantages of being in a buying group. Usually these groups have between 8 and 30 members—less than 8 cannot generate enough volume to get significant discounts and more than 30 tends to be unwieldy and less effective. Usually groups meet quarterly and stay in contact by e-mail in between meetings.

You can find a buying group or start one yourself in several different ways, including:

- Talk with your vendors and suppliers and ask if they can put you in contact with other accounts not in your area.
- Attend a trade show and ask suppliers to introduce you to retailers from other parts of the country.
- While at a trade show, talk with other attendees who are not in your area but sell the same products in other areas to find potential members or possibly a group already in existence.

Sometimes you may see an ad in a trade journal for a buying group, but that is rare. Most of these groups add members through referrals from other members or manufacturers.

Associations

As a retailer, you spend most of your day working with customers, vendors, suppliers, and employees and have little contact with other business owners. Memberships in trade associations give you an opportunity to meet periodically with other business owners and share information or bounce off ideas for improving their sales or operations. You will also find opportunities for training and education that target your specific industry.

When it comes to retailing, the granddaddy of all trade associations is the National Retail Federation (www.nrf.com) as we mentioned earlier. The association represents more than 1.6 million U.S. retail establishments with more than $4.7 trillion in 2006. It also represents more than 24 million employees—about one in five American workers.

The research and education arm of the NRF is the NRF Foundation, which conducts industry research, develops education and workforce development programs, and promotes retailing as a career. Its research provides industry and government leaders with analysis about public policy decisions and their impact on consumers, retailers, and the economy. The Foundation operates NRF University *wired* to encourage professional development and excellence in retailing. Courses are available online for retail associates, executives, and business owners.

Another key association leader is the National Restaurant Association (www.restaurant.org) for retailers in the restaurant business. The association represents over 300,000 restaurants and provides education and research of value to its members.

Each industry has at least one trade association, so seek out an association for your industry. As an association member you will find …

- Workshops and certification programs that can help you and your employees develop professional skills.
- Networks of business owners who operate similar businesses in other areas of the country. Through networks you can share information and get ideas for ways to build your business or solve a problem you've been having with your store.
- Marketing ideas that were used in another area of the country that you can adapt for your market.
- Representation in Washington, D.C., or in your state legislature, for issues that impact your store.

While being a business owner can sometimes leave you feeling isolated, you can break out of that isolation by joining trade associations and buying groups. You can develop networks, get additional training, and find specialized consultants that can help take your business to the next level.

The Least You Need to Know

- You must follow laws and regulations or your business can be closed down. Get to know the laws and regulations that directly impact your business.
- You can save money and exchange ideas by joining or forming a buying group.
- Trade associations offer you opportunities for education and training, as well as access to key research and government representation. Seek out and join trade associations related to your retail business.

Part 3

What You Can Imagine, You Can Achieve

How do you come up with an idea (concept) for a new store? Look at what's missing or what's there but not done well. This could be a product, a service, a consumer segment, or an experience that is not being met or fulfilled in your area today.

Once you've pinpointed your unique concept, you have to decide how you are going to differentiate yourself from the competition. Then you must translate your concept into a concrete plan with clear steps for how you are going to execute your idea. In this part, I help you sort out your concept and give you the basics for building a plan.

"No—we create the market. One dove wearing a bathing suit in Cosmopolitan Bird *and then everyone will want one."*

Chapter 6

Define Your Vision and Determine Your Strategy

In This Chapter

- Concepts that worked
- Identifying your niche
- Realizing your vision
- Developing your strategies

Your idea for your retail store may be based on your passion or your expertise, or you may just think it's a good concept. However, you must define the vision for your store and determine the strategies you will use to build your business. Your vision and resulting strategy will be the foundation and the glue that holds your business together.

In this chapter, I introduce three successful retailers who built their retail businesses based on their passion or expertise. They found their niches and built successful businesses based on those niches. After taking a brief look at what they did, I will take you through the steps of articulating your vision and determining your strategy.

How Some of the Most Creative Store Concepts Came to Life

Every successful store starts with a person's, couple's, family's, or group of friends' idea about what they think people want but don't currently get in the existing retail environment. Three very successful retail businesses—Healthy Back, Build-A-Bear, and Crate & Barrel—all started with one small store in one community built around the visions of their founders. Let's take a look at how each started.

Healthy Back

Anthony Mazlish founded Healthy Back in March of 1994 because he wasn't able to find the products for relief from his own back problems. He became frustrated with the lack of options available. None of the existing products being offered helped to relieve his pain. He realized that the world needed a store that specializes in the sale of a variety of ergonomically designed products that help to relieve back and neck pain, and improve daily comfort.

The first Healthy Back store opened in Rockville, Maryland, in 1994 and exceeded all expectations. The first store's success was so good that the company opened additional stores in the Washington, D.C., metropolitan area. The first prototype store for national expansion opened in Raleigh, NC in 1996. Healthy Back then acquired a back retailer based in San Diego in 1998 to continue its expansion. Today the company runs 17 stores, an online shopping store at www.healthyback.com, as well as a mail-order catalog.

Anthony Mazlish identified his niche while trying to solve his own problem—a problem that became his passion and helped him develop a successful retail business.

Build-A-Bear Workshop

Maxine Clark started Build-A-Bear after a 25-year career with May Department Stores. Her passion for retailing started when she was a girl growing up in Miami. When designing Build-A-Bear, she wanted to create a magical entertainment place for children with a carnival atmosphere. She started Build-A-Bear with $750,000 in personal savings and opened her first store in St. Louis, Missouri, in October 1997.

Maxine wanted to build an interactive entertainment retail experience. Each store is built around the teddy bear theme with original teddy bear fixtures and artwork. As children build their own bear (or other stuffed animals, such as frogs, bunnies, cows, dogs, cats, and ponies), store associates (known as Master Bear Builders) help the children (known as guests) throughout the bear-building process. Today the company operates over 190 Stores in the United States and Canada with revenue over $300 million. It is listed on the New York Stock Exchange as BBW.

Maxine Clark used the expertise she learned working for others for 25 years, as well as her passion for building an interactive entertainment environment for children, to create a successful retail experience. But remember it all started with a lifelong vision and one store in St. Louis in 1997.

> **Savvy Retailer**
>
> You can learn more about how Maxine Clark built her successful Build-A-Bear Workshop business by reading her book, *The Bear Necessities of Business: Building a Company with Heart* by Maxine Clark and Amy Joyner published by Wiley in 2006.

Crate & Barrel

Crate & Barrel was started by Gordon and Carole Segal in 1962 when they returned from their European honeymoon. While in Europe they bought all kinds of unique, functional, and affordable items for their home. When they got back to Chicago, they realized that no one was selling the great designs they found at reasonable prices in Europe. So the idea of Crate & Barrel was born.

Their first store was opened in an abandoned elevator factory because they couldn't afford to lease anything else. The walls were old brick and they had no budget for drywall, so they nailed up crate lumber to cover them. They stacked shipping crates and filled barrels as display fixtures. Their lack of funds ended up creating the well-known retail environment that you find in their stores today. This environment created by financial necessity helped them to come up with a unique name for their stores, "Crate & Barrel."

Their first store opened in December 1962 with one employee and the Segals operating the store. The store showcased affordable gourmet cookware and contemporary housewares that could not be found elsewhere in the United States. According to the history on Crate & Barrel's website, the Segals were so excited about their new venture they forgot to buy a critical item—a cash register. So they used a box with a lid. Today Crate & Barrel operates 150 stores nationwide.

The Segals had little experience operating a retail business and started their store based on a product line that they knew was unique, but thought others would want.

They developed a retail environment that you can still find in their stores today that was built on necessity—they just didn't have the money to do anything else.

Identify Your Passion or Your Expertise

So what is your passion? Do you believe your expertise is something around which you can build a successful store?

There is no way that I, or anyone else, can create a vision for your store. Your vision must come from you. You have almost total freedom to create your business as long as it is based on a service or product that the public needs.

What I can do is help you to clarify your vision and create the type of retail business you want to build. The best way to get started is to pretend that you are your store's first customer on opening day. You are standing outside the new store that you have never seen before. Within a matter of seconds you will decide whether or not to enter that store.

Through the eyes of this customer, what do you see that makes you want to open the door and enter the store? What does the store look like? What do you see when you first enter the store? Take the time to develop your answers to these questions as you try to fine-tune your vision.

Picturing your business in your mind is a crucial process in which you literally close your eyes and spend hours seeing, hearing, touching, tasting, and smelling the business you are about to create.

Discover Your Secret Weapon

You also must find your secret weapon. That will be the hook that gets customers to come to your store rather than your competitors'. You should choose your secret weapon based on the needs of your customers.

Selling Points

Remember this important lesson from Marketing 101: customers do not need to buy drills to have them, they buy them so that they can make holes. You should not think about why customers want to buy a particular product, but you must think instead about how that product solves a particular need that the customer has.

For example, if you decide that your vision is to run an eyewear store, your secret weapon might be the fact that you are an artisan who can custom-design eyewear. Instead of just talking about "glasses," you would talk to customers about "unique, hand-crafted frames that complement [their] unique personality."

This statement appeals to both the apparent need, which is glasses, and to a deeper need, which is individuality—something that the store's secret weapon can deliver effectively. Then you must ask whether there are enough customers who need both the glasses and individuality for this eyewear store to be successful. More to the point, the big question is: are there enough customers who need both your product and the deeper need that your secret weapon can deliver? In Chapter 3, I discuss how to evaluate your idea and customer base.

Can you identify the secret weapons for the three successful retailers just discussed? For Healthy Back the secret weapon was finding ergonomically designed products for the neck and back and selling an assortment of these products all in one place. For Build-A-Bear Workshop it was designing a unique interactive shopping experience for children of all ages. For Crate & Barrel it was offering European-style gourmet cookware and other obscure household items at an affordable price in a themed retail shopping experience.

As you develop your vision, visit successful retail stores around you and try to identify their secret weapons. As you begin to identify other secret weapons, you will find it easier to develop your own secret weapon and find your own niche. In Chapter 4, I discuss how you get to know your competition.

Articulate Your Vision

You need to think carefully about four critical questions as you try to articulate the vision for your store. Your ultimate success or failure could literally depend on you finding good answers.

- Why should a customer shop in your store?
- What is the role of price competitiveness in your store?
- What is the range of merchandise assortments in your store?
- What is the level of service in your store?

Use this worksheet to help you develop a clear vision for your store:

Developing a Clear Vision Worksheet

Exterior and exterior sign: ______________________

____

Window displays: ______________________________

New experience or "same old": _____________________

____

General atmosphere: ____________________________

Overall visual appeal: ___________________________

General organization: ___________________________

____

Color and texture: ______________________________

Mood set by lighting: ___________________________

____

Everything visible from the front door: _____________

Spotlights highlight merchandise: __________________

____

Front-and-forward displays: ______________________

____

Displays with props, related merchandise: ___________

____

Brand names evident: ___________________________

____

Merchandise in departments: ______________________________

____

Presentation tells a story: ______________________________

____

Printed product information: ______________________________

____

Price tickets and signs: ______________________________

____

Consistency of interior signs: ______________________________

____

Sign holders: ______________________________

____

Number of sales associates: ______________________________

____

Staff appearance and identification: ______________________________

____

Level of in-store service: ______________________________

____

Level of product knowledge: ______________________________

____

Type of shopping experience: ______________________________

____

Price range: ______________________________

____

Price competitiveness: ______________________________

____

Value: ____

____

Merchandise quality: ____

____

Special sales: ____

____

Speed of checkout: ____

____

Payment methods: ____

____

Delivery service: ____

____

Returns policy: ____

____

Type of music: ____

____

Neat and clean: ____

____

Other: ____

____

As you try to complete this worksheet, you may find that you are not able to fill in all these details. Come back to the worksheet after you've finished learning more details about running your store in Parts 4 and 5. You can then refine and expand your vision in Appendix C, which also has a copy of this worksheet.

Build Your Strategies

After you've articulated your vision, you will need to make some fundamental strategy decisions about where your retail business fits in the broad spectrum of retail alternatives that are available in your area. One key part of this decision-making process is your strategy for adding value to the products that manufacturers create.

To be successful, every retail business needs to add value to the products it sells by adopting one of three basic strategies:

- Offering the greatest or newest assortment of products
- Offering the lowest prices
- Offering the best or fastest service

Although these strategies add value, each one meets the needs of different customers. The challenge you face in retail is to be at least competitive in all three areas and to clearly exceed your customers' expectations in one of them. In the following chart, I summarize the impact of these three strategies.

The greatest-assortment strategy involves "dominating" a product such as toys, office supplies, or furniture. To adopt the greatest-assortment strategy, a retailer must be among the largest in the country—able to purchase huge quantities and introduce efficiencies that the vast majority of retailers can only dream about. Another component of this strategy is to have the best "edited" assortment, one that your customers find perfect for them.

The lowest-price strategy involves economies of scale (buying cheap by ordering large quantities) and driving every possible cost out of the business. To adopt the lowest-price strategy, a retailer also must be among the largest in the country—able to purchase huge quantities and introduce efficiencies that the vast majority of retailers can only dream about.

In today's retail world, the big-box retailers "own" these first two strategies. You would need a megastore of 100,000 square feet and millions of dollars in inventory just to play in their league. That is why they are sometimes called "Category Killers," because they can kill a category for other retailers whether it is toys, electronics, or clothing.

With assortment and price taken, the only option left for you is the best-service strategy. Although this strategy comes to you by default, it can be very successful and profitable. Indeed, we believe that this is the future of owner-operated retail in North America—if you are prepared to "walk the walk" and make service the heart and soul of your business. The service strategy also can be found in convenience stores. Here the strategy is providing a service that is both fast and convenient.

Strategies to Add Value

	EXCEEDS CUSTOMERS' EXPECTATIONS BY PROVIDING THE ADDED VALUE OF:	DEVOTED TO:	CHARACTERISTICS:	CUSTOMERS SAY:
GREATEST/ NEWEST ASSORTMENT	Exceptional range or breadth and novelty of product assortments Unique selection of products in relation to a specific lifestyle	Product differentiation	Creative selections Special assortments Leading-edge products	"Their assortment is awesome. If they don't have it, no other store will."
LOWEST PRICE	Price savings and an efficient shopping experience	Operational efficiency Elimination of operational waste and costs	Best price No-hassle shopping No mistakes	"You just can't beat their prices. They are the absolute lowest, every day."
BEST/FASTEST SERVICE	Customer intimacy based on personalized relationships and individual responsiveness that saves customers shopping time and anxiety Specialized products to meet the needs of individual customers	Anticipating and solving customers' problems Taking responsibility for results Focusing on only those customers who place a premium on this type of service	Customized Responsive Personal relationships Speedy	"After we bought it, the sales associate called to see if it was working to our satisfaction." "They are always available to me."

You may find it easy to answer the question, "Why should a customer shop in my store?" with great-sounding words but, as anyone who has ever tried to deliver good service knows, the "talk" is much easier than the "walk." To start, you need to structure your business so that everything you do—and every strategy, merchandising, buying, personnel, sales management, technology, and customer service decision you make—is focused clearly on service.

We are not suggesting that you can ignore assortment and price as you start to develop a "strategic framework" for your business. To the contrary, you cannot have great service if you do not have what your customers want. You also won't have many customers if you have what your customers want but your prices are 30 percent higher than the prices at your competition.

You need to think carefully about your range of merchandise assortments. As the buyer for your business, you could, in theory, buy anything that you wanted to buy. In practice, however, you need to act as a selector of merchandise for your customers—and to understand who those customers are.

Once you do, the merchandise assortment you need to carry in your store will become clear. It will have a focus—that comes from your knowledge of your customers' *needs* and *wants*.

def•i•ni•tion

Needs relate to the basic necessities of life—food, clothing, shelter, and so on. You must have these products to live.

Wants relate to the items that a customer desires but does not absolutely need to live. Often, as retailers, unless you are selling the basic necessities of life, you are selling to customers wants, which are driven by emotion.

You also need to think carefully about your pricing policies. You can't ignore the fact that customers know and understand the retail marketplace. The people that shop in your store will also shop on the Internet, go to the best retailers in cities they visit, see your competitors' advertisements, and generally have a good sense of what items should cost. This is especially true if the item has a relatively high purchase frequency. If somone only buys something once every few months or years, he is not as familiar with the price as he would be for a gallon of milk.

Most of all, you need to think carefully about your level of service. Eventually, you will find yourself having to decide how many people to schedule for what could be a slow day. Will you decide based on the cost of staffing your store that day or on the level of service you have promised your customers you will deliver? In other words, how much of your business will be "talk" and how much of it will be "walk"?

Savvy Retailer

In my consulting work, I often meet owner-operated retailers who are trying to follow a strategy of being good at everything, but this approach does not work well today. Too many smart, aggressive retailers are offering customers shopping alternatives that are distinctly superior on one important aspect of their business—assortment, price, or service—while being at least competitive on the other two. You must pick one of three to excel in, but don't forget the other two. A good example of a highly focused assortment retail strategy can be found at Design Within Reach (DWR), a retail and online furniture company selling classic furniture and accessories. The company focus is very clear: select and offer an assortment of furniture and accessory classics all under one roof. Today, you can find those pieces online, as there are dedicated online retailers selling bits and pieces of that assortment, but DWR is the only bricks-and-clicks retailer carrying such a large assortment of classic furniture.

When you adopt a specific marketing and operational strategy, you give your store a competitive advantage that adds value to the products you sell and differentiates your store from the competition in a distinctly superior way.

This ability to focus resources in a single strategic direction is the reason why some stores succeed while others fail. The successful stores know where they are going and how to get there. The others lack a viable strategic plan to achieve their goals and wind up being average at everything—which does not differentiate them in customers' minds or meet customers' needs and wants.

There are two rug stores across the street from each other where I live. They both carry very similar oriental rugs, most of them priced at $4,000 and higher. Their retail strategy is the same: discount their product all year round. Signs are in their windows saying "70% off" or "Blowout Sale" every day of the year. The questions become, "Why should a customer choose one store over the other, when they both try to appeal to him or her in the same way?" and "What's unique about their offering?" Also, they carry high-quality items, yet they are always on sale. Is the quality of their products not that good, hence the big discounts? Are the original prices not real to begin with? Are the sale prices really regular prices in disguise? Mind you, that's a very common strategy amongst oriental rug stores, but then what makes these stores stand apart from each other? Nothing but the color of their sale signs. Around the corner and down five blocks from my home is an incredibly successful rug store that promises the highest quality and design services. This store's rugs are seldom on sale, and the store has a loyal customer base.

Here is a good but incomplete strategic framework for an owner-operated retail business. It's incomplete because it does not describe the store's secret weapon, but that's the part only you can add after you've figured it out.

> My store will be competitive in price with other stores in the market, but I will not meet discount-store prices. I will shop my competitors regularly and make sure that I am never more than 20 percent higher than the lowest price in the market.
>
> I will carry assortments that are important to my customers and never be out of stock on basic items, but I will not dominate any merchandise classification.
>
> I will earn my margins and truly amaze my customers by providing the best "extra mile" service they can find. This will include detailed product knowledge, a pleasant atmosphere, after-sale service, free delivery, and a make-it-right returns policy.

Your strategy for service, price, and assortment may be slightly different than the previous one, but be sure to think about how you will deal with all three types of strategies in your framework. When you add your secret weapon to this basic strategic framework, you'll have a good strategy upon which to build your business. In Chapter 7, I talk about how you develop your vision and strategy into a solid business plan.

The Least You Need to Know

- Every successful retail business starts with a person's, couple's, or group of friends' vision and builds from there.
- Discover your secret weapon—the unique product, service, or concept that will drive customers to buy from you rather than your competitors.
- Articulate your vision in detail so you will be able to build a successful business.
- Develop your strategy based on customer service, but don't forget the other key basics—price and assortment.

Chapter 7

Develop a Solid Business Plan

In This Chapter

- Knowing the rights
- Writing the plan
- Getting the SCORE

Failing to plan is planning to fail. This is an old adage that is as true in business as it is in every aspect of our lives. A business plan is your roadmap to success. A well-thought-out plan includes where you want to go, how you plan to get there, the obstacles you expect to face, and how you plan to overcome them.

You need a business plan for yourself, the banks, your landlord, and any investors you might approach for money. In this chapter, I explore the key elements that should be part of your business plan and introduce you to the resources available to help you build one.

The Six Rights of Retail

You probably know the basic premise of how retail works. You buy an item at *wholesale* and sell it for more than you paid for it. Sound simple? Well there's more involved. They are what retailers call the "six rights of retail."

def•i•ni•tion

Wholesale is the selling of goods in large quantities to retailers who then sell them directly to customers. The wholesaler is essentially the middle man between the manufacturer and the retailer.

To be successful, you must have: the right item, in the right place, at the right time, in the right quantity, at the right price, with the right service.

Remember these six rights as you build your business, and your business plan and you will be on the road to success.

Developing a Business Plan

You've articulated your vision and your strategy (see Chapter 6), you've evaluated your ideas (see Chapter 3), you've evaluated your competition (see Chapter 4), and you know the industry in which you plan to work (Chapter 5). Now it's time to put all those pieces together into a business plan that will give you a roadmap to building your successful store.

Writing a business plan is not just a fruitless exercise so you have something to show the bank, your landlord, or potential investors. Don't just buy a fill-in-the-blanks business plan off the shelf. Take the time to really own this plan by writing it from scratch so it reflects your vision, your goals, and your dreams for the future.

Most business plans are developed for a five-year period, but you should review your plans at least annually and update them based on your store's actual performance and any changes in the marketplace.

Cover Page and Table of Contents

The first page of your business plan should be a cover page that gives your audience an overview of your business. You should include:

- **The title.** This should start with "Business Plan for …" You don't need to be creative about the title. Your audience doesn't have time for it.
- **Your business name.** The name of your company.
- **Your store's name.** If different than the name under which you plan to legally do business.

- **The names of owners and key employees.** You should include a brief bio that describes your and your employees' backgrounds. Be sure to include information relevant to the type of retail store you plan to operate. For example, one owner may have strong experience operating retail stores in another industry, so talk about his or her retail background. Another owner may have extensive experience in the industry, but no retail experience, so focus on his or her industry background.
- **Your business address.** If you don't yet have a store, use your home address.
- **Your contact information.** You should include your phone numbers (home, cell, and fax), your e-mail address, and your web address, as well as your street address. You definitely should have a web address even if all that is on that address is a one page document about your soon-to-open store.

Your second page should be a table of contents that gives your audience a list of what is included in the document and on what page the item can be found. You need to make it as easy for your readers to use the document as possible. Most bankers or investors have very little time to spend on your business plan, so make it easy for them to jump to the information that is most crucial for them to make a decision.

Executive Summary—You and Your Vision

Your executive summary is where you want to introduce yourself and your vision to your reader in a concise manner. Whether or not your reader will go any further in reading your plan will be determined by how well you present the concept in this brief summary.

I'm sure you are aware that many people make up their mind about you in the first few seconds that they meet you. Well that's true for a business plan as well. A potential investor or lender will decide whether or not they are interested in pursuing a relationship with you based on the minute or two it takes them to read your executive summary.

You need to excite your audience about both you and your vision for the business. Your executive summary should include a brief discussion of these items:

- Explain who you are, what your company is, and what your business concept is.
- Expand on your business ideas and why anyone would want to buy your products from you. Talk about your competitors and what you plan to offer to make customers choose you over your competition.

- Discuss how you plan to market your business and be sure to include the four "p's" of marketing—price, product, place, and promotion. You should also discuss how your store will operate, such as self-service, full-service, discount, or full-price. You also should review your potential customers and how you will attract them to your store.
- Briefly discuss your financial plans. Include information about how much you expect to spend, how much you expect to sell, and how much profit you expect to make.
- Talk about your management plan. Include who will run your business and the manager's qualifications for the job. You also want to briefly discuss how your business will operate day-to-day.

End your executive summary with a few sentences that summarize very briefly what you just said, but be sure to get across why you think your business idea is a great opportunity. This will be your last chance to get the reader to want to read further.

Your Business Idea and Strategy

Hopefully by this point you've got the reader on the hook and she will take the time to read more about your business in detail and how you plan to build that business. In the next section of the report, you'll take the reader through the structure and vision for your business, review your target customer base, discuss your service and price levels, explore the industry in which you'll operate and its trends, and review your competition.

Your Business Structure and Vision

First you should discuss how you will structure your business—as a sole proprietorship, partnership, limited liability company, or corporation. This information is critical for any financial institution or individual investor who may be thinking about funding a portion of your business start-up or ongoing cash needs. In Chapter 9, I talk about the different business structures and help you sort out the possibilities.

You also want to take the reader further into the vision you have for your store. In Chapter 6, you complete a Developing a Clear Vision Worksheet. Pick the information on that worksheet that you think will help you make the case for your store. Explain why your store concept is unique and how it will draw customers.

Your Target Customer

Your next section should talk about your target customer. In Chapter 3, I talk about the type of customers you might decide to target based on key demographics, such as age, ethnicity, and economic status. Describe the demographics for your target customers and how you will design and market your store to meet the needs of these customers. Also discuss how your marketing plan will attract these customers to your store.

Your Service and Price Levels

After discussing your target customers, you must talk about the level of service you plan to give your customers, such as self-service or full-service. Give the reader of your business plan some idea of what the customer experience will be like when he walks into your store.

You also need to discuss how you will price your goods, such as discount pricing or full retail pricing. Be sure your price levels match the service you plan to give. For example, don't state that your customers will serve themselves, if you expect to charge full retail prices. That's not a logical business model. Customers expect a much higher level of service if they pay full retail prices.

Your Industry

Explore the industry in which you plan to operate. Talk about your industry's trends and how you will develop your store to take advantage of these trends. In Chapter 5, I discuss how to research your industry and its trends. Use those resources to develop your industry section and talk about the trends you see developing in your industry and how you plan to use them to beat your competition.

Your Competition

Review the assessment you completed regarding your competition. I give you the tools to do a competitive analysis in Chapter 4. Talk about both your direct competition and your indirect competition in the area.

Give a more detailed assessment of the three direct competitors you identified. Use the information from your SWOT analysis developed in Chapter 4 to give your readers a good overview of your store's strengths, weaknesses, opportunities, and threats.

Discuss how you will use your strengths and overcome your weaknesses to compete head on. Also discuss the opportunities you identified to help make your store successful and beat your competitors.

Penetration Strategy—Making Your Store a Success

After discussing your SWOT analysis, you are ready to discuss how you plan to penetrate the existing marketplace and implement your strategy. In this section of your business plan, you discuss how you plan to position your store against your competitors and how you plan to market it. In Chapter 15, I discuss how to develop and implement a marketing strategy. Use the key points you develop after reading that chapter to write the marketing section of your business plan.

Positioning your store in the minds of your customers is one of the most difficult things you can do. Essentially you want to discuss how you will get your customers to think about your store as the best place to get the type of products you sell. For instance, one of the best examples of product positioning was done by Xerox. How often do you say you will "Xerox" something rather than "copy" it?

Whatever products you sell, you want to position your store so customers think to come to you first. For example, if you are opening a candle shop called Lucy's Candles, you want your customers to think of Lucy's Candles any time they need to buy candles. Discuss what you will do to position your store successfully in the minds of your customers.

The Forecasts—How and When You Are Going to Make Money

All vendors, financial institutions, and investors that read your report will want to know how you plan to make money and how much you plan to make. In fact, don't be surprised if your readers jump to the financial section immediately after reading your executive summary. At least you've got them hooked and now they want to see if your financial planning is feasible and sound.

In Chapter 20, I show you how to develop profit and loss statements and balance sheets. For a start-up business plan, you won't have any existing accounting records from which to develop these key statements, so you'll need to project the numbers based on the sales you expect to generate, the prices you expect to charge, and the costs you expect to incur.

Remember all businesses take time to develop their customer base. You need to realistically sit down and think about (your best guess) how many customers you expect will enter your store in the first month and how quickly you think you can grow that customer base. Your cash flow projections and financial statements should be based on the growth you expect to see in the first five years of operation. Plan it month to month though in the first year or two, because growth will likely vary greatly each month as word-of-mouth spreads for your store.

Try to make this as realistic a projection as you can, because you will be using the business plan to raise capital. You don't want to be too optimistic, which means you will project more cash inflow than you actually receive and you will not seek to raise enough capital and fall short. You may even have to close the store because of lack of funds before you have a chance to grow the business.

You don't want to be too pessimistic with your numbers either. If financial institutions and investors think your store will take too long to be self-sustaining because you were too pessimistic in your projections, you may not be able to raise any capital at all.

After developing your financial statements, calculate the key financial ratios or profitability and liquidity. If your ratios don't look good, you do need to review your financial statements and determine what you can do to make them look better. But don't fabricate the numbers just so you'll look good on paper. You will need to perform close to those numbers to satisfy the financial institutions and your investors or they may cut off your funding down the road.

The Players

Your final section should give your readers a good overview of the people on your team. Include biographies (three to four paragraphs) for each of your key players, such as your partners, the store manager, key sales or technical personnel, marketing director or consultant, and any key advisors. Also, you want to include background and contact information for your lawyer and your accountant.

Resources to Help You Build a Business Plan

If you've never run a business or developed a business plan before, don't try to go it alone. You can get free help from SCORE volunteers (www.score.org). SCORE is America's premier source for free and confidential advice for small business owners. Since it was formed in 1964, SCORE has assisted over 7.5 million small business owners with counseling, training, and advice.

You probably will be able to find a SCORE chapter close to you because there are over 375 SCORE offices nationwide. You'll also find a lot of helpful "how to" articles and business templates on SCORE's website. If no chapter is near you, contact SCORE through its website. Volunteers also help small business owners by e-mail and phone.

SCORE volunteers, who are primarily retired business owners and corporate executives, share their business acumen and lessons they've learned over the years in business. You can get help developing your business plan, improving your marketing plans, managing your cash flow, and many other critical issues you will face as you try to start your business and keep it alive.

Another great resource to help you develop your business plan and then when your store is up and running is www.allexperts.com. I am a member of this service and a volunteer expert and I regularly answer questions and provide advice to retailers on concept development, business planning, and operational issues.

After you've got your business plan in hand, you can start to raise capital for your store. In Chapter 8, I talk about ways to raise money.

The Least You Need to Know

- Remember the six rights of retail as you develop your business plan and your store.
- Write a brief and concise summary of your vision and strategy in the executive summary of your business plan that entices the reader to read further.
- Develop a solid business plan focusing on your vision, your strategy, your marketing plans, and your profitability.
- Don't hesitate to seek help from SCORE and other free sources in both developing your business plan and your business.

Chapter 8

Raising Capital

In This Chapter

- Measuring your cash
- Seeking help from family and friends
- Partnering up
- Getting money from the SBA
- Seeking venture capital

You can have the best idea in the world for a new retail business. But if you don't have enough money to get it started and keep it running until it's profitable, your business will not succeed. Many good retail ideas fail because the owner just didn't have enough cash on hand to get the store going.

In Chapter 7, you learned how to determine how much cash you need by developing a solid business plan. In this chapter, I talk about assessing your own cash position and how to raise the additional cash you need to build your business by asking friends and family members, finding a partner, getting a loan through the Small Business Administration (SBA), or, if you have an idea for expansion, seeking venture capital.

How Much You Have

Once you have your business plan finished and know how much cash you will need to build and grow the store over the next five years, you will need to assess what you have on hand and how you will get the rest. Few people starting a business for the first time have the cash to fully fund that business for five years, and in most cases, it takes at least two to three years for the business to be profitable enough to pay yourself a significant salary.

So you will need to think not only about how you will fund the expenses for opening your new store, but you will also need to think about how you will pay your monthly living expenses, including your mortgage, your food bills, your utility bills, your clothing, health care, and any other basic necessities you need for your family. You should expect that the income from the new store will not be enough to cover all of your personal expenses for at least two to three years.

If you start your business without enough money to fund the store, as well as your personal needs, you will have to make choices that will result in failure. Many new business owners get so caught up in trying to make ends meet and covering just the basic expenses that they don't have enough money to wow their customers and open a store that truly presents the vision they have for the store in their minds.

When you don't have enough capital upfront, you will be unable to take the financial risks that may be necessary to attract customers, respond to their demands or complaints, or even implement suggestions you might get from customers to improve your store. You may have to make choices not to do things that could make more money, because your cash is too tight.

You need to break down your business plan into month-by-month cash needs and match that with month-by-month plans for raising that cash. As you create your idea in your head, start socking away money for your dream store in the bank just as you would for your retirement. Some people decide to take on part-time work while building their store to keep cash flowing. Others will draw funds from their retirement savings, especially if they have a sizeable nest egg built up from working in a traditional job for 20 or 30 years.

Taking money from a retirement fund can be very costly, though. If you do plan to draw money from a retirement account, be ready to pay a lot of money to the tax man. Retirement funds taken out before you are 59½ will be penalized 10 percent in addition to regular income taxes you must pay on the money taken out. Expect to pay about 40 percent or possibly more (depending on your income bracket) of what you draw from your retirement accounts in taxes.

Another common way people raise money is to take a second mortgage on their home. Be very careful choosing that route, because you do put your home at risk if you are not able to make the additional mortgage payments.

For many small business owners, credit cards end up being their primary financing strategy. In fact, according to the National Small Business Association's 2007 Small Business Survey, 44 percent of small business owners financed their capital needs with credit cards and 43 percent used the earnings of their business. Only 29 percent indicated they were able to get bank loans and 22 percent used private loans or other sources. When you look at the financial statements for larger companies, you will see that they can depend on bank loans, but smaller companies often cannot.

Savvy Retailer

According to the 2007 Small Business Survey, 71 percent of the retailers who use credit cards as their source of financing carry a balance month-to-month, and the number of small businesses carrying a balance on credit cards is increasing, from 64 percent in 2000 to 71 percent in 2007. Small businesses also indicated that terms of credit have gotten worse for credit card users over the past five years.

If you do decide to use a credit card for building your business, be sure that you get a separate card just for the business. Any interest you pay on business expenses is tax deductible, so it's best not to mix personal and business expenses on a credit card.

Forty percent of small business owners said in the 2007 Small Business Survey that they were not able to grow their business or expand operations because of lack of access to new capital. Some were not able to increase sales and some had to reduce the number of employees or employee benefits. If capital were available, 77 percent of the respondents said they would take advantage of the new capital by investing in advertising, hiring more employees or improving employee benefits, and buying more equipment.

While you may be very excited about your new store, do think carefully about whether you have enough cash to get started now, or whether you should wait a year or two and save up enough money so you can give your store the jump start it needs.

Loans from Family and Friends

Another possible route for finding funds could be loans from family and friends, but tread carefully. Borrowing from family and friends can result in a loss of relationships you treasure if your business goes belly up and you can't pay them back. If you do decide to seek private loans from family and friends, put it in writing, spell out the terms, and keep to those terms to avoid problems down the road.

Your family or friends likely will be more tolerant if you need to delay a payment than a bank would be, but don't take advantage of this kindness too often. Treat this loan as you would any other business loan.

Seeking Partners or Not

If you have a great idea, but just don't have the funds to get started, you might consider finding a partner. Many small businesses do start up with a general partner, who runs the business day to day, and one or more silent partners (often limited partners) who share in future profits by providing cash upfront.

If you do decide to find a partner, be sure you work with an attorney to draft a partnership agreement. This agreement should spell out the answers to the following:

- How will you divide the profits of your store among the partners?
- How can your partners decide to get out of the business and get back their investments?
- What will happen with each partner's investment if the business does not succeed?
- How can each partner's family member sell their share of the business if a partner dies or becomes ill?
- How will the partnership dissolve if one of the partners decides she wants out?

You should make these decisions upfront before you start the business. They will be much harder to make if the business faces a crisis and you want to end the partnership.

You can have two types of partners in any partnership arrangement—the general partner and the limited partners. The general partner runs the business day to day and will be held personally responsible for all business activities, no matter how much he personally invested in the business. Limited partners are passive owners of the business and are not involved in its day-to-day operations. If a claim is filed against the business, the limited partners can only be held personally liable for the amount of money they actually invested in the business.

Deals with Vendors, Suppliers, and Professionals

As you identify vendors, suppliers, and professionals who you want to work with you in developing your store, you may find that you can negotiate deals to delay payment in exchange for something else down the road. For example, you may be able to work a deal with your supplier to pay them after you've gotten paid with a premium tacked on. You can offer to pay more than negotiated if the supplier will wait until you have the money from sales. This is known as trade credit from suppliers. Note that this type of arrangement with merchandise suppliers is very rare, however, with professionals such as store designers or fixture suppliers it may be possible.

You may be able to work out similar deals with other professionals who help you structure the business. Your accountant or attorney may be willing to wait for payment if you promise them some portion of initial profits. As noted before, make sure that these deals are in writing and both sides understand the terms and timing.

Depending on the leasing environment in your area, you may be able to cut a deal with your landlord as well. If there are a lot of retail vacancies, you are more likely to have success cutting a deal. You may be able to negotiate a lease that permits you to pay less for rent during the start-up phase and pay more once your store is profitable. Some landlords may also help with a contribution to store construction and build out if they really feel that your concept will bring a lot of traffic and be successful.

Better Not!

If you do find you have a cash flow problem, don't just ignore your bills or avoid your vendors and suppliers. Negotiate with them instead. You are more likely to work out a deal with vendors or suppliers when you talk with them about a problem instead of making no payments at all and ignoring their calls. For example, many suppliers will happily take post-dated checks that extend payment beyond normal terms.

Small Business Administration Loans

Once your business is off the ground, you may be able to get a loan from the U.S. Small Business Administration, but be ready for a lot of paperwork. You will need to be able to show the SBA that your business is profitable, so don't even think about applying for an SBA loan in the start-up phase of your business, unless you already run a successful business and the money you need is for a new store or any other form of business expansion.

The application process, which is done with a local bank that is authorized to make loans for the SBA, can be overwhelming. The SBA looks closely at a number of key credit factors before even considering a loan. These include:

- **Equity investment.** You must have a significant amount of money invested in the business, which can include personal funds and borrowed, but there will be a careful examination of your debt-to-equity ratio ("debt" meaning the amount borrowed and "equity" meaning personal investment). The SBA determines whether your level of debt is appropriate in relation to the investment you have in the business, as well as the earnings you expect to make. The stronger you make your case for projected profits, the more likely your loan will be approved.
- **Earnings requirement.** You must be able to show that your cash outflow will not exceed your cash inflow for an extended period of time. How you will manage your cash must be clearly spelled out, and you must be able to show that you will have cash on hand to adequately support your business operation at the right time and in the right amount. In other words, you must be able to show that you will be able to pay your bills as well as your loans.
- **Working capital.** Working capital is the excess of current assets (which can include cash, bank deposits, accounts receivable, and inventory) over current liabilities (any debts you must pay over the next 12 months). You must be in a strong working capital position to qualify for an SBA loan.
- **Collateral.** Collateral can include assets that are useable in the business, as well as personal assets outside the business. For SBA loans, personal guarantees secured by personal assets are required of every owner who gets an SBA loan. How much of a personal guarantee will be required depends on the assets owned by the business and the amount to be borrowed.
- **Resource management.** Your ability to manage is another critical element. When making its final decision about whether or not to give you the loan, the SBA will look at your past managerial experience, your education, and your motivation.

Selling Points

You can find out more about the U.S. Small Business Administration's loan process at www.sba.gov/services/financialassistance/index.html. The SBA has other financial programs for small businesses including disaster assistance and grants.

Venture Capitalists

If you've developed a successful store idea and decide it's time to expand regionally or nationally, you may need a large infusion of cash. Venture capitalists are often the only way to grow your business for this type of risky endeavor.

Venture capital funds are investment groups that pool their money to fund new or growing businesses. In most cases, a venture capital fund will offer you the cash your business needs in exchange for shares of ownership in the business. Often business owners must give up as much as a 40 percent ownership in the business in order to attract venture capital.

In most cases, you seek venture capital when your plans are too risky for banks or capital markets (such as corporate bonds or stocks). You also will get managerial and technical assistance from the venture capital fund managers as you build your business. Venture capitalists usually require you to appoint one or more of their choices to your board of directors. If you do decide to seek venture capital, remember you are entering a type of partnership and not just getting funds. Note that in the past few years, smaller retail endeavors have not been favorites of venture capital firms due to high risk and relatively modest returns.

Now that you've got your money in hand, you're ready to run your store. In the next part of the book, I take you through the key day-to-day functions of running a store.

The Least You Need to Know

- You will need to invest significant personal capital to open a retail business. Be careful about how you raise that capital and what it will mean to your personal life.
- You can borrow from family and friends, but treat this as a business loan and take responsibility for paying the money back.
- You may decide to find a partner who can help fund the new business venture, but be sure to lay out all the partnership details carefully in a written contract.
- The U.S. Small Business Administration does make loans to small businesses, but don't expect to qualify for one when you are in the start-up phase of your retail business.
- You may want to think about venture capital funding if your business is successful and you are ready to expand regionally or nationally, but remember, you will need to give up a significant portion of ownership and control to get the money.

Part 4

Running the Store, or Wearing Many Hats

Running a store means wearing multiple hats: one for every task that needs to be accomplished. Even if you are assisted in these tasks by a lawyer, an accountant, a store designer, and so on, you are still in charge of making the final decision on what's right and best for your store.

This part will help you develop an in-depth knowledge of how to effectively run a store and wear the retailers' many hats, including selecting the right location for your store, designing a store environment and displays that will attract customers and maximize your sales, and selecting the right product for your store at the right price and in the right quantity.

"I'm supposed to open my doors in three weeks, but my shipment from Bali still isn't here and my manager just flew off with one of the new hires!"

Chapter 9

Structuring Your Business and Protecting It

In This Chapter

- Structuring your business
- Knowing the laws
- Insurance decisions

You will need to pick a legal structure for your business and its retail stores. Deciding on a sole proprietorship, for example, instead of a corporation structure or other legal structure will impact your operating costs, tax obligations, and your personal liability. In addition, you need permits, registrations, and a business license. If you don't follow all the rules, your store could be shut down.

In this chapter, I review the pros and cons of each legal structure from a cost, taxation, and liability perspective. I also discuss the key permits, registrations, and licenses you need.

Structuring Your Business

Not all businesses are structured the same way. You have a number of types to choose among—sole proprietorship, partnership, limited liability company, and corporation. Let's take a closer look at each.

Sole Proprietorship

If you're just opening your store and will own a 100 percent interest in the store, a sole proprietorship is the easiest form of business for both tax purposes and record keeping. As a matter of fact, the IRS will assume a sole proprietorship if your business has only one owner unless you've actually incorporated the business under state law. In other words, you don't have to do anything legally or financially to get started as a sole proprietor in the eyes of the federal government.

In fact, the sole proprietorship isn't a separate taxable entity. All your business assets and liabilities belong directly to you—the business owner. You report the business on a Schedule C, "Profit or Loss from Business," or Schedule C-EZ, "Net Profit from Business." Both forms actually become part of your individual tax return. The net profit or loss is reported on the first page of your 1040, and you pay taxes on the income based on your current individual tax rate. You also must pay Social Security and Medicare taxes on your net profit.

Better Not!

The biggest downside of sole proprietorship is that it isn't a separate legal entity and all debts or claims are made against the individual who owns the business. To protect your personal assets, you may want to get business liability insurance.

Partnerships

If you plan to open your store with one or more partners, you can set up your business as a partnership. There are two types of partners—*general partners* and *limited partners.* The IRS considers any business with more than one owner a partnership unless you have incorporated under state law or you elect to be taxed as a corporation by filing IRS Form 8832, "Entity Classification Election." We talk more about corporate tax issues later in this chapter.

Partnerships file their own tax returns using IRS Form 1065, "Partnership Return." These forms are actually information returns that show income, deductions, and other tax-related business information. This return must also include the names and addresses of each partner and each partner's distributive share of taxable income. The return must be signed by a general partner. If the partnership receives no income and doesn't pay or incur any expenses in any particular tax year, Form 1065 does not have to be filed.

def•i•ni•tion

General partners, who actively run the business, are subject to the same personal liability for partnership debts and claims as sole proprietors, even if the act that caused the claim to be filed was carried out by one of the other partners. Be careful who you partner with, especially if you plan to be the general partner with all others being limited partners.

Limited partners don't take an active role in the management of the partnership. Their liability is limited to their investment in the business plus any obligations they may have to make additional investments in the business. For example, a partnership agreement may specify that each partner put a set amount of money into the business each year for the first five years.

In addition to filing the information Form 1065, partnerships must file a Schedule K-1, "Shareholder's Share of Income, Credits, Deductions, etc.," for each partner. This form is used to report the income or loss of each of the partners, which will then be taxed as part of each partner's individual tax return. Like a sole proprietorship, the partnership itself is not a tax entity. Even if the partnership doesn't actually distribute the cash and decides to hold some of the money for future company needs, the individual partners—not the partnership—will still have to pay taxes on the income.

Partnerships are the most flexible form of ownership if more than one person is involved in the business, because income and losses can be distributed as determined by the owners, such as 40 percent to one owner and 60 percent to the second owner. Any split is okay, as long as it is based on a business purpose and not solely for the purpose of tax avoidance. Other business entities, such as corporations, must distribute their income and losses based on the percentage of ownership or investment in the business. We'll talk more about this later when we explore the other types of business entities.

Partnerships offer a major tax advantage for new businesses because you can write off losses. Generally, new businesses have losses rather than net profits due to start-up expenses and the time it takes to build a client or customer base. Partnerships provide a mechanism to write off these losses against other income. There is one catch, though. You can't write off a loss that exceeds your personal investment in the business; however, if you increase your investment in future years, you can then write off the loss.

Partnerships face the same liability issues as sole proprietorships because the managing owners can be fully liable for any debt or claims. The rest of the business structures limit the liability of the owners.

Limited Liability Companies

A partnership or sole proprietorship can be set up as a limited liability company (LLC). This is actually a hybrid somewhere between a corporation and a partnership or sole proprietorship. An LLC is a state entity organized under state laws, so any protections against liabilities depend on the state in which the company is formed. However, generally an LLC is given the same protection from liability given to traditional corporations.

LLCs are treated as partnerships or sole proprietorships (if only one person owns and runs the company) when it comes to filing federal income tax forms, unless a Form 8832 is filed to classify them as corporations. State laws for filing tax forms vary on a state-by-state basis.

While limited liability may sound great because it protects individuals from many business liabilities, when it comes to borrowing money, sole proprietors or partners may still be required to give personal guarantees to get the money, especially if the business is first getting started. Few financial institutions will make loans to new businesses that don't have much in the way of business assets.

Liability limitation may be helpful when it comes to protecting yourself or your partners from claims of malpractice or other related issues. Again, this will depend on your state and how it set up its LLCs.

Corporations—C and S

Your greatest liability protection as a small business owner comes from using the business structure known as a corporation. A corporation is a separate legal entity, and individuals are protected from getting sued for the corporation's actions or facing collections from the corporation's creditors.

Many legal advisors recommend that a sole proprietor or partners incorporate if the business is particularly "risky"—in other words, if it faces a strong possibility of being sued. Corporate structures can also make it easier to raise needed investment capital to grow the business.

There are actually two types of corporations for tax purposes—C and S. The C corporation is the standard kind of corporation that most large businesses are structured as, and it is subject to corporate income tax. A small company just getting started can avoid corporate taxation by filing with the IRS as an S corporation. Whether you file as a C corporation or seek the special IRS designation as an S corporation, it is still the same legal entity.

All corporations have a board of directors (even if it's just you alone, or you, your wife, and your children) and shares of stock that represent ownership. Most small businesses have privately held stock that is not traded on any public exchange.

To qualify as an S corporation, you must meet all of the following conditions:

- Your corporation must be organized under the laws of the United States or one of its states or territories that is taxed as a corporation under local law.
- All shareholders must agree to the S corporation election.
- Your corporation may have only one class of stock. C corporations may have *common* and *preferred stock* for example.

def•i•ni•tion

Common stock is a portion of ownership in a corporation that includes the right to vote on key corporation issues and entitles the owner to share in the company's success, usually through dividends or increase in stock value.

Preferred stock usually has a specific dividend that must be paid prior to the dividends paid to common stock holders. This type of stock usually has no voting rights. If the company fails, these shareholders will get their share of the assets before common stock holders.

- Your corporation may not have more than 75 shareholders (corporations formed before 1997 were limited to 35 shareholders). So S corporations are only for small business entities.
- Shareholders may not include a nonresident alien or a nonhuman entity, such as another corporation or partnership. There are some exceptions to this. A shareholder can be a trust or estate authorized as an S corporation under tax laws. Also, certain tax-exempt organizations, such as qualified pension plans, profit-sharing plans, or stock bonus plans, can be shareholders.

The S corporation is treated similarly to partnerships for tax purposes. Profits and losses are passed through to the owners and taxed at their individual income tax rates. The key difference when it comes to taxes is that the profits and losses of an S corporation must be allocated based on actual stock ownership.

Better Not!

The biggest disadvantage for a C corporation is that income is taxed twice, once at the corporate level and again at the individual level for any distributions to the corporation's stockholders. In other words, if you are a small business owner, you could end up paying taxes twice on the same money.

Remember, partnerships have more flexibility because their distributions can be done by any formula the business owners decide makes business sense. For example, if one partner has a lot of cash to put up front while the other partner is primarily offering his or her unique knowledge, a partnership could more easily adjust for this difference. S corporations can pay out salaries to owners as a business deduction. Partnerships cannot pay salaries to owners. Any payouts to owners are a distribution of profits.

Business write-offs and salaries may offset the negative of double taxation, though. Corporations are taxed as a separate tax entity and the shareholders are taxed on dividends or other distributions from the business. Business owners are allowed to pay themselves a reasonable salary (reasonable based on industry standards within the industry that the company operates) and avoid the corporate tax level on the money paid as salary.

I'm not going to delve deeply into C corporations because their tax rules are complicated and go beyond the scope of this book. If you're thinking of establishing your business as a C corporation, you definitely should seek good legal and financial advice—don't try to go it alone!

Just so that you have an idea of corporate tax rates, here's a table that shows the current rates:

2007 C Corporation Tax Rates

Taxable Income Over	But Not Over	Tax Rate
$0	$50,000	15%
$50,000	$75,000	25%
$75,000	$100,000	34%
$100,000	$335,000	39%
$335,000	$10,000,000	34%
$10,000,000	$15,000,000	35%
$15,000,000	$18,333,333	38%
$18,333,333	-	35%

Making Your Choice

Now that you know the choices for structuring your business, let's look at what might make sense for you. Of course, every situation is unique, and I strongly suggest that you seek guidance from legal and financial advisors to figure out what is best for your company.

Most small business structures are taxed at your individual tax rates, even S corporations, but they offer different levels of liability protection. The key difference as you move from sole proprietor to partnership or corporation is how earnings and distributions are treated for tax purposes. Also, when you get to the highest level, a traditional C corporation, you must pay both corporate and individual taxes on dividends paid to shareholders.

Basically, if you're a sole proprietor and want to keep things as simple as possible, there are very few tax advantages to organizing as anything other than a sole proprietor. Your lawyer may see some reasons to incorporate from a legal perspective if you would be subject to frequent lawsuits. If that's the case, a limited liability company might be the best solution for you, but be sure you consider your state laws and state tax provisions for LLCs before going that route.

A sole proprietor may consider establishing an S corporation as a way to limit liability, but taxes will never be simple to file again; be certain that you understand the liability advantages before taking that step. Although you may be able to pay yourself a salary and avoid employment taxes on your share of corporate income above a reasonable wage, you need to be certain that the tax savings are worth the additional legal, tax, and other financial expenses of maintaining corporate status. Perhaps business liability insurance, discussed later, would be more cost-effective and offer the protection you need.

If you have partners, setting up as a limited liability partnership (LLP) probably makes the most sense. It provides the maximum amount of flexibility, allows a single level of taxation, and gives you liability protection as well. Organizing as a corporation is a good choice if you plan to produce or manufacture a product and want to build the company into a major nationwide or

Selling Points

The government runs two excellent websites for small business owners. One is the main site for the Small Business Administration (www.sba.gov), and the second is a website for women business owners (www.sbaonline.sba.gov/womeninbusiness). Both websites offer a wealth of information about starting up and running a small business.

worldwide business. You don't have to make the decision right away. You can wait a year or two or elect S corporation status initially before taking the plunge into the more complicated tax structure that requires you to pay taxes twice.

Don't try to make the decision about business structure on your own. You definitely should seek advice from an attorney or tax advisor before making major business decisions, and take it slow.

Laws and Regulations

Anyplace you want to set up your retail business, you'll find there are registrations, licenses, and permits you must have before you can open for business. In all cases, these involve the desire of local, state, or federal government entities to put in place protections for the public from unqualified or unscrupulous businesses.

- Registrations involve filling out government paperwork so the public knows who owns the business and what type of business it is. How you register your business will depend upon the type of business you open. The registration process for a corporation is much more difficult than that for a sole proprietorship.
- Licenses involve proving that you have the professional credentials to operate your business. For example, a hairdresser must get a license to open a shop and cut hair.
- Permits specify what type of business can operate in a location, as well as the regulation of the buildings a business operates to be certain the business is operating safely.

Business Licenses

Once you know the type of business you plan to operate and where you want it to operate, you should contact your town, city, or county clerk and apply for a general business license. You will need to supply:

- Structure and type of ownership of your business.
- Federal Tax Identification Number (if you don't have one, you can call the IRS at 1-800-829-4933 to apply for one).
- Business name (DBA—doing business as) or the name the public will see, if different from what you registered your company as.

- Mailing address where you want any licenses, reports, tax returns, and other governmental correspondence to be sent.
- Location of business operations and location of business records. You may have two locations—one for the store and one for where you will keep your business records (in many cases for a small business, this could be your home office).
- List of all owners, partners, and managers.
- Nature of your business, which is a description of your business activities, products to be sold, and services to be offered.

You need to post your business license in a visible place in your store. You may need other specialized licenses as well as a general business license, depending upon the type of store you plan to open. For example, if you plan to serve liquor, you must also get a liquor license.

Permits

Some types of business must also get a permit to operate their store in the location selected or to put up a sign. You also will likely need police and/or fire department permits and building permits. Here are some key permits you likely will need:

- **Zoning permits.** All local governments have zoning laws that specify how a particular property can be used. If you are opening your store in an established shopping center, you won't have to worry about getting a zoning permit. But, if you want to set up your store in a location not normally used for business, you need to get a zoning permit. You also may find that the type of business you plan to operate cannot be opened in certain locations. For example, suppose you want to open a convenience store that sells alcoholic products. The zoning ordinance in your town may restrict how close that type of store can be to a church, synagogue, or school.
- **Sign permit.** Before ordering your signs for you store, check to find out if any special permits are needed for signage. Many towns regulate size, color, type of material or lighting that can be used, and how the sign must be hung. You may also find that certain information is mandatory on the sign, such as your store's street address. Often neon signs are banned completely. Check with your town, city, or county clerk's office or building department to find out what type of sign regulations are in place and whether or not a permit is needed for the sign you plan to use.

- **Police and/or fire department permits.** In most cases, these types of permits involve regulations regarding alarm systems, such as fire alarms and sprinkler systems. If you do put in a security system that automatically alerts the police department, you may get charged after a certain number of false alarms. Check with your local police and fire departments to find out what regulations are in place regarding fire and security systems and whether or not a permit is needed.
- **Building permit.** Any time you plan to do construction on your store, you need a building permit. This includes remodeling and renovations. You need to get your plans approved by the building department before you start work and the building department will send out inspectors to check on the work during construction. In most situations, the contractor you hire will apply for the building permits. When the work is completed, your contractor must also get the building department to sign off on the work of each trade, such as plumbers and electricians. When the building department has signed off on the work, it will then issue a Certificate of Occupancy (CO). You must have a CO to furnish and open your store.

Better Not!

You may be tempted to save money and hire a contractor who says he can do the work cheaper if he doesn't go through the hassle of getting a building permit. Don't do it. Not only would this be illegal, but it can result in your store being closed when the local government entity finds out, and you also may be hiring a nonlicensed contractor whose work is not up to par.

Insure Your Business

You'll spend a lot of hours building your business and can lose it all in a matter of minutes if disaster strikes. You can protect your assets by being certain that you carry the right types of business insurance. Business insurance falls into three categories: business liability, business property and casualty, and worker's compensation (if you have employees). All your expenses for insurance are fully deductible as a business expense.

Business Liability

You certainly wouldn't go without liability insurance for your house in case someone got injured on your property, and definitely not for your car in case of accident. So why wouldn't you think of getting liability insurance for your store?

I briefly review the various types of liability insurance available, but your best bet is to sit down with an insurance advisor whom you trust and determine what makes sense given your business plans and its liability risks.

First, there is general liability insurance. This covers a business against accidents or injury that might happen on its premises. If you will be providing professional services as part of your store operations, then you should consider professional liability insurance, which protects you against claims arising from your business activities, including errors or omissions when providing professional services.

Selling Points

If your company has a board of directors, you may want to consider purchasing directors' and officers' liability coverage. This protects your top executives and board members from personal liability in case the company is sued.

Business Property and Casualty

Business property and casualty insurance protects you from a loss if you experience loss, damage, or theft in your store. Two kinds of business property and casualty insurance are available:

- **Named-peril.** This protects against losses that are specifically named.
- **All-risk.** This is much broader and protects against all perils.

Named-peril insurance is cheaper because the coverage isn't as broad, but if a loss occurs because of something not named in your coverage, you get nothing. There are also three forms of coverage:

- **Basic form.** Covers damage from common perils, such as fire, lightning, windstorm, vehicles, aircraft, and civil commotion.
- **Broad form.** Covers all the basic perils plus others such as water damage; collapse; glass breakage; weight of snow, ice, or sleet; and sprinkler leakage.
- **Special form.** Covers all perils except those specifically excluded. Exclusions can include flood, earth movement, war, wear and tear, insects, and vermin.

When you buy insurance—whether it is for your business or home—make sure you know what perils are covered. You certainly don't want to find out that you don't have coverage after a major catastrophe happens.

You also can select two different reimbursement options:

- **Replacement cost reimbursement.** This pays you the cost of actually replacing the lost property.
- **Actual cash value reimbursement.** This pays you based on the replacement cost minus the physical depreciation of the property.

The actual cash value reimbursement option might cost you less upfront, but you'll also collect a lot less if you have a loss.

Special-named perils that you may want to consider, depending on your specific business situation, include the following:

- **Crime.** This protects you against burglary, robbery, embezzlement, employee theft, and disappearance or destruction of property because of criminal acts. The cost of this coverage depends on the size of your company and its risks of needing to file claims.
- **Cargo.** This protects you against loss of inventory or goods while on a company truck.
- **Business interruption insurance.** This covers losses incurred because your business operations are interrupted by an act beyond your control. It provides resources so that you can continue to pay utilities, payroll, loans, and other obligations until your business is up and running again.
- **Product liability insurance.** If you produce and sell a product, this insurance covers you if you are sued related to a problem with the product's performance. Service businesses can also be covered under this type of insurance for services performed.
- **Inland marine insurance.** This insurance covers high-risk, mobile items that have a high stated value not covered by your other commercial property policies. This can include valuable tools, artwork, or jeweler's inventory.
- **Fire and extended coverage policies.** This covers losses from hail, windstorm, vandalism, or fire beyond the normal coverage of commercial liability. This can include protection for your accounts receivable records, computer files, currency, securities, and valuable papers.
- **Flood.** If your business or home is in a flood zone, you will need a flood insurance policy to be sure your assets are protected.

Worker's Compensation

If you have employees, you might need worker's compensation insurance. This insurance pays benefits to your employees if they are hurt on the job. Coverage includes medical bills, a part of lost wages, vocational rehabilitation, and death benefits.

Whether you need to carry this coverage depends on state law. If you fail to carry it when state law requires you to, not only will you be subject to covering an employee's costs after an accident or injury, but you also may face severe fines and even jail time for violating the law. You can usually purchase this insurance from your state or through various private companies.

Better Not!

Five states require that you purchase worker's compensation insurance from them: North Dakota, Ohio, Washington, West Virginia, and Wyoming.

Premiums for worker's compensation are based on the size of your payroll and the risks involved in the work. For most retail businesses risks are low, but if you offer services where there is a high risk of injury, your insurance costs might be higher.

The Least You Need to Know

- You will need to decide on a legal entity. This decision will impact your store operations, your liability, your costs, and the taxes you'll have to pay.
- Check with your town, city, or county clerk and be sure you get all the registrations, licenses, and permits that are required before you open your store.
- Don't skimp on insurance. You need to protect the business you build.

Chapter 10

Finding the Right Location and Its Costs

In This Chapter

- Evaluating your location options
- Locating near customers
- Determining costs
- Negotiating contracts

Picking the location for your store can be one of the most exciting tasks and definitely one of the most important. I'm sure you've heard that "location, location, location" are the three most important decisions in any real estate transaction, but in retail it's even more crucial. Today, there's no guarantee that customers will come unless you locate your store where they are or where it is convenient for them to go.

In this chapter, you find out how to select the right location considering your store concept as well as the area's demographics, competition, and security. We'll explore your options from a mall location to a main street one. Finally, we'll review the key things you need to know to get the best deal from your landlord.

Store Location Can Make or Break You

A good location for your store can be much more valuable than any advertising you do. Over the course of a year, you'll find that it's cheaper to pay the rent required for a good location than to pay for the extensive advertising needed to pull people into a poorer location—if you can get them there at all.

If it's hard for your target customers to get to you, if there's no parking near you, if the area is not safe, or if the building you are in does not reflect your image, you won't draw the kind of customers you want no matter how much advertising you do.

Your Goals

Your goals in finding the perfect location for your store should include a location that:

- Drives customer traffic (foot and commuter traffic).
- Attracts employees.
- Projects the right image.
- Ensures your competitiveness.
- Allows you to run your store efficiently.
- Meets your budget.

As you find the many available options, choose only those that help you meet these goals.

Recruit a Real Estate Partner

You may need help finding the best location, so you shouldn't hesitate hiring a real estate professional who understands small business needs or, even better, who understands the retail industry and your target customers. Ask business or retail owners you know for recommendations of a good agent, especially if they had great success with someone who helped them find their location. If no one you know can recommend someone, you can also look for real estate professionals with either the Society of Industrial and Office REALTORS® or the CCIM Institute.

Selling Points

If you don't know a real estate professional, you can use many sites on the Internet to find a local professional such as www.allcommercialproperty.org or www.loopnet.com to find both properties and companies that can help you.

Be Near Your Target Customers

Your first question when looking for a location is: "Can I be anywhere or do I need to be located in a particular area?" Generally, if you have been in business for some time and have a great following, you can open a store—your second or third store—"anywhere" and become a "destination" for your loyal customers and their friends.

But if this is your first store and customers don't know you yet, your location becomes more important. Customers are not going to seek out your store unless you are right where they are or where it's easy and convenient for them to get to.

Examining Demographics

You need to know where your target customers are located. Pick an area where your target customers live or work. If multiple options are available to you, get to know each area's demographics including age, gender, ethnicity, occupation, household composition, and income.

Knowing an area's demographics can help you find the right location. Only locations with a customer base like the one you are targeting should be considered. For example, you shouldn't open a store in an affluent neighborhood if your store carries low-price, average-quality merchandise and offers limited service. This type of store would be more successful in a low- to mid-income area where customers are more interested in saving money than service or high-quality products. Or, if you plan to open a gourmet food store specializing in Eastern European imports, you are more likely to succeed in a community with a high concentration of Eastern European residents.

Affordable Demographic Data

You can get a good sense of the community surrounding your target store location by looking at basic data from the Census Bureau. Census demographic information can tell you the numbers and types of people who live in a certain geographic area, classified by age and sex. It can also tell you the number of households, the average household size, and the average, median, and per capita income levels in a given area.

Selling Points

Looking for access to demographic data for free? One good source on the Internet, FreeDemographics.com, lets you create customized market analysis reports for any geographic area.

For a monthly fee or annual subscription, you can also access demographic reports and maps from Claritas (www.claritas.com), a marketing company which helps gather demographic data and target marketing information about the population, consumer behavior, consumer spending, households, and businesses within any specific geographic market area in the United States. Another website, www.mapinfo.com, has a great retail site selection component you should check out.

To Be or Not to Be ... Near Your Competitors?

You may think it's best to locate somewhere your competitors aren't, as long as your research indicates there's a market for your products or services in that area. You won't have to share customers with your competitors because you are the only choice for them. Also, you won't need to compete on price. While these are all good reasons for locating your store where you are the only "game in town," most retail experts will tell you it's better to be closer to your competitors.

There are many reasons for this argument:

- Some competitors choose to "cluster" in close proximity because they are selling unique, but similar, items. By clustering together, they can draw more customers. For example, art, jewelry, and high-fashion clothing and shoe stores often find it advantageous to be close to their competitors. Customers who shop at these kinds of stores tend to go where they have numerous stores to browse.

- While foot traffic is obviously important, landing the "perfect" customer is far more crucial. By being close to your competitors, you can benefit from their marketing efforts. Successful competitors chose their locations based on the ideal demographics of a particular area. In many cases, they've also devoted large portions of their advertising budget toward driving traffic to their locations. You'll likely find they have already conducted the necessary market analysis and you won't need to spend more money on this.

- Competitors can make you better. Because survival of the fittest is the game, you are always striving to do more and better for your customers to entice them to shop with you instead of your competitors.

To succeed with this strategy you need, of course, to be confident enough in your product to outsell your competitors.

Other Business Neighbors

Another successful strategy for picking your location is to find a spot near indirect competitors—stores that do not carry similar products to yours. Opening your store near stores that cater to the same clientele with different products allows you to draw from their customer base. These stores are very often called "magnet" or "anchor" stores, which refers to their ability to attract a large number of customers. A good example of a magnet store is a large grocery or department store.

Savvy Retailer

A large wine and spirits store I worked with a few years ago opened a store right off of a major highway exit in a complex that had a Staples store and a large empty store space next to it. The landlord announced that the empty space was going to be rented out to Trader Joe's, the grocery chain. Our retail client wanted to oppose the deal, fearing that Trader Joe's wine department would compete with his business and take customers away from him. I explained to our client that the proximity to a grocery store was the best thing that could happen for a number of different reasons. First, Trader Joe's draws incredible foot traffic. Second, Trader Joe's has the same customer base—mid- to high-income people who love to entertain and love wine and food. Third, Trader Joe's wine selection is bargain wines primarily and my client offered better quality wines for great values at the mid- to high-price level.

If you locate close to a magnet store, you can maximize your benefits from their traffic by planning your store hours to coincide with those of the magnet. If possible, you should even think about opening your store a little earlier and closing it a little later than the magnet. This way, your store can benefit from customers arriving before the magnet opens, as well as shortly after the magnet store closes. Depending on your store, the magnet store's employees could be among your early and late customers.

You should also try to coordinate your promotional and sale activities to those sponsored by the magnet. As a small business owner, you normally have the flexibility to make on-the-spot marketing decisions. For instance, if you see that the magnet store is holding a major sales event starting on Monday, you can go in over the weekend and set up your sale. If the magnet is not a competitor, you may be able to get advanced notice of these events, and have time to advertise your sale as well.

You should also consider other types of businesses or schools when picking a location, such as office parks, schools, colleges, and hospital complexes. All of these can help generate much-needed foot traffic (or commuter traffic). For example, if you wanted to open an art materials store, the best location for your store would be next to an arts college. You'd have a lot of your target customers shopping at your store, including college students, professors, and artists.

Convenience Above All

A great location must be convenient for your customers. Your store must be easy to find with ample parking spaces and street visibility. Also, you should be near reliable public transportation, so your employees can get there. In addition, you want to have a hassle-free commute.

Ready Access for Customers

You need to make sure that your chosen location provides easy access to enough potential customers to support your business. This is why many retailers choose a location that puts them in the midst of heavy car or pedestrian traffic.

If your store depends in large part on drive-in or walk-in customers, even the side of the street you are on can make a difference. If you are on a street where most of the commuter traffic goes one way in the morning and the other way in the late afternoon, you'll probably do better with a location that's on the return-home side of the street. But if a large part of your business involves the sale of items to be consumed at, or on the way to, work—such as coffee and donuts—you'll do better on the other side of the street.

Easy Access for and to Employees

For many small retailers, the ability to attract and retain qualified employees can be critical to their success. You should carefully consider the availability of qualified employment prospects within a half-hour drive of your location. You also must look at public transportation access and service because it is very likely your employees will be using it.

If good public transportation is not available, your employees may be late regularly or get frustrated with the commute and quit. If your store is located far from public transportation and the only way for employees to get to your store is by car or cab, you might have difficulty finding people who want to work for you.

You Count, Too

While your key location questions will be based on financial considerations, don't forget to meet your own personal needs. Remember, part of the lure of store ownership is the ability to control not only how much you make, but how you make it.

If you are like most small business owners, you can expect to spend a large chunk of your time at your store. Quality of life issues are as relevant to the location choice as you wish to make them. Don't forget to ask yourself these key questions:

- If you have a choice of locating the store in several different locations, which of them would you rather spend that much time in?
- How long are the commuting times between your home and the various choices?
- If one location is in a place where you really don't want to be, but it appears to be the best choice from the point of view of business efficiency and profitability, would you be prepared to sacrifice some profit to obtain your desired business lifestyle? If so, how much?

Selling Points

While it might be tempting to locate a new store in your own community—it is convenient plus you already know the demographics—you need to look at what it's going to cost you to operate in that community. Other locations might be a better business choice because of lower sales taxes, lower rent, lower wages, and utilities cost.

Parking, Please!

Customers, employees, yourself, and anyone else visiting your store all need adequate parking. How many times have you given up in despair when there was no parking to be found near the store you wanted to visit? As a store owner, you face diminishing profits every time a potential customer can't find a parking spot.

If you are considering a space located in a mixed-use neighborhood (such as residential and retail), you should check out whether the parking lot is used by local residents without permission. If it is, you may have problems with the neighbors, some of whom may be your customers, if you want the parking only for your customers.

Community Considerations

In addition to convenience and parking, you also must consider community services, access to credit, and available utilities.

Community Services

When planning to buy a personal residence, you carefully consider the quality of the community's social services including police and fire protection, education, and health care. When choosing a retail location, these issues should be important, too. You need good police and fire protection, as well as easy access to emergency health care. In addition to the human costs, you must think about the dollars-and-cents costs for legal liability and attorneys' fees, theft, and higher insurance costs.

But other community services such as education, health care, and welfare services can be significant to your location choice as well. A quality local school system can give your business an available pool of well-educated potential employees. Local community colleges and high schools can be resources from which your business can draw to encourage employees (possibly through tuition reimbursement programs) to improve and enhance their job-related skills.

Access to Credit

The availability of credit can also be important. Traditionally, financial institutions are more likely to grant loans to small retailers who locate in the same community or neighborhood as they are. This means that if you choose to locate your store in an area that is not well serviced by several financial institutions, you may have difficulty obtaining credit at a reasonable rate.

Available Utilities

No matter what kind of store you are opening, the efficiency of your store operation will be negatively affected if utilities such as power, heating fuel, telephones, and water are not reliably available at reasonable prices.

You might want to consider having an emergency power generator at your store. Although such a system probably wouldn't be sufficient to keep your whole store operating, it might be useful in some situations. For example, if severe damage to business equipment or inventory (such as computers or perishable goods) could be avoided by maintaining temperature control in a small area, having such a back-up generator might avoid costly losses. Even having an uninterruptible power supply for your computers can save you days of trying to reconstruct files if the power goes out in the middle of a backup or sale.

Better Not!

If power outages would result in big losses to your business, you might also be wise to consider adding power interruption coverage to your business insurance policy.

Safety Matters, Too!

A convenient and profitable location should not be your only concern. You also want a location that is safe for your customers, your employees, as well as yourself. Crimes against people and crimes against property can significantly add to your cost of doing business. Shoplifting, employee theft of inventory (also called "shrinkage"), and theft of business property are all too common and costly. Crimes against business owners, employees, customers, and others who enter your store are less common, but can be more tragic and traumatic when they occur.

While you'll never be completely free of crimes against your store, there are decisions that you can make about your location that can lessen the likelihood and impact of crime on your store. Primarily, these decisions concern store location and building security.

If you locate in a high-crime area, you'll likely need to invest in more store security features than if you locate in a low-crime area. The benefit of locating your store in a high-crime area is that they usually offer significantly cheaper rent. By saving in rent, you have the money to buy a reliable security system. Another consideration is that high-crime areas are often underserved by retailers and other businesses. Some small business owners have found they can make a good living by accepting the risks of operating in a particular neighborhood where there's little or no competition.

The kind of security features that you need will depend on the kind of store you operate, and on how severe you think the crime threat to be.

Common building security features include:

- Steel security doors, particularly in areas of the building that are away from public view.
- Security alarm systems: motion sensors, breaking glass detectors, window and door alarms—all of which may or may not be hooked up to security monitoring services or the local police department.
- External lighting on all points of access into the building, the dock facility, and parking lots.
- Fenced, limited access parking lot and company vehicle storage areas.
- Security cameras, hooked up to a video recording system or monitored by an on-site security guard, and trained on entry points and other areas where theft is most likely to occur, such as the sales floor and the loading docks.

- Lockable cash offices, equipped with secure safes.
- Bullet-proof security glass (needed in high-threat areas, and where large quantities of cash or extremely valuable products are kept).

You may also consider hiring security guards. You can either employ these guards directly or contract with private security service companies for them. Although you can have a guard stationed at the site full time, most small stores that use security services choose a guard that only periodically checks the store after hours.

Better Not!

Before you decide to use security guards on your business premises, ask your insurance agent about how this affects your liability coverage. You should be particularly careful about this if your guards will be armed. The last thing you want is to end up paying a legal judgment to a burglar.

Pros and Cons of Various Locations

You will find pros and cons for each type of shopping location. The following table outlines the strengths and weaknesses of the various location types that you may want to consider for your business.

Location	Strengths	Weaknesses
Downtown	Most central Big draw Office market A lot of service and culture	Parking problems Distance from suburbs Quality of location varies
Regional Shopping Center	Drawing power Good parking and access Mass market	Distance may be too great for "convenience" merchandise High base rents

Location	Strengths	Weaknesses
Community Shopping Center	Close to market Parking Good traffic from food stores	May not specialize Can be hurt by downtown and regional centers
Strip Malls or Street Locations	Convenience Low cost base Can specialize	Local traffic only Small geographic base of shoppers Transit or parking problems
Warehouse or Industrial District	Low cost Budget image	Location not typical for shopping: low traffic Requires heavy promotion

Consider Your Neighbors

Your neighbors should be a big factor in your location decision. You not only want to look at the general character of the neighborhood, but also the kind and appearance of nearby stores and neighbors. Just as you should never disregard the appearance of your facility, you should not completely overlook the effect that the appearance of surrounding businesses and neighbors may have on how your store is perceived.

How Much Space Will You Need?

When selecting a facility for your store, you need to think of your internal and external space and operational requirements. For example, if you are selling high-end products, your customers likely will expect a spacious and elegant sales area, so you'll need a bigger space in a high-end area of town. If your store relies on low prices to beat out the competition, a luxurious facility may work to your disadvantage. Cost-conscious customers may feel that your prices couldn't possibly be all that low if you can spend big bucks on your facility. In fact, some successful businesses that target the low-end use the fact that their stores look cheap or are in low-rent, out-of-the-way areas to promote their low prices.

If you are setting up a store for the first time, I strongly suggest that you map out your facility needs in some detail. That way you will be able to gauge how much space you'll need to rent more accurately. You definitely don't want to rent a space too small or too large. Both can be a problem. You won't be able to set up the type of store you planned if the space is too small. If the space is too large, your store could look barren and give the impression that you are not successful.

Internal Requirements

You need to think of how you are going to operate your store and what space requirements you will need to meet. Ask yourself these key questions about store operations:

- Will you need a separate office for individual consultation? If you are opening a high-end jewelry store, that is something that you might want to offer to your customer.
- Will you need a separate room for demonstrations, events, and classes? If you are opening a wine and food store, you might want to think about offering classes and cooking demonstrations to your customers. You will therefore need a separate area to accommodate tables, chairs, and maybe a demo kitchen.
- Will you need washrooms, changing rooms, etc.?
- Are you opening a furniture store or other large items type of store? Then, make sure the receiving dock is set up to accommodate deliveries.
- Will you ship product from your store? Will you have a stockroom? Again, you need to make sure that you are set up to perform these functions efficiently and effectively.
- Will you have 30 or more employees? A lunch room for your staff should be included in your plan.

When looking at the inside space, you also need to determine if it could be constructed or decorated to provide the best look and feel consistent with the image that you are trying to project.

Making Modifications

You may find the perfect location, but the building doesn't meet your requirements for size, layout, or appearance. Or you may find the building is almost perfect, but you must change one thing before you can use it. For example, you may need to add or widen access doors. Or you may need to increase the capacity of the ventilation system.

Don't jump to rent this almost perfect facility, before you consider these factors:

- How much would it cost to make the modifications? Get a detailed estimate of how much the additional work would cost. You may be able to get price (if you plan to buy the property) or rent concessions from the seller or landlord.
- Will the change be allowed? You'll need to investigate what type of permits may be needed to do the work and whether you would need a zoning or building code variance for the modifications you plan.
- How long would it take? You may need to delay your opening or open while the modifications are being completed, which could have a negative impact on the operations of your business.

Planning to Grow?

Your best bet may be to rent a location that can accommodate potential future growth, but cost often makes that impossible. A location that offers more space or features usually costs more. You'll have to decide whether you want to take on the additional costs now in order to have the benefits of easier expansion later. Or do you want to rent a less desirable space knowing that you may have to move when expansion is needed?

You should consider a larger, more expensive space only if you reasonably believe (not just hope) that you will need the extra space in the future. You also must be sure that your additional costs for this extra space will not be a drag on your current business operations.

Savvy Retailer

Most small business advisers suggest that start-up businesses keep a tight rein on costs. Business plans can be put together that envision additional facility requirements, but acquiring the additional space should probably be put on hold until business activity and profits justify taking on the added expense.

Do It All Within Budget

Don't forget your budget when looking for space. If you are not able to purchase or rent your facility at the best price, your store will be at a long-term disadvantage. If you spend more than your budget for space, these costs will be an ongoing drag on your company's profitability.

During the start-up phase, you may not have the money you need for other critical expenses, such as design, signage, or fixtures. Long-term overspending on the facility will make your company's profit-and-loss statement less attractive, so you may have difficulty borrowing money if needed.

Buy Or Rent?

Should you buy or rent your facility? Tax and cash management issues play a crucial role in the buy or rent decision, so many retailers seek the advice of their accountant or attorney when making this decision. You may also wish to do so. Generally in a start-up situation, money that would be used for a down payment to buy is needed to operate the business, so buying a location is often not desirable or even possible.

In addition to these tax and cash management issues, you also should consider other critical questions, such as: If you choose to rent, what happens when the lease term ends? Will you be forced to move or will your rent go up to a level you can't afford? You won't have these problems if you buy, but what if you decide another location works better for you once the business is successful? Will owning the property make it more difficult for you to make a strategic move?

If this is your first venture into the retail business, there's no decision here. Rent your space until you have a going concern, know your customers, and can be sure you've got the right location. You can also somewhat protect yourself with an option to extend the lease or even an option to buy, which is sometimes possible.

Estimate Costs

Rent may not be your only cost when you pick a location. Be sure to ask the landlord if you'll be required to contribute to maintenance, property taxes, or building insurance. Costs also can differ greatly if you choose a mall location versus a street location.

Mall Location

In a mall location, your rent is usually stated as a minimum guaranteed rent per square foot of lease area and a certain percentage of sales. In most cases, the percentage is between 5 and 7 percent of gross sales, but this can vary by type of business or other factors. If the percentage of your sales is higher than the minimum rent, you pay the percentage of your sales. If the minimum rent is higher, then you would pay that rent.

In addition, you may have to pay dues to the center's merchants' association, minimum advertising commitments, and be required to pay for maintenance of the common areas. So total rent could be your minimum guaranteed rent, merchant's dues, one or two ads, and maintenance of the common areas. Be sure you can afford total rent costs, not only the base rent costs.

For example, your guaranteed or base rent could be $10 per square foot. Suppose you plan to rent 1,500 square feet. Your monthly guaranteed rent would be $1,250 (1,500 square feet times $10 equals $15,000 per year, or $1,250 per month). Your percentage of gross sales could be 6 percent. Suppose you sold $10,000 in your first month, then your percentage based on gross sales would be $600, so you would have to pay $1,250 (your base rent) that month. You would need to top $21,000 a month in sales before your gross sales percentage would be more than your base rent.

You'll also need to design and finish the space. You pay for the light fixtures, counters, shelves, painting, floor coverage, and installing your own heating and cooling units. You may be able to negotiate with your landlord for a cost allowance toward finishing your retail space. This is known as a tenant allowance and can be used toward storefronts, ceiling, and wall coverings. The allowance will be spelled out in a dollar amount on the lease.

Street Location

In most nonshopping center locations, rent is a fixed amount that is not related to sales volume. But you will be responsible for the upkeep of both the inside of your store, as well as the exterior of your store. While in a mall location maintenance of the common area is provided, that's often not true for the external area of your street location. Some landlords may give you a percentage-only rent deal. If you can get that, it is the safest way to go because no matter what your sales, you only pay a fixed percent. If you can get this type of deal at less than 6 percent, it would be hard to say no to if the location meets your needs.

Negotiating with the Landlord

Once you've narrowed down your target areas, then it's time to get the details from the landlord. In many communities, there's an abundance of space, so a landlord may need to provide you with information to lure you to his spot. This should include:

- Blueprints, a site plan, and the space available if you are considering a location under construction.
- Information about the trade area to give you an idea from where your customers will come.
- List of other tenants, so you know both your competition and the other stores that complement your products from which you can draw customers.
- Estimated total expenses for the space you are considering.
- Names of surrounding cities and towns and their population demographics.
- Information about population growth and trends.

Information You Must Provide the Landlord

You also need to provide information to the landlord before she will be willing to lease to you. This information includes:

- Your business plan.
- Your space requirements and plans for your space.
- Pictures of the products you plan to sell and stores that are designed similarly to the one you plan to open.
- Financial statements.
- Funding commitments.

Signing the Deal

Once you've found the right location, you'll need to sign a lease. Ask your attorney to help you negotiate a lease that is fair and equitable. Your attorney can also help you understand everything in the lease agreement. Be sure you understand all the details very well.

Everything in a lease is negotiable. An attorney with years of experience in negotiating leases will know the common terms that are negotiable and what the best possible deal could be.

Think carefully about the length of the lease you accept. If you make the term too short, you could end up with a dramatic increase in rent or possibly the loss of space just when your business is taking off. But if you make the term too long and your business fails, you could face significant costs to break that lease.

You also may want to make your lease contingent on the continuing presence of a key major anchor. If the major anchor leaves the mall, you may want to add a provision to your lease that you have the option to leave as well without any penalties.

Another key term is the transferability of the lease. Can your lease terms be transferred to someone else if you decide to sell the business? Obviously, if you've found a great location and developed a thriving business, it will be worth more to a buyer if he can keep the same lease terms—as long as you did a great job negotiating them up-front.

You also may want the right to sublet some space, especially if you are initially taking on a larger space then you need, but want the additional space for future expansion needs. Subletting part of your space may help you defray some costs during your business start up, but be sure your contract allows you to do it.

If you are renting space in a mall and are quoted a price on the common area maintenance, you need to realize that this price is an estimate. If the mall has a lot of vacancies, your actual cost will be higher because there are fewer merchants contributing to the upkeep.

So, without a doubt, location is key, but the actual location is not your only crucial decision. Consider what types of stores are around you and how well they will help you build the kind of traffic you want in your own store.

The Least You Need to Know

- A large part of your store's success depends on its location. Seek professional help in finding the right one.
- Pick a location that is convenient not only for your customers but also for you and your employees.

- Costs for stores inside malls are very different than street locations. Be sure you understand your total costs before signing a deal.

- Negotiating a lease can be critical to your store. Work with an experienced attorney who can help you get the best deal.

Chapter 11

Buying the Right Stuff at the Right Price

In This Chapter

- Buying secrets
- Determining price points
- Buying terms
- Picking suppliers
- Supplier relationships
- Knowing how much to buy

You can make some mistakes in running your business, but as long as your product is right, you can still make money. How do you make sure that your product is right? You must buy products that your customers want. Sounds obvious, but it's not as easy as it sounds.

In this chapter, I discuss the key points you need to remember when buying the products you plan to sell, how you should select and work with your suppliers, and how you should negotiate with them for the best deal.

The Secret of Buying

As the buyer for a retail store, you have to get out of the habit of viewing products through your own eyes and start viewing them through the eyes of your customers. You must remember that you are really just a "proxy" for the hundreds of customers who will later stand in your store and pick the items they want.

Your role as a buyer is one that fulfills your responsibility to your customers. Accept your role as a proxy and move beyond your personal tastes. Develop a genuine respect for the items that your customers will like and ultimately buy.

> **Better Not!**
>
> Thirty-five years ago, retail buyers had the luxury of believing that their tastes somehow "matched" the tastes of their customers. They could afford to make some buying mistakes because times were good and their businesses still made money. A few retailers can still operate this way, but the vast majority cannot. Don't waste your time trying this tactic.

Understanding what your customers will like and ultimately buy is going to be a constant challenge as long as you own your retail business. Customers' tastes change over time. You will always need to consider that they may have moved on from an item in your store that they liked just a week ago to an item that you do not carry.

Great retailers are students of their customers—they constantly study them to better understand their likes, dislikes, dreams, wishes, and aspirations.

Develop Your Price Points

As you decide on the merchandise you will carry, you also need to think about how you will price the goods you plan to sell. These are known as price points. Develop a price point discipline by deciding in advance that you will carry only specific price points within a given merchandise classification. This will enable you to offer your customers a clearer in-store presentation and make your buying much easier.

Although many successful stores use just three price points in a classification—often called good, better, and best—you may elect to use four or even all five of the following in some situations:

- Your *opening* item price point might be $29. This would be a specific low-end product that you buy to match the low-price leader in your trading area. Depending on the philosophy of your store, you may choose to ignore that competitor instead of battling on price.

- Your *good* price point might be $39. This would be an entry-level product offering good features and quality for a good price.
- Your *better* item price point might be $49. This would be a slightly better product offering somewhat more features and quality for a somewhat higher price.
- Your *best* item price point might be $79. This would be a noticeably better product offering significantly more features and quality for a significantly higher price.
- Your *top of the line* item price point might be $100 or more. This would be a specific product that you buy to offer your customers the biggest, the fastest, or the nicest. You would stock only a few of these very special items.

In planning your merchandise mix, you need to be careful that your lowest price point in a classification is reasonable in relationship to your highest price point in that classification.

If the spread is too great—for example, you stock one wristwatch at $29 and another at $299—a customer who is looking for either one may not enter your store simply because you carry the other price point.

A $299 wristwatch in the window will give a "high price" message about your store to a customer who is shopping for a $29 wristwatch. At the same time, a $29 wristwatch in the window will give a "low quality" message about your store to a customer who is shopping for a $299 wristwatch.

The only way to avoid this situation is to plan your merchandise mix thoroughly. You need to decide exactly what customers your business will exist to serve, because attempting to be "everything to everyone" is a fast route to bankruptcy.

Credit Realities for New Retail Businesses

As you start to do your buying, you should not expect merchandise suppliers to give you favorable payment terms. Your business has not yet established a "credit history" with those suppliers. Knowing that most new retail businesses fail due to inadequate financing, suppliers will be leery of giving you 30 days or more to pay for the merchandise you order initially.

For most of your orders during your first year of operation, you may expect to pay the entire cost of each order before delivery. Some suppliers will accept as little as 50 percent of the entire cost in certain situations, but you should not expect it.

However, do expect a cash discount. When you pay COD, you should get at least a 2 percent discount if not even higher. In this case, there is absolutely no risk for suppliers and they have their cash right away.

Whether you must pay the entire cost of each order or just half of that amount, it is clearly in your best interest to establish a good credit history as quickly as possible. Doing so could take from six months to a year, but you should then be able to negotiate at least 30-day payment terms with most of your suppliers.

This is not as much of a break as it may at first appear. The "clock" starts ticking on those 30 days as soon as the supplier produces an invoice—which most suppliers do on the same day as they produce the "picking tickets" that remove the inventory from their warehouse.

If the supplier produces an invoice on Tuesday, the order will probably be "picked and packed" on Wednesday and moved to the shipping dock on Thursday. Depending on how far away the supplier is from your store, you may not receive the merchandise until the following Friday. It could then take you several days to open and count the shipment, enter the items into the computer as inventory, add price tickets, and move everything to the sales floor.

In other words, it can easily take half of your 30-day payment term just to get the merchandise to the sales floor so that your customers can see it. So see if you can negotiate the invoice date to be "arrival in store" and not "invoice creation date." This could buy you up to 15 more days to sell the merchandise and significantly increase your cash flow.

Setting Buying Terms

The terms you negotiate with a supplier are often more important than the price you actually pay for a product. All terms are negotiable, so be aware of what the key terms are and think about what you might want to change. Key terms you may negotiate include:

- Who pays for getting the product to your store? (You may be better off negotiating prepaid freight at a slightly higher cost as the supplier may pay a lower freight rate than you would.)
- The number of days you have to pay the invoice.
- Allowances and rebates that relate to the size of your order. (Some suppliers give a volume rebate that is calculated over a 6- or 12-month period.)

- Provisions for "co-op advertising," where the manufacturer shares advertising costs with you. The money for co-op advertising can be more important than the price. Every year, most manufacturers set aside a certain portion of their advertising budget for co-op advertising. They use this money to subsidize retailers' advertising campaigns that include their products, brand names, and logos.

Co-op advertising is a win-win for both the supplier and the retailer. Suppliers know that placing some of their advertising dollars close to the point of sale will lead to higher sales of their products. Retailers can offset the cost of their advertising campaigns, and their advertising budget can go much further.

You can get creative about negotiating co-op advertising dollars. Let me tell you a story of one owner-operated retailer—a golf store owner—who was able to put together a major golf tournament because of his creative negotiations for co-op dollars. Rather than approaching just one supplier with a "like everyone else" proposal for a quarter-page newspaper ad that would include the supplier's logo, this retailer dared to be different. He approached 10 of his suppliers with a creative proposal for a high school golf tournament, one in which his suppliers, his customers, and his store would all win.

Selling Points

Retailers often do not ask for co-op advertising as part of the terms of their purchasing agreements. That leaves much of the money sitting unused in the suppliers' coffers. Don't forget to ask for those co-op dollars.

His idea was to invite 500 golfers from 17 area schools to the tournament. The golfers would compete over several weeks and, at the beginning of the tournament, each participant would receive a gym bag containing golf balls, tees, a glove, and other promotional gifts from the suppliers. People who finished in the top 10 would receive golf clubs, golf shoes, and other significant prizes.

The suppliers responded to his proposal by donating a total of $80,000 worth of merchandise to the event. What did they ask in return? Mostly they wanted photos that they could use in their newsletters—and a chance to support the tournament with co-op advertising dollars again next year.

For the suppliers, this tournament was a chance to put their product directly into the hands of 500 young people who could well become loyal customers and buy their products for the next 50 years—as well as their parents who appreciated the efforts put forth. For the customers, this tournament was a chance to play a game they enjoyed and bask in the sunshine of a little VIP treatment. For the store, the tournament was many things, including an advertising and goodwill campaign that will reap benefits for years.

In short, everybody won because the owner-operated retailer understood that negotiating for co-op advertising dollars could add more to the bottom-line profitability of his business than any price breaks he could negotiate with his suppliers.

Suppliers who support co-op advertising will often give you up to 20 percent of the value of your order in co-op advertising dollars. Many will pay 50 percent or more of the cost of an ad that features their products, brand names, and logos. These amounts are usually negotiable.

There are many other terms that you can negotiate with suppliers. No deal will contain all of these, but you may be able to negotiate five or six of them with your best suppliers.

- FOB, or Free on Board, terms, which relate to the shipment of product to your store and who pays for what. You can negotiate who pays the costs as well as who owns the products when in transit. Ownership can be a critical point if the product is damaged, lost, or stolen during shipment.
- The terms for return when a product is damaged or returned by customers, including who pays the shipment cost for returning the goods.
- The cost of some markdowns (reduction in price) to move the goods if they do not sell at regular price in three to six months.
- The frequency of visits by your suppliers' reps and have them count stock and provide sales support.
- Preticketing, so you won't have to ticket all the items when you get them at the store. They can go right on the shelf/rack.
- Fixtures for displaying product.
- Packaging that makes it easier to display and sell product and may be different from your competitors.
- Selling aids including tags for the products and instruction sheets, if appropriate.
- Promotional material (package stuffers).
- Rebates, such as quantity discounts.

- Sample items for demonstration purposes.
- In-store demonstrations.
- Product knowledge training for your employees done by the manufacturer's reps.
- Free mannequins.
- Vendor-paid trips to trade shows for you and your key employees.
- Vendor-paid ad for the Yellow Pages.
- Link on the vendor's website to your site.

Think about which of these terms would be most beneficial to your store and negotiate for them during the buying process.

Buying Effectively

Negotiating terms is not the only critical issue that you should consider when planning to buy for your store. Where you buy and when you buy are crucial as well. When you buy for your store, you should follow some proven guidelines that will help you buy effectively, including:

- Do your buying in your own store whenever possible. This lets you "play the game" on your home field in comfortable and familiar surroundings. If you do your buying by telephone, the same strategy applies: play the game on your home field by preparing all of the information you will need in advance and placing the call at your convenience. If you negotiate by e-mail, never answer an e-mail without printing it out and thinking about it for at least an hour. Looking at something on hard copy versus the screen has a profound impact on how your brain processes the information.
- Understand that when you go on an out-of-town "buying trip," you are giving up the home-field advantage. The best thing you can do in this situation is to set a modest schedule of appointments that leaves you plenty of time to think and plan—as well as visit and shop for "good ideas" at the leading retail stores in the area that you are visiting.
- Always take your open-to-buy budgets with you on a buying trip. You will need to know exactly how much you have to spend on each merchandise classification if you intend to control your inventory and run a profitable business. I talk more

about open-to-buy calculations later in this chapter. You will find an open-to-buy worksheet in Appendix C.

- Never buy an item when you first see it. Instead, take some time to consider the big picture before you place an order. This could mean seeing everything that is available for the coming season before placing any orders (if you sell fashion items) or reviewing the items you have already bought or could buy (if you sell nonfashion items).
- Invest in a compact digital camera and photograph every item that you buy or are considering seriously. These images will help you remember what you have already bought so that you can coordinate colors and avoid buying items that are too similar. They will also be useful in product-knowledge training for your sales associates as the delivery date approaches.
- Always be honest and ethical with your suppliers so that you can build long-term, win-win relationships with each of them. Your reputation both as a business owner and as an individual is something you should enhance, protect, and defend. Pay your bills on time, and if you are going to be late, let them know how late and when you will be paying. Silence is not good when it comes to bills.
- When you agree on terms with a supplier—but before you sign a purchase order—confirm your understanding of the agreement by restating the deal verbally and in writing: "You are going to do this and I am going to do that, right?" Then ask any questions you may have: "Can I get additional quantities if I need them? Will they be at the same price?" and take note of the answers.
- Keep a supplier book and refer to it often. This does not need to be fancy, just a loose-leaf binder in which you can make notes on every contact you have with your 10 biggest suppliers. Make this a complete record of your telephone calls, meetings, and any other contacts you may have. You will be surprised at how often you need to refer to this information.

No matter what you are buying, you should always have an alternative to buying that item from that supplier in that place at that time in that quantity and at that price. The alternative may not be as fast or as easy—and it may even require you to learn something new—but an alternative does exist somewhere. Don't rush to buy something if the deal is not what you planned either in price, quantity, or other negotiated terms. Take time to think about alternatives.

Better Not!

If buying the name brand from the name-brand supplier is the only alternative you can see, you may have put yourself in a trap. But if you have five suppliers from whom you can buy a given product, you can no doubt buy more effectively. Perhaps the alternative is to live without the name brand, or to develop the sales of another brand.

The trick to buying is making sure that you always have an alternative so that you can push away from the negotiating table and say, "I'm sorry, we can't do this deal."

Evaluate Potential Suppliers

Just as you compare your competition, you should also systematically compare the suppliers from whom you plan to order. Take a copy of the checklist that follows when you talk with suppliers and find out which of these services each of them offer:

Products Offered by Supplier

_____ Demand: a wanted brand name item, line, title

_____ Recognition of product lines: ease of sell-through

_____ Packaging: effectiveness, helpfulness, environmental appropriateness

_____ Quality: high quality, long lasting, no returns

_____ Units: singles, six-packs, dozens

Service as It Relates to Stock

_____ Delivery: on time

_____ Bar coded: carton, package, and product bar codes

_____ Quantity: as ordered, all at once, no substitutes

_____ Peak-time support: will train staff as required

_____ Returns: accepted on defective/returned products

_____ Special orders: prompt filling

Service as It Relates to Sales

_____ Sales force: calls regularly or as requested

_____ Knowledge: knows about my problems and the product

_____ Information: knows industry, sector, and store performance figures

_____ Review: conducts quarterly and annual reviews

Promotion

_____ Advertising: creates shopping demand for products

_____ Co-op advertising: available and flexible

_____ Promotion: wide range of promotional items available

_____ Support: will help with demonstrations

Finances

_____ Pricing: consistent, good value

_____ Discounts: offers closeouts to present customers first

_____ Terms: will offer net-net or extend payment

Communication

_____ Problem solving: sales representative can do it all

_____ Executive: can reach someone in a crisis

In Appendix C ,you will find the "Checklist to Evaluate Potential Suppliers." As you talk with suppliers, check off which of the listed items they offer. Before you pick your top 5 to 10 suppliers, complete the checklist so you can easily compare your potential suppliers and find out which ones offer you the best combination of these services.

After you've worked with your suppliers for about six months, review your initial checklist comparison and verify that the suppliers you are using lived up to the promises made when you initially negotiated your agreements. Some will not, and it may be time to consider replacing those who do not perform to your expectations. Remember, you are the customer!

Building Supplier Relationships

Your first priority after you pick suppliers and vendors for your store is to build a person-to-person relationship with each of your chosen suppliers—one that can be a win-win relationship for both parties. This is a different kind of relationship than the "us versus them" adversarial relationship that is too common in the industry. While it's true the big retailers wield a lot of power because of the size of their orders, small retailers who develop the right kind of relationship with a supplier can do even better.

> **Savvy Retailer**
>
> When I was a product manager for one of the largest casual-wear suppliers in North America, my customers included some of the biggest retailers in the country, as well as hundreds of owner-operated retailers from coast to coast. The large retailers bought huge quantities of merchandise, of course, and the owner-operated retailers bought smaller quantities—some even less than $15,000 a year. Month after month, however, the supplier's distribution facility filled the orders from a select few of the small owner-operated retailers first. How did these "small fish" get their orders filled first even before the biggest retailers in the country? They established a win-win relationship with the supplier's product manager and invited him to lunch whenever he was in their cities. They realized he was a human being who also took pride in his job, recognized the importance of owner-operated retail accounts, needed the consumer information they could provide, and wanted to sell his products. These retailers' initiatives got them the best allocations and the most complete shipments possible.

Many suppliers welcome owner-operated retailers today. As the retail business has consolidated, suppliers find themselves with fewer but larger accounts. The loss of any one of these accounts could have a significant impact on their bottom line.

Suppliers are rediscovering that small is beautiful. That it makes good business sense to have 100 or 200 good, healthy, owner-operated retailers as customers. These suppliers want to develop strategic win-win relationships with owner-operated retailers who will present their products well and provide the end-customer feedback that they need.

Take advantage of this changed perception and work to increase your "perceived legitimacy" in the eyes of your suppliers. Even something as small as the purchase order you use in your initial buying can help you look like a true professional—or not.

As you prepare for your first buying trips, you will need to decide whether to use your supplier's standard purchase order or create one of your own. If you use the supplier's purchase order, you will not only give up some of your perceived legitimacy but also give up control of the relationship.

Print your own purchase order and include your terms and conditions—the standard deal that you negotiate with suppliers—on the document. Think about this from the other side of the negotiating table. As a supplier, would you be more impressed by a retailer who comes to the meeting asking to borrow some paper or by one who presents a professional-looking document that spells out his standard purchasing terms in full? Probably the latter.

Most office supply stores sell preprinted purchase order forms that can serve as a model for your "personalized" design which would include your store name and logo. You terms should include:

- Standard purchasing terms of Net 60 or even Net 90. That means you will pay for the merchandise either 60 or 90 days after you've been billed.
- Order-cancellation date of no more than 30 days after the preferred shipping date. Every order that you write should have an in-store cancel date clearly indicated on the order; if it is not there, you may be legally responsible to receive the merchandise even if it is several months late.

Even if you choose to use your supplier's standard purchase order, you may be able to alter the terms on that form. As with any contract, either party can change the terms of a purchase—if the other party agrees. But be certain both you and the supplier initial those changes so they will be legally binding.

Open-to-Buy Calculations

How much can you plan to spend and what do you need to spend? You should know the answer to these questions before you even talk to your suppliers.

You figure this out by doing an *open-to-buy* calculation, which is the amount of money at retail value that you can spend buying merchandise. Although you will be paying at "cost," I always recommend that you do your buying at "retail"—always ask yourself what the customer is willing to pay for your items.

def•i•ni•tion

Open to buy relates to the amount of money you can spend or the amount of product you can buy in a product category.

For example, if you know that you have $3,000 of open to buy in a certain category; you should go to market with a plan to buy merchandise that you can sell for $3,000. As you shop, you will need to convert things mentally back to cost in order to understand the impact of the purchase on your profit margin and cash flow, but do this after you evaluate the items at retail value, just as your customer would when they look at them in the store.

The formula you use to calculate open to buy is: determine the inventory you need for the following month plus sales and markdowns for the month minus beginning of month inventory and products on order. You will find a blank Open-to-Buy Worksheet in Appendix C, but to give you an example of how it works, I've included a completed one below:

Open-to-Buy Worksheet

	Inventory Required for Following Month	$9,200	Beginning of month for March
+	Sales	2,100	February plan
+	Markdowns	200	February plan
=	Inventory required	11,500	
-	Inventory on hand at the beginning of the month	8,000	February plan
=	Open to Receive	3,500	
-	On order	0	February on order
=	Open to buy	$3,500	

To manage your retail business effectively, you will need to calculate an open to buy for every merchandise category in your store for every month of the season. Although your open to buy is the amount of money that you can spend buying merchandise, we suggest that you always "hold back" about 10 to 20 percent. This is especially important if you operate in a segment of the retail industry where store owners get calls from suppliers offering closeouts or clearances "if you act today." By holding back part of your open to buy, you will be in a position to take advantage of these offers if you wish.

As a hard and fast rule, however, you should not buy any merchandise if you do not have sufficient open to buy in the appropriate merchandise category. This rule applies no matter how great a "deal" your supplier offers. Special deals seldom provide you with more total sales from customers. Instead, they tend to sell in place of items that you already own.

Better Not!

You should never buy more than a three-month supply of any item. Buying a two-month supply would be better, and buying a one-month supply would be best. The world changes rapidly in retail, and you will significantly lower your risk if you buy closer to your needs. The farther in advance you buy, the more risk you are taking.

As an adjunct to this rule, the fact that you may be "overbought" in one category does not mean that you should stop your buying in other categories. For example, if you are in the hardware business, the fact that you are "overbought" in hammers does not mean that you should stop buying nails. The two are not interchangeable in your customers' minds—and destroying your nail selection would do nothing to sell your surplus hammers.

Most retailers plan their buying based on two six-month seasons: February to July (spring/summer) and August to January (fall/winter).

This came about because the clearance markdowns that most retailers take after the busy month of December rightly belong to the fall season. They take the markdowns to clear that season's merchandise and these markdowns, or losses, should be applied to the season that caused them.

Beyond this, at some time and in some way, every retailer needs to take a "physical inventory." This is a complete count by quantity and price of all the items in the store. For most retailers, the end of January is the point at which they have the least inventory to count and the fewest customers to interrupt their counting.

Reaching the Sell and Buy Point

Your goal on your road to profitability is to reach what is called the *sell and buy point.* This is when you sell items to your customers before you have to pay your suppliers for them. If you could do this with most of your merchandise, you would have a healthy business indeed. You would then be what is called "cash flow positive" as you would never need to borrow any money to pay for merchandise. In rare cases, you could even earn interest by investing that money until it was time to pay your suppliers.

def•i•ni•tion

The **sell and buy point** is the point at which you sell your products to your customers before you have to pay your suppliers for them.

While most owner-operated retailers cannot achieve sell and buy based on their size, you can and should structure your business with that goal in mind. The payment terms that you negotiate with your suppliers become critical to reach the sell and buy point.

When buying, you may be able to choose between various payment alternatives. For example, you may be able to choose between paying "2 percent 30" and "Net 60." The first means that you get a 2 percent discount for paying the invoice in 30 days. The second means that you get no discount, but have 60 days to pay. With sell and buy in mind, I recommend that you choose the Net 60 option.

Anyone who understands interest rate math would argue against this advice. They would tell you that it just does not make financial sense to pay more than you have to for an item. And this is true if you look at the transaction from a short-term perspective.

I still recommend Net 60 because those terms will help you approach sell and buy. You will pay a little more for the item, but you will stand a much better chance of paying for it with your customers' money. The higher price makes sense if you look at the transaction from a long-term perspective. As a bonus, it will be much easier to return an item to your supplier if you find a hidden defect before you pay the invoice.

When it comes to payment terms, you really need to decide whether you are in the cash-management business or the retail business. If you are in the cash-management business, have significant cash available to you, and can earn more money by taking advantage of quick-payment discounts, take the 2 percent net 30. But if you are in the retail business, you should focus on turning your inventory quickly and trying to reach sell and buy. The biggest and best retailers in the world play the game this way, and they are hugely successful. We believe you should follow their lead and take the Net 60 when given the choice.

Now that you know how to buy, in the next chapter I look at how to manage and organize the merchandise you bought.

The Least You Need to Know

- When buying for your store don't buy based on your tastes—buy based on the tastes of your customers.
- Know your price points before you go out to buy your products.

- You can negotiate terms with your suppliers. Get to know the key terms and decide which ones are the most critical for you.
- Interview potential suppliers and compare the terms and services they offer. Don't lock yourself into one supplier. Always have alternatives in mind.
- Build a win-win relationship with your suppliers to get the best terms and the best service.
- Know what you need for your store and only buy products you need. Don't get caught up in a "good" deal if you don't need the product.

Chapter 12

Managing Your Inventory

In This Chapter

- Planning framework
- Merchandise mix
- Pricing right
- Knowing your seasons

After you decide who you want to buy your products from and what products you want to buy, you then must figure out the right quantities, at the right price points, and in the right assortment. Merchandise management is about deciding how much of each product to carry, making sure it's exactly what the customer wants, when they want it, and at the price that they are willing to pay.

In this chapter, I review the basics of merchandise planning and how to determine the right mix of merchandise. I also discuss how to avoid over- or under-buying, as well as how to manage the goods when they arrive. Finally, I discuss markdowns and the lessons you learn from them.

Merchandise Planning: A Framework

First, you need to come up with a merchandise plan. A merchandise plan gives you a roadmap for profitably managing what your store will carry for the next season based on the six rights of retail:

- The right product—inventory and assortment.
- The right place—where to display the product in the store. If you have multiple stores, you need to determine at which stores it is going to sell the best.
- The right time—the delivery time required to get it to the store when the customer wants it. For example, ordering the newest style of running shoes that arrive after the beginning of the marathon running season will be too late and you'll lose a lot of sales.
- The right quantity—determining the right amount of merchandise to order so you don't end up with too much merchandise left on the shelves after the end of the season or too little merchandise to satisfy your customer's needs during the season.
- The right price—set a price that will sell the article and return a fair profit to your store or company.
- The right service—you must have the right people with the right training to effectively sell it to customers or it won't sell.

Determining Departments and Classifications

To help you develop your merchandise plan, you first need to understand how to group the items you plan to sell into "departments" and "classifications," also called "categories." That's the only way you'll be able to manage your inventory in a profitable way. Computers make this management much easier today. To help you understand how departments and classifications evolved into what is used in stores today, let's look at how we got here.

If you had started your business in 1950, you would have run it with little or no structure. With the adding machines that were used then, you would know that you made a total of $500 worth of sales, but you would have no idea what items you sold.

Departments

In the 1970s, things got easier. With the evolution of cash registers, you could track your sales by department. At the end of the day, you would know from the cash register tape that you had made a total of $1,500 in sales—and that you had sales of $500 in department one, $650 in department two, and $350 in department three.

As you think through the selection of merchandise you will offer in your store, keep in mind that you should have fewer departments rather than more. Each department should account for at least 10 percent of your business. Therefore, the maximum you mathematically should have in your store is 10 departments. Some successful stores have only one, whereas most have three or four.

Department totals, by themselves, do not provide enough information. You really need to understand what you are selling at a deeper level, as well as what is not selling. You may even want to see these numbers every hour.

Since the 1990s, retailers have been able to use computers to take charge of the merchandise management part of their businesses and structure their inventory to a very high level of detail. Using the right program (I discuss software programs in Chapter 19), you can know your numbers in detail at the end of the day—or whenever you want during the day. For example, your computer system would tell you that you made a total of $4,500 in sales. And that you had sales of $1,500 in department one, $1,950 in department two, and $1,050 in department three. You can even dig deeper into the details and find out what you sold. For example, an electronics retailer could find out that he sold 12 widescreen DVDs and 8 full screen DVDs of a particular movie title.

I often remind retailers that customers "vote with their wallets." By this, I mean that the most valuable market research you will ever have is the behavior of your customers. You can do all kinds of research to ask customers what they would like to buy in your store, but their answers will all be "in theory." The only answers that really count are the ones that customers give when they put their money on the counter to pay for their purchases.

Better Not!

If you do not count the votes of your customers through their purchases, you will not last long in the retail business. You cannot afford to ignore the crucial information that people will give you every day through their buying behavior.

Classifications

The extra information you can get by using computers to manage merchandise is available as long as you develop your merchandise plan with an extra level of detail below departments. The detail can be called either *categories* or *classifications*. Both words refer to the same thing: a grouping or assortment of merchandise that the customer views as interchangeable.

def•i•ni•tion

Both **categories** and **classifications** refer to the same thing in retailing—they are a method of grouping or sorting your merchandise. Hard goods retailers such as hardware or office supply stores tend to use categories, whereas soft goods merchants such as clothing or cosmetics retailers tend to use classifications.

Think about how your customers will shop in your store to define your classifications. For example, if you are a hardware retailer and sold out of hammers, a customer will not buy a can of paint and use that to pound nails instead. Paint and hammers would be in different product categories. Or, if you are a women's fashion retailer and sold out of dresses, a customer will not buy a bathing suit and wear that to work instead. Dresses and bathing suits would be in different product classifications.

As you try to develop your product classifications, remember that when a customer comes into your store looking for a particular item, several items from the same product classification can often meet their needs, but never items from other product classifications. The same rule of thumb applies for a classification as applies for a department: each classification should account for at least 10 percent of your business in that department. Therefore, the maximum you can mathematically have in each department is 10 classifications.

The actual number you choose will be a trade-off between your need for accurate information and your ability to digest that information in a meaningful way. You may decide that different departments need to have different numbers of classifications.

The key here is to let the customer be your guide. If you have too many classifications, some will inevitably represent only a small percentage of your total business. The customers will be telling you clearly that they do not believe you are the right store at which to buy items in that classification.

Sub-classifications or sub-categories are further definitions of a classification or a category. For example, if you are a menswear retailer who does a good business in your dress-shirt classification, you might want to have two sub-classifications—one called long-sleeved dress shirts and another called short-sleeved dress shirts.

Within each sub-classification, you might want to divide things further into lines, items, and stock keeping units or SKUs—the finest level of detail at which you can define an item. For example, here is how a retailer would take a long-sleeve shirt down to the SKU level of classification:

Classifying Items to the SKU Level

Department:	Menswear
Classification:	Dress shirts
Sub-classification:	Long-sleeved dress shirts
Line:	Arrow brand long-sleeved dress shirts
Item:	Button-down collar, white, 100 percent cotton Arrow brand long-sleeved dress shirts
SKU:	Size 16½—34, button-down collar, white, 100 percent cotton Arrow brand long-sleeved dress shirt

To be a successful retailer, you need to recognize that you cannot be everything for everybody. "I am sorry, but I don't carry that item," is one of the hardest things you will ever say to a customer—but you must say it to certain customers. For example, if your business is a shoe store, you may decide that you will not carry shoes for children, not stock athletic shoes, or not offer wider sizes.

Assuming that you have a good point of service (POS) system, which I discuss in Chapter 19, it will be much easier to understand the exact merchandise that your store should carry after it has been open and operating for six months. You will then be able to start tailoring your inventory to match the votes that you got from customers during the first season.

Carrying what your customers want to buy is one of the most critical things you can do to become an important source of that merchandise for them. This is why structuring your business around classifications makes sense. By analyzing your sales at the classification level, you will learn that customers prefer some classifications to others, and that they want to spend a certain amount of money in each classification. Then you can buy accordingly and give them more of what they want the following season.

For example, if you were the menswear retailer selling dress shirts, you might learn that 80 percent of the votes in your dress shirt classification went to items priced between \$50 and \$60. You might also learn that 90 percent of those votes went to your long-sleeved dress shirt sub-classification. And that 50 percent of those votes went to the Arrow brand.

Here is how the math for that calculation works:

> 80 percent of your total dress shirt votes went to the $50 to $60 price range.
> 0.80 × 1.00 = 0.80
>
> 90 percent of that 80 percent went to long-sleeved dress shirts (72 percent).
> 0.90 × 0.80 = 0.72
>
> 50 percent of that 72 percent went to the Arrow brand (36 percent).
> 0.50 × 0.72 = 0.36

So looking at that calculation, where should you put 36 percent of your dollars when you buy dress shirts for next season? Arrow brand long-sleeved dress shirts would be a good place to start. Assuming the price for the shirts is in the $50 to $60 range and will probably increase to between $55 and $65 in the next season, that's what you should plan to stock. If you tracked your information to the SKU level, you could take this analysis down to the size, style, color, and fabric that won the most votes from your customers.

Without this knowledge, you could easily put 50 percent of your dollars into shirts priced at $100 and face huge "markdowns" next season when they do not sell. Worse, you could put 50 percent of your dollars into shirts priced at $60 or below and face an entire season in which you can match your unit sales from the previous year but not your dollar sales.

While this level of detail is great information you could base your decisions on, there is a limit to this. You will sell thousands of different SKUs each day or week, and analyzing sales at the item, line, and sub-classification levels will probably be overwhelming. That is why I suggest that you just look at classifications.

In fact, if you manage the entire merchandise management side of your business at the classification level using the right technology, you will achieve a level of information and control that most owner-operated retailers only dream about. At the end of every day, you will be able to look at your sales by department to see if you are meeting your goals. If you are, everything is fine and you can go home to rest.

If you are not meeting your goals, you will be able to "drill down" to the classification level and find out why. Perhaps you will find that within a certain department, classifications one and two are performing well but classification three is nowhere near budget. Once you know that, you can go home—with a clear understanding of what you need to look at first when you come in the next morning.

Maintaining the Right Assortment

In addition to picking the right products, you also need to carry the right assortment of those products. Assortment dimensions include sizes, colors, styles, price ranges, fabrics, and lifestyles. The process of assortment planning is complex. Most retailers take years to learn how to do it properly. The complexity is due to the fact that you are dealing with a process that has many dimensions or components. When buying merchandise for your store, not only must you select an appealing range of products to buy, you also need to make sure that there are choices of colors in each of the styles. In addition, you have to have low-, moderate-, and high-priced items for different customers. And you most likely need to have different materials or fabrics. Finally, you need the product to appeal to different lifestyles. When you take a total quantity of 1,000 different products and begin to break them down by all these dimensions, it gets quite complex.

In analyzing your sales to determine why certain items sell well whereas others don't, you need to look at your stock based on the many dimensions that you used when you created the assortment in the first place. If you want to know why one item is not selling, you must look at last season's sales and markdowns by size, color, lifestyle, and so on, and then decide to remove not the entire item from your assortment but only specific colors or sizes that do not sell.

Most retailers find they have winners in their inventory that customers buy a lot and they just did not have enough items in inventory to satisfy their demand. Similarly, they find that a majority of their inventory is not selling as well and is therefore unprofitable.

Assortment planning helps you focus on the 20 percent of your most profitable stock with the goal to increase it to ensure improved sales. In order to develop a well-balanced and profitable merchandise line, you must follow some important rules:

- Purchase the core merchandise on a regular buying cycle. This frees up dollars for investment into new merchandise and seasonal offerings to build incremental sales.
- Construct the merchandise mix first by category and then by sub-category.
- Avoid the creation of duplicate styles and fashions. Duplicate styles and fashions can cause confusion in your assortment if there are too many similar items in the same sub-category. The more duplicated lines you buy, the more you must reduce the depth of sizes in each line.

- Have a meaningful range of prices in each sub-category. The number of different prices should reflect the type of merchandise and how wide the range is of the selection. For example, you should not include in the same sub-category items that have a price range of 10 times the difference between items. If the lowest priced article in the sub-category is $30, the highest price should not be above $300. Finally, the price range should not have similar items where the prices have small differences, i.e., $70, $71, $72, $73, $74, etc., because this will cause customers to challenge the reason one item is one dollar more than another one.
- Try to achieve a good-better-best "trade up" in a category. Have a low price point that is competitive in your market, then a better item at a higher price (heavier cotton, more durable imprinting, etc.), and finally, a much higher price point (the highest) that has the best wood, the best design, and the best of all features. This will give customers a clear reason the prices are different and often they will "trade themselves up" to the higher priced item.
- Have quantities in standard customer sizes and extreme sizes for a particular item if you sell clothing or shoes. When determining the quantity by size for an order of a jacket, for example, you should consider both standard customer size profiles for the jacket and also oversized jackets if you have many customers larger than XL. You should use an average of the sales by size to date.
- Specify in every merchandise plan how the assortment is to be developed in terms of the number of core items that will be bought and the seasonal merchandise required to satisfy local market conditions.
- Keep in mind how the customer will view the assortment. In addition, you must be clear on your store concept and image, and work up from there to build the assortment.

Looking at the past is key. However, it might not work every time. For example, if you are running a clothing store, last season's markdowns on certain styles or fabrics might not have anything to do with this year's performance of similar products. It might be that a style that will sell this season was bought too early last year and is just now catching on. Or a fabric like cotton will be back "in," or denim will make a dramatic turnaround. You must look at the past but not be a slave to it. Customer behavior is just a rear view mirror. It does not always predict the future.

Pricing Strategies

We all need to become better at identifying the true market value of the products we sell and understanding that there are customers who will generally pay more if the product is right, customers who will pay more at certain times, customers who will never pay more, and customers who simply are not influenced by price at all. I know that you are asking yourself where you can find more of the latter! But the truth remains, price is an important factor to many of your customers, and how you set your merchandise prices is critical to your business strategy.

If you don't have a clear price policy, you are flirting with disaster. Whatever your price policy is, you must always be prepared to explain it to your customers.

If something doesn't sell within at least three months of your putting it on the shelf, you do want to mark down the price and move it off your shelf so you can make room for items that are selling. When you take a markdown, not only must you learn something from the action, but you must also be able to explain to your customers why you are doing it. If you fail to explain to your customers that this is a markdown for the end of season, because products are damaged or defective and so on, then you run the risk of your customers not believing any of your prices and turning each interaction with your customer into a mini auction.

Can you imagine a return to the days when every transaction with a customer was a negotiation? What would your store be like if every item was open to negotiation by the customer? Yet this is what is possible and is already happening on the Internet today. You need to move your customers away from a price only concern. Here are five suggestions that will help keep you out of the price only game and will give you a strategy for your price policy:

- Control your inventories (never buy more than you can realistically expect to sell in eight weeks). Remember that scarcity increases demand.
- Always try to get exclusives so you are not being shopped on an apples-to-apples comparison basis. If you cannot get total exclusivity, then get time (first three months), geographic (only one in your city to sell it), or channel (only gift store). Even if you can just get different packaging that will make it look less like the others, it can work.
- Nurture your customers who do not shop you on price alone. Send thank-you cards and maintain close relationships with those good customers. Help them by creating gift registries, remembering important dates for them, becoming more than an item provider in their lives. Add value to what you do for them.

- Always keep your markdown items at the back of the store where the customer has to search to find them. Drag customers through the total store and tempt them with your good items before they see the markdowns.
- Remember, the price you paid for the item has nothing to do with the markdown price. Your first markdown is the cheapest. If you take a markdown (and make sure you *never* take a markdown without knowing the cause) and the item sells out immediately, do not regret the fast sale. Pat yourself on the back, you paid your tuition. Now don't make the same mistake again.

Managing Markdowns

Just as you plan and budget everything else in your business, you need to plan and budget your markdowns. Retailers use two kinds of markdowns: *regular* and *promotional.*

Regular markdowns are the ones you take to reduce permanently the book value of certain items in your inventory. For example, you might reduce a particular line in which you have only broken sizes, colors, or assortments from $49 to $39. You will actually cross off the old price on the price ticket and write the new price using a red pen.

Promotional markdowns are the ones you take for a specific event such as a "weekend sale." You might, for example, plan to sell 50 of a particular item at $19 instead of $24 during that period. You need to include a promotional markdown of $250 (50 units × $5) in your plan, but you will only record a markdown for the items that you actually sell.

def•i•ni•tion

Regular markdowns are when you permanently reduce the value of certain items in your inventory.

Promotional markdowns are when you temporarily reduce the value of items in your inventory for a special purpose, such as a weekend sale.

In the case of promotional markdowns, you do not permanently reduce the price of every unit you have in the store. After the sale, the remaining items are still in your inventory at regular price.

It is vitally important that you record and track every change from the original ticket price of every item you bring into your store. Computer systems can do this automatically if you change the price in the computer at the same time as you change the price of an item. If you do not have a computer inventory system, you must manually record each price reduction on a markdown form.

If the price change is only temporary and the item will return to "regular price" after that—such as a promotional markdown for the "weekend sale" described previously—you will only record a markdown when you sell an item. The promotional markdown list that you keep beside the cash register for those three days might look like this:

Promotioinal Markdown List

Date of sale: ______________

Class	Item	Description	Regular Price	Sale Price	Markdown Amount	Quantity Sold	Total MD Dollar

You can fill this in for each promotional markdown you take at the cash register. Most stores fill in the names and stock numbers of the promotional items in the morning and just enter the units sold with hash marks as they go through the day. I filled in a sample promotional markdown list below to show you how that looks:

Promotioinal Markdown List

Date of sale: October 3 to 5

Class	Item	Description	Regular Price	Sale Price	Markdown Amount	Quantity Sold	Total HD Dollar
3	17395	Women's shoe	$89.95	$79.95	$10.00	6	$60.00
8	19990	Women's hose	$5.00	$4.00	$1.00	10	$10.00

To record regular markdowns—also called "permanent" markdowns because the selling price will never go back up—you should use what is called a "laundry list." You use this list to record a batch of markdowns, completing one line as you change the price of each group of items. Here is what a regular markdown "laundry list" might look like:

Regular Markdown "Laundry List"

Date: October 1

Class	Item	Description	Original Price	Markdown Price	Markdown Amount	Units	Total HD Dollars	Reason
3	11122	tie	$17.00	$8.50	$8.50	10	$85.00	Wrong style
2	98773	shirt	$45.00	$35.00	$10.00	8	$80.00	Too small

By using both a promotional markdown list and a regular markdown "laundry list," you can keep track of every markdown you take. You will constantly be updating your inventory value and tracking your reductions. You can then use this information to identify bad vendors, colors, materials, or sizes so that you do not make the same buying mistake again. In Appendix C, I include a "Regular Markdown Laundry List" that you can use to keep track of your markdowns.

When you take regular markdowns, you should ignore the cost of the items. Remember that your customers do not care in the least what you paid for an item. They only care about what they must pay for it. The whole point of taking regular markdowns is to adjust your inventory to "market value"—the price your customers will pay.

You should always take your regular markdowns on the first day of the month, so you have the maximum number of days in which to record a sale to offset the markdown. Because you record your regular markdowns by month and by classification, it is quite possible to have markdowns that exceed your sales in some months. This is not something to fear if you clean up a problem and learn from the experience.

As we mentioned earlier, "Your first markdown is the cheapest." This suggests that when you recognize you have made a buying mistake, you should deal with it. Try to eliminate the problem with the first markdown instead of reducing the item's price a little at a time, thus keeping your mistake "front and center" for weeks or months.

A number of formulas purport to tell you how much to take as a first markdown, but I do not really trust any of them. Instead, you should determine the appropriate price reduction by looking at your original quantity, your rate of sale, and your stock turnover goals for the classification. The idea is to calculate how long this particular item would likely be in your store if you did not take the markdown.

For example, if you originally bought 25 of an item and still have 17 of them left after eight weeks, the rate of sale is one per week. This means that you have at least a 17-week supply if you do not take the markdown and possibly longer because size, color, and assortment factors may slow the rate of sale even more. When you sell the last piece, that item will have been in your store for almost the entire 26-week season.

If you have a turnover goal in that classification of more than two turns per year—it should be at least three and preferably four turns per year—you should "bite the bullet" and cut the price. You likely paid for the item after 30, 60, or 90 days, so you are looking at your own money, including all of your potential profit, when you look at those 17 pieces.

If you choose the right markdown price and sell the 17 pieces in a week or two, do not second-guess yourself. Understand that you took the right action and chose the right price. Just be certain that you learn from the experience. Decide which of these mistakes you made:

- You priced the item too high and you cannot expect that high a margin the next time. If your margin wasn't that good to begin with, you either need to find a supplier who can provide the item at a lower price that matches what your customers are willing to pay or you discontinue the item.
- You bought an item that did not fit the mix of merchandise in the store, and you should not buy that item again.
- You bought a color that your customers didn't like, and you should not buy that item in that color again.

You may determine a different reason for the mistake. Whatever the reason, be sure to note it on your markdown laundry list so you can avoid making the mistake again.

If you find yourself in a position where you have more items to mark down than you have markdown budget available to do it, this could be the result of many factors, including:

- **Buying based on incomplete records from past seasons.** Without a good road map to guide you, it is easy to end up just about anywhere.

- **Buying based on the availability of co-op advertising or favorable dating.** You should always consider terms when you buy, but these should never be your reason for buying.
- **Overpaying, which leads to overpricing.** If the customer feels they can get a lower price—read "a better value"—somewhere else, they will probably shop there.
- **Buying too many.** By nature, most retailers are optimistic that tomorrow will be better than today. It might turn out to be, but you should never buy based on optimism.
- **Buying from too many vendors.** You should not put all of your eggs in one basket, but neither should you spread them out too thinly. You need to have several vendors for whom you are an important account.
- **Bringing in items too early.** If the customer sees an item before they are ready to buy, it may become "old news" by the time they are ready. For example, if you stock a new shoe style before the shoes are "in," customers may ignore it. When the item catches on, though, it may be seen as outdated because you've had it on the shelves too long.
- **Bringing in items too late.** As tough as it is, you need to enforce delivery dates and cancel late orders. This matters a lot, because you build all of your sales, staffing, and advertising plans around having merchandise at the time you expect it.
- **No plan to sell.** You need to plan exactly how you will sell any merchandise you buy. This plan could include advertising, point-of-sale signing, or perhaps special staff training.
- **Repeat orders on fashion merchandise.** You should make it standard practice never to order additional quantities of a fashion item that sells well. By the time you notice the "hot seller," write a repeat order, and receive the new shipment, you will probably be well past the customer's peak interest in that item.
- **Broken sizes, colors, or assortments.** When you see any of these, it is probably time for a markdown because you no longer have a good selection to show your customers.
- **Competition.** The price is lower down the street, and you have to match it.
- **Soiled or damaged goods.** Items in your store get shopworn as people look at and examine them. I describe this as getting "older and moldier."

- **End of season.** As you get close to each new selling season, you should try to sell every single piece of nonbasic merchandise from the current season.
- **Poor or hidden display.** Every item that you buy should have at least one "moment in the sun" during the prime selling season. Your customers have to see it to buy it.
- **Last in, first out on "basics."** A fundamental rule of merchandising basic items is that you should place new products on the shelf behind any old products you still have.

Making It Seasonal

In an ideal world, owner-operated retailers would follow a "seasonal" philosophy when it comes to taking markdowns. This philosophy says that you should give merchandise in your store extended exposure at full price, taking markdowns only at the end of the season. In practice, this usually translates into a commitment to hold your price for at least 16 weeks.

By following a seasonal markdown philosophy, you will give your customers time to see your full merchandise assortment. They will be able to see how various items fit together and get comfortable with any new ideas. You will be able to tell them with confidence that it is okay to buy at full price today because everything will not be going on sale tomorrow.

In fact, under a strict application of the seasonal markdown philosophy, all of the merchandise from a season would go on sale at once—in the last six weeks of the season. This strict application would make sense if you could buy perfectly, but no retailer has ever been able to buy perfectly. That is why I recommend that you take regular markdowns.

And when you take these markdowns, you should move the items to a special rack or area near the back of the store. You should never contaminate your regular-price selection or highlight your buying mistakes by placing them at the front door. Customers who want discount prices will gladly walk through your regular merchandise to find the "bargains."

To help make things clear for your customer, you should always adjust sale items to specific price points instead of to percentage discounts. This will let you create a $10 table, a $20 rack, or whatever. With experience, you will learn the "sale" price points that work best in your business and can work those into your plan.

As an owner-operated retailer, you need to build a reputation for quality. Which means that you need to protect your integrity and not play the sale game. Your prices should fluctuate based on a week-by-week plan that you create at the start of the season—although there will always be minor modifications due to competitive conditions.

Once you start moving toward the discount arena, you will find yourself competing against the category killers and big-box retailers, and you will almost certainly lose.

If you need to lower your prices in order to meet your weekly or monthly sales goals, something is drastically wrong somewhere in your business, and you should seek professional guidance immediately.

Once you know your departments and classifications, you're ready to think about designing the layout of your store. In the next chapter, I introduce you to store design.

The Least You Need to Know

- Develop your merchandise plan and keep your eye on the six rights of retail.
- Develop departments and classifications for your merchandise so you can track your performance and quickly identify any problem areas.
- Your customers vote for products they want at the prices they are willing to pay by their buying behavior. Track how your customers are voting and plan your future merchandise purchases based on what you know about your customers' preferences.
- Don't hesitate to consider a markdown if your products sit on your shelves unsold for more than three months.

Chapter 13

Designing the Store to Optimize Sales

In This Chapter

- Crafting your store's unique design
- Creating the right in-store experience
- Making your store sell as good as it looks
- Choosing materials, fixtures, colors, and shapes

Choosing the right look and feel for your store is as important as choosing the right product for your customers. Whether you do it yourself or you work with a design or architectural firm specialized in retail spaces—and I highly recommend that you hire a professional firm to help you—your goal is to choose a store design that entices customers to enter, purchase, and come back for more. Store design gives you the opportunity to create a retail environment that is unique, comfortable, and convenient, as well as one that makes you stand out from the competition.

In this chapter, you learn how to select the right look for your store based on the image that you want to project, your products, prices, service level, and customer profile. You explore how different colors, shapes, materials, and every other design component may affect your customer's perception of your store brand and how to choose the right design elements for your store. You learn how to design a store to maximize your service and sales potential.

Choosing the Right Design

You create an image for your store with the design you choose. You can communicate this image to your customers using various design elements. Store design can be your best form of advertising, but to be effective and truly stand out, the look and feel of the store must convey this image in the customer's mind. It must be compelling, clear, consistent, and competitive. For example:

- A compelling design gives a reason to the customer to initially come in and then to buy from you. Think about what would make you want to walk into the store as you plan your design.
- A clear and consistent design ensures that you attract the right customers and deliver a uniform message. For example, don't surprise them with high prices if the store looks low end. Also don't try to impress customers with an upscale design and then have low-end goods in the store.
- A competitive design is a design that is not just another undistinguished image in an already overpopulated scene. Create a look for your store that is noticeable and truly different from your competitors.

What Your Customers Want

Consumers demand more and more every day. They either want fast service, quick delivery, and to pay as little as possible, or they are looking for a really special product or unique shopping experience.

Fast and cheap is what the big boys like Wal-Mart, Target, or Amazon.com offer. You can't compete with that, so you need to focus on a unique experience. That's what most specialty retailers are focusing on today, and what you should likely aim at, as well.

Store design (and visual merchandising) can help you deliver to your customer an extraordinary experience. But before we see how, let's find out more about customers' expectations.

Customers like to be happy. And if they are happy, we know that they are more likely to buy. Can a well-designed store make them happy? Yes it can! Think of ways to make the customer, or his/her shopping companion, want to stay in your store and shop. Nordstrom, for example, does it simply by providing a nice sitting area for people who prefer to relax while their companion shops their store.

Savvy Retailer

When my wife shops at Nordstrom, the department store chain, her favorite part of the store is the shoe department. I often go with her, and although I know that it's not going to be a fast shopping trip, I do it willingly. Why? Because they have couches for me to relax on while she shops. A few chairs, a few magazines, even some coffee or water, which don't cost that much. Yet, these simple amenities are well worth the small cost to make people comfortable and keep them in the store longer. If I am comfortable and enjoying a magazine (make sure to have a good mix in your store and that they are current issues), I am less likely to put pressure on my wife to leave. That translates directly into better sales.

Customers also have social needs that they want satisfied. Social needs refer to our need for love, friendship, image, status, self-esteem, recognition, and lifestyle. We try to satisfy these needs every day through our interactions with the rest of the world and yes, also when we shop in a store. A diamond ring in a Tiffany box is not just a ring. It is a way to satisfy a status and recognition need both of the giver and the receiver.

Customers want to be transported to a different world. Shopping is no longer just about picking up essential products. It's about temptation, attraction, and creating a memorable impression that encourages the customer to come back over and over again. That's why more and more stores today are built to deliver compelling and distinctive experiences for the customer.

And finally, customers sometimes want their shopping experience to be fast and easy. A well laid-out store with optimum space and paths through it makes it easier for a customer to purchase by having the merchandise readily accessible. It also guides customers efficiently through the store.

Better Not!

There's a difference between too much and not enough convenience. You don't want to make it too easy for the customer to rush through the store and miss out on some of your best displays. And you don't want to make it difficult and time-consuming for them to shop. Determine how you want your customer to walk through the store and design a path that will take them past your best merchandise and displays. But carefully balance convenience and your desired path. If you make it too difficult, customers may leave in frustration.

What You Want: Sales, of Course!

A store that looks and feels good is not only great for the customer, but it is great for you, too, provided that your customers buy what you're selling. When selecting your store design elements, make sure that the store not only looks good but also maximizes your service and sales opportunities.

I believe that a good store layout can mean up to 40 percent more business. Good design tends to attract more and better customers, which means more profit. You can also reduce the amount of inventory you need to purchase.

def•i•ni•tion

Markdown refers to a reduction in the selling price of your product. Markdowns are usually applied to slow-moving or old inventory or to promote an item to increase sales.

Proper fixtures often require less stock on them to look full. Good design can also help decrease your *markdown* rates. In a well-organized and well-designed store, where all the merchandise is in "its own place," slower moving items become apparent much earlier and can be auctioned with a markdown faster.

Your Service and Price Level Factors

In deciding the layout and design for your store, there are two important factors that you also need to look at: service and price level. You need to choose from three service levels—full-service, high-price; assisted self-service, mid-price; and self-service, low-price.

If You Are Full-Service, High-Price

If you are a full-service store, you need sufficient staff to greet, welcome, and service your customers. Your customer-to-staff ratio should be three customers (or less) to one staff. This is often the level of service of higher end stores, such as Tiffany or Nordstrom.

The type of fixtures and store layout that you should select for this store must reflect the high level of service that you are providing to your customer. Desks, chairs, tables—all must be conveniently located for the customer and the staff to use. You should also choose deluxe materials and design for your store such as marble, brass, exotic woods, luxurious textiles, complex color palettes, and fine-detailed workmanship.

If You Are Assisted Self-Service, Mid-Price

If you offer assisted self-service, your customer-to-staff ratio should be about five customers (or more) to one staff. Staff are there generally to answer questions that some customers may have, but most customers are allowed to wander the store and look at and select merchandise by themselves.

Store layout and fixtures must be designed to make it easy for customers to find what they need and help themselves. Materials used will range from basic shelves and tables to more custom-designed display units. This is the level of service generally offered at mid-price stores such as The Gap or Barnes and Noble.

If You Are Self-Service, Low-Price

If you offer self-service, your customers will almost entirely be on their own from the moment they enter the store (except at checkout). This is generally the business model of mass merchants and lower price stores such as Wal-Mart, Target, or a supermarket.

In this kind of store, every store element is key in providing the service that the customer needs without relying on store staff. You also tend to select plastic, chrome, Formica (which resembles marble), simple color palettes, and minimal detail for your store as indicators of low-price.

Crafting Your Store's Unique Image

The old saying that we judge a book by its cover is also true of a store. Your design choices, from the wide variety of options available to you, have a major impact on how your customers view your store and the experience that they have in it.

Your Store Name and Trademark Logo

Your store name is a key component of your image and overall look. You can use your first or last name, or a foreign word, an exotic name, the name of your core product, or something entirely different. The best store names manage to capture the essence of the store's unique identity—what the store is about. Whatever name you choose for your store, make sure it is easy to pronounce and remember. Here are some successful naming examples:

- Whole Foods (the organic food grocery chain)
- Lightology (a lighting store)
- 7/11 (the 7 days a week, 11 hours a day convenience chain)
- Modernica (a modern furniture store)
- The Children's Place (the children's clothing chain)
- Just Grapes (a wine store)

> **Better Not!**
> Don't design your trademark logo yourself unless you have some experience. Hire a designer to make sure it looks professional and reflects your brand as well as your target customers' taste. Then, consult a trademark lawyer to have it registered so no one can duplicate it.

A trademark logo can be a color, a picture, a style, a shape, a symbol that is unique to you and that you want your customers to associate with you. So, even when the store name is not present, customers can still recognize it and know that it's your store. Think of the bull's-eye of Target, the apple of Apple computers, or the blue-and-yellow color of Best Buy.

Store name and trademark logos must appear on everything—packaging, letterhead, signs, ads, price tags, receipts, and so on.

Eye-Catching Storefront and Interior

Use your storefront to make a powerful and eye-catching statement that causes the customer to stop and look. You want customers to notice your store when they are close and also from a distance. And you want them to want to come in to see more of what they saw outside.

The store's interior is a vital element of the storefront and should be as exciting as the storefront. For many stores today with an open front, as most mall stores have, the interior of the store becomes a part of the exterior as it can be clearly seen from outside.

Matching Building Exterior and Store Sign

If the building you are in doesn't match your store image, you might want to consider making some changes, such as adding or removing some architectural features in keeping with your image. Sometimes, it doesn't take much. If the building is too plain, just put some planters outside. Or install stylish (or traditional, depending on your image) light fixtures to illuminate and add some drama, particularly at night.

The store sign is a key component of your image and one that you should pay a lot of attention to. Why? When people look for you, you need to make it easy for them to find you. Signs don't have to be big to be noticed.

> **Better Not!**
>
> Don't go out and buy a new sign before consulting with your local municipality. Oftentimes, city ordinances impose limits on the type, size, and position of the sign, and it is a good idea to check.

Outdoor signs should be bright. They also need to be placed where they can be visible from every possible angle the customer may be approaching from. If you use a sign that is lit, make sure the light is always on.

Parking Lot

Your customers' perception of your store and their experience start even before they enter it. If the experience they have in the parking lot (or on the street where your store is located) does not reflect the image that you are trying to project, they will often not return.

If you are all about personalized service, make sure the parking lot is safe, clean, and easy for them to access and use (and there are sufficient spots). Even when you have no control over the parking area which you may share with other businesses, you can still exercise some power with the landlord or the parking attendants and expect them to do a proper job.

Traffic-Stopper Store Windows and Entrance

Store windows are as important as your storefront. They are among the first things that passersby see, and if they like what they see—their first impressions are good—chances are that they will come inside.

Store windows must project your unique image and identity. So, if you are about luxury and exclusivity, make sure the windows are a reflection of everything in life that is exclusive and luxurious. For example, if you are selling high-end bedroom and bath accessories, create a luxurious bedroom or bathroom in your storefront window.

Never turn your window's lights off, even after you are closed. You can also highlight a key section inside your store that is visible from the street by leaving your lights on in that section. This will encourage window shopping even when you are closed.

Your store entrance should be inviting and easy to enter. If the customers have to work to get in, they are much less likely to even try. Once you get them in, you are halfway to a sale!

Be sure your entrance is wide. Make it easy for a mother with a stroller or a person in a wheelchair to come in.

An inviting entrance is an entrance that has no obstacles, displays, or other barriers and offers a completely open view of the entire store.

Seating Area, Bags, and More

Remember earlier when I talked about Nordstrom's couches, and how I liked shopping there with my wife because I can just sit and relax while she shops? Nordstrom is not the only store that understands the importance of making the environment comfortable for a customer. Most bookstores today offer the same comfortable chairs and couches that naturally attract people and cause them to stay.

True, you don't want customers to sit there all day, but as we said earlier, the longer they stay in a store the more they spend. By placing chairs strategically, you can also guide customers through key areas of the store and have them face product areas that are important to your business.

Bags and all packaging materials in your store are also part of the store design and must reflect your brand's identity and deliver the same brand message to the customer. Bags aren't expensive and can be an effective form of advertising for your store because people often reuse them and carry them around to other places.

Business cards, fliers, event cards, postcards, and anything else in your store also add value to your image. So be sure to use a consistent image on anything you do related to your store.

Identifying Your Store Layout Hot Spots

Layout is about creating a path for your customers to shop your store effectively, efficiently, and to make sure that they are exposed to your best merchandise. Fixtures and other store elements will be located strategically according to your layout.

To help you decide on the best layout for your store, here is a list of the most valuable areas in a store where studies have demonstrated that most customers are naturally drawn to:

- **Entrance area.** This begins just after the transition zone, about 5 to 7 feet beyond the *lease line* and extends in a semicircle about 26 feet into the store.
- **Right side of the store.** More than 90 percent of customers will turn right upon entering a store. Place your fixtures for your best items here in sight of the customer as they turn in this direction.
- **Thirteen- to twenty-six-foot semicircle area just inside the entrance.** This is your "prime real estate area," or, in other words, the most valuable section of the store. It is called prime real estate because almost 100 percent of your customers are exposed to it. Again, you should place your display units for your best offerings and impulse items here.

def•i•ni•tion

Lease line is where the public space ends and your store begins. It is generally where the store entrance door opens.

- **Cash wrap or checkout area.** This is where you hope that every customer will stop! It is your last chance to make sure your customer has the total solution. You need to place fixtures near or behind the cash wrap, where you showcase accessories, maintenance products, and impulse items.

Effective layout also means creating an environment where customers can get around easily and not get frustrated with clogged aisles, narrow paths, and poorly lit areas.

Turning Your (Best) Lights On!

Lighting is a critical design element. You can have the best display and product in the world, but if you don't light your store and merchandise properly, your customer will not be able to appreciate the quality of your products.

Lights are not only used to make a product look good (and show the true color). Be sure that they also make the customer look good, too. This is particularly important in changing rooms, if you have them, and where mirrors are located.

Like color, music, and scent, light also contributes to setting the mood. If the mood is right, customers will be more inclined to stay and buy more.

Better Not!

We do not recommend using fluorescent lights unless they are the new energy efficient bulbs that mimic incandescent lights. Even though fluorescent lights are inexpensive to operate, they look cheap, provide very harsh light, and they are mainly used in low-end stores.

Selling Points

Use quality lighting for better results. Consider the use of halogen lamps whenever possible. They will last longer than standard incandescent lamps. They are more expensive, but they tend to provide a whiter and truer light.

Here are some lighting options for you to consider:

- **Spot track lighting (also called accent lighting).** Use this type of lighting to draw attention to merchandise, displays, windows, signs, or particular areas of the store by providing a focused path of bright light.
- **New high-efficiency fluorescent recessed lamps (also called floodlights).** Use them for ambient or background lighting.
- **Recessed incandescent lamps to mark traffic flow.** These lights are effective in guiding the customer through the store.
- **High bay lighting.** They are a type of lighting used in high-ceiling areas to light surfaces more than 15 feet away. This type of lighting is often used in warehouses as well as warehouse-type retail stores.
- **Wallwasher lighting.** This type of lighting is ideal for providing even lighting to wall displays, particularly where there's heavy vertical merchandising. For maximum accent and to create a visual backdrop, you may want to include halogen focal point lighting along the same track.

Choosing Floor, Ceiling, Fixtures, and Wall Treatments

When choosing your store floor treatment, ceiling and wall finishes, and fixtures you need to consider these three things:

- The look you want to create—materials and shapes must reinforce your brand message and enhance your product, not compete with it.

- The cost to buy and replace them.
- The requirements of local building codes.

Here are some options that are available to you and some recommendations about when to use them.

Floors

The most common choices are ceramic tiles, limestone or marble (real and faux), carpeting, hardwood floors, and polished concrete.

Ceramic tiles, marble, and limestone are usually found in high-end stores. While a very good choice from an aesthetic point of view, they may be expensive and may scratch or crack. One good alternative to stone or marble are stone and marble imitation flooring. Although they might cost the same as the real options, they can cost half the price to install and they last longer.

Hardwood flooring is also common in mid-price to high-end stores. It adds elegance and warmth, but it can be pricey and tends to scratch easily. Newer forms of engineered hardwood are a lot more reasonable and may stand up to heavier traffic better.

Carpeting is widely used. While it can stain, you can remedy that by using carpet tiles that are easily replaceable when they get dirty. The good thing about carpet is that customers and staff find it a comfortable surface to walk on. It's also reasonably priced and rarely represents a large investment.

Finally, there is the latest look in store floors. It is simple polished concrete. Stores from Costco to Urban Outfitters, Old Navy, and even some high-end designer stores have found that it is a simple, easy-to-maintain look that works very well. If you do concrete, make sure you provide mats in areas where your staff spends a lot of time standing.

Walls

Your options for store walls are multiple, including paint, wallpaper, paneling (wood, glass, metal, or plastic), and wall systems.

Most stores use paint. It's more versatile and you can change and redo it easily with limited cost. Many stores also use slat wall because it is considered one of the most flexible and versatile of all wall systems. With slat wall you can have a painted finish, a wood finish, mirror, or almost any material you want. The benefit of slat wall is that you can easily add shelves, bins, hanging arms—any type of merchandise presentation system you require—and change it daily if you wish.

Ceilings

Ceilings are truly an active component of your overall interior design direction. So, for example, for an industrial look and feel, choose exposed ceiling to complement the look. Also, if you have a high ceiling, paint it a dark color to lower it, whereas if you have lower ceilings, paint them a light color to give a feeling of height.

Fixtures

The only purpose of a fixture is to sell merchandise. They are there to hold and present merchandise and should not be the central focus of your store. That's why good fixtures are almost invisible, because what you should see is the product and not the fixture.

> **Selling Points**
>
> Flexibility when it comes to fixtures is key. As customer interests change, so will the product lines you carry. Be sure your store fixtures accommodate these changes as well.

At the same time, fixtures also communicate image, and they need to reflect your store's unique identity. If you're trying to create a particular time or place, the more authentic the materials and details, the better the effect will be. Or, for example, if you sell handicrafts, select wooden displays and furniture, whereas if you sell computers you may want to consider glass and chrome. What you sell dictates your choices when it comes to fixtures. Your goal is to make the product stand out and sell.

Peripherals Matter, Too

Peripherals, also called atmospherics, are generally colors, music and video, scent, and cleanliness. They are used to promote the desired image and provide the right experience to your customer.

Choosing the Right Colors

It is estimated that in visual communication, 80 percent of the impact of the message results from the use of color.

When deciding on the color for your store, I recommend that you consult with a professional designer to make sure you choose what's right for the type of experience that you want to give to your target customer.

Here is a list of some rules for using colors in a store:

- Colors must be subordinate to the product. Background colors should be a soft neutral tint particularly with colorful products and if your merchandise is going to change color every season. This will allow the product to stand out. At other times the background could echo a common color of the merchandise.
- Choose one or a very few dominant colors for principal displays.
- One strong color used with subordinate colors is better than too many strong colors. If you use too many strong colors in combination, you may create confusion. Conversely, if you choose one strong color in combination with subordinate colors, you create order.
- Choose lighter tints to deepen the space. Color affects depth perception. For example, in window spaces, darker colors seem to shorten the space, bringing the background closer, whereas lighter tints deepen it.
- Choose colors that have the desired impact on your customers. While bright colors may attract a customer into a store, prolonged exposure to a large amount of bright color can make a customer uneasy and can also divert attention from the merchandise. If you want to use bright colors, do it in graphics and other areas away from the product.
- Choose colors and hues based on price and size. Choose vivid hues for lower-priced merchandise and go for more refined and/or currently fashionable hues for exclusive merchandise. Also use bright colors for small areas, combined with a very soft second color. The more intense a color, the smaller the area it should cover and the softer the second color used in combination with it should be.

Playing Your Customer's Preferred Music and Videos

Strictly speaking, music and videos are not visual elements. But they are usually part of your store design because they are an integral part of the store's image and the shopping experience, so they should reflect your primary customer's taste and preferences.

I recommend using soft music in most cases. Soft music slows a customer's pace, resulting in sales increases, whereas very loud, fast music can deter customers from entering or remaining in a store.

Selling Points

If permitted, music could be used outside to create excitement, creating a mood and drawing customers into the store.

This is obviously very different if you are a music store or a fashion store for teenagers or young adults. In that case, blaring music is a must as customers identify with that lifestyle and are often happy that the music is a "barrier" to their parents!

When using videos, make sure that they are consistent with the image of your store. They should feature the brands and products you carry, narrate your history, or talk about your services, events, or promotions. They should feature the lifestyle of your target customer. They should entertain, amuse, and educate, and above all, they should always be working—so no blank video screens in your store!

Draw Customers with Scent, Cleanliness, and Professional-Looking Staff

Scent, if appropriate, can be used to draw customers into the store. If inappropriate, though, it can discourage them from entering it. That's why the scent should be that of the products carried in the store and not the one coming from the street or from the store next door. So, for instance, if you are an aromatic candle store, the scent in your store should be that of the candles you sell, not the donut store next door.

Selling Points

Restrooms (highly recommended if you encourage long visits) and any area of your store that the customer may have access to are an extension of your store and must project the same image. Be sure that they are always clean, with enough supplies, and working properly.

Lack of cleanliness can deter a customer from shopping in your store. If your store is untidy, dirty, and disorganized, customers will find it distasteful and will not want to shop there. Dust every day and clean shelves, floors, doors, mirrors, glass tops, props, and your products regularly.

Your store staff should be dressed appropriately for your store image. Their behavior toward others, both customers and colleagues, should be a true reflection of your brand image and message.

Designing a Store That Deters Shoplifters

Shoplifting is one of the biggest headaches for retailers. Training your staff regarding how to spot shoplifters is one way you will combat shoplifting. Designing your store to help deter shoplifters from stealing is another way.

Locate your registers so that customers must pass them before exiting the store. Also avoid high fixtures or displays that obstruct your view of the entire store. Place ceiling mirrors in corners where shoplifters might hide merchandise. And, above all, maintain adequate lighting everywhere in the store.

The use of security equipment such as closed-circuit television is also recommended if you sell very expensive items. If you own a very large store, hire a uniformed security guard.

And finally, don't forget to check restrooms and dressing rooms regularly for empty hangers or discarded packaging.

The Least You Need to Know

- Create a store design that is compelling, clear, consistent, and competitive.
- Know what your customers want, and design an exciting environment that meets their expectations.
- Map out your store so customers see your best stuff, but don't create a path that is inefficient and slows down your customers.
- Light your store well, and keep the lights on your key merchandise, even when the store is closed, to encourage after-hours window shopping.
- Use colors, floors, walls, and fixtures to help create the image you want for your store.

Chapter 14

Creating Product Displays That Sell

In This Chapter

- Craft displays for high impact and sales
- Create buying appeal
- Use signs and graphics effectively
- Tell a story

Visually, you want to present your products on the sales floor and in the windows to create maximum impact and generate top sales. There's a difference between creating good looking displays (art) and displays that sell (science).

You might have a knack for displaying product attractively and yet not know how to do it to encourage customers to buy more. Or you might know technically what it takes to create a presentation that sells but lack the artistic sense to do it nicely. The truth is that you need to have both, and if you don't, you need to hire someone who does.

In this chapter, you explore techniques for how to display product in your store. You discover how to use different sections in your store to tell powerful merchandising stories. You also learn how to make it easy for your customers to shop in your store and browse it in its entirety.

Why Visual Merchandising Is So Important

Store design is like a cover of a book that encourages your customers to look further. Product displays tell the story inside the book that makes your customers want to stay. In order to do so, your merchandise must be presented to excite, entice, and encourage the customer to buy.

Research tells us that 80 percent of purchases today are made on impulse. This means that 80 percent of your sales depend on how well you present your product to the customer and whether or not your presentation encourages the customer to buy on impulse. You tap into this impulse with exciting displays that make it easy for your customer to find the product.

Good layout and visual presentation enhances the feeling of service and makes your customers feel good. Atmosphere, comfort, convenience, design excellence, discovery, interactivity, involvement, and store cleanliness are all factors that enhance your customers' shopping experience.

Visual merchandising can help you …

- Sell more to existing customers.
- Get them back more often.
- Attract new customers.
- Increase profit margins through adding value to your offer.
- Keep customers longer in the store—the longer they stay, the more they buy.

Staging Your Product on the Floor and in the Windows

Think of it like a production. Place your main characters—your best products—front and forward. Make sure your customers see them first. Then place your other characters in the less prominent spots.

In a store, there are what we call hot spots—strategic areas that represent your best opportunity to capture impulse buyers and to showcase exceptional merchandise with exceptional presentations.

Here are the key ones to remember:

- Transition area from the entrance to inside the store (first 6 to 10 feet). Don't put too much there. Customers need space to decompress from the outside environment.
- Right side of the store—the direction most customers turn.
- Front 20 to 30 percent of the store (13- to 26-foot semicircle area just inside the store). This is the section in your store that most customers are exposed to, including those who just come in to quickly find out what you are about and then decide to stay or leave based on what they see in those first 13 to 26 feet.

Savvy Retailer

In his book *Why We Buy: The Science of Shopping*, Paco Underhill warns against placing any product in the first 5 to 15 feet of a store (called the "decompression zone"). When customers enter a store, they are decompressing from the outside to the inside environment and they are unable to see or notice any product that is in the decompression zone.

Covered in the following sections are other hot spots where you want to feature your best merchandise.

Power Walls

Walls are used to tell a single, eye-catching story, such as Back to School, Fall Scents, European Best Sellers, New Arrivals, Rare Rugs, Oprah Winfrey's Selections, and other special-selling seasons or sales.

A customer should understand what a wall is saying in about two seconds. Wall displays therefore should be visually easy to understand and not contain too many different colors or uniquely shaped items.

Focal Points

Focal points are the areas at which a customer naturally looks after entering a store or turning in an aisle. Here you would feature desirable items with a strong sign, a graphic, a display, or lighting to help direct the customer's eye.

Store Windows

Store windows should never be used as your stockroom! Windows are integral in creating a positive impression and impulse buyers, because they offer an opportunity to begin telling your store's unique merchandise story immediately. When the story is told well, people decide to walk in your store's door.

> **Selling Points**
>
> When it comes to windows, less is more. Simple, linear, and uncluttered displays go a long way in delivering a clear and powerful message. The more merchandise you try to jam in your windows, the less value and impact that merchandise has.

The store window is the place where you can showcase one single product, a season story, a special offering, anything that tells a story about the quality and value of the products carried in the store, and the excitement that the customer will find inside.

When economically possible and applicable, try using a video screen or multiple screens to make your windows more exciting and unique. Movement of some type in your windows will be much more enticing to potential customers than just a group of your best products.

The ABCs of Visual Merchandising

Visual merchandising is the science part of product presentation. It is based on years of observation and analysis of how people shop.

The result of these studies is a series of recommendations about how to make it easy, convenient, and effective for customers to find and buy what they need. This includes how to departmentalize your inventory, place your fixtures, present product for buying appeal, design signs and graphics, and create displays that tell a story.

Start by Departmentalizing Your Inventory

Effective merchandise presentation starts with a proper departmentalization and classification of your inventory. You departmentalize and classify your inventory by putting all of the same products in one area. This makes it easier and more logical for customers to find what they want.

For example, one department in a shoe store could be women's shoes. Within that department, a category or classification could be casual shoes and another category could be dress shoes. In a gift store, a department could be frames, and within the frame department, a category could be wooden frames and another category could be metal frames.

Placement of Your Fixtures

After organizing your product by departments and categories, you will then need to position your store fixtures based on traffic flow and sight lines. Fixtures, however, should never be placed where they will impede the traffic flow. Fixtures can include tables, cubes, countertops, shelving, and slat walls.

The customer should be able to move freely throughout the store. Even if you have limited space, leave enough area to properly display your products so your customers can see them.

By all means, avoid what is often called the *butt brush*. This happens when a customer is examining an item, making a buying decision, and someone walks by and brushes her from behind because of the narrow aisles. This is death to a deliberation buy. The recommended aisle width is 36" minimum and 48" would be ideal.

def•i•ni•tion

Butt brush, an expression introduced by Paco Underhill in his book *Why We Buy: The Science of Shopping*, involves the likelihood of a shopper being brushed from behind. In repeated and close analysis of his extensive videotape library on shoppers' behaviors, Paco concluded that the likelihood of a woman's being converted from a browser to a buyer is inversely proportional to the likelihood of her being brushed on her behind while she's examining merchandise. So he recommends that store aisles and sections be wide enough to avoid any butt brushing, especially when it involves merchandise that requires time to inspect.

Fixtures should also not block sight lines to other parts of the store or create hidden areas where shoplifting can occur. Chairs or benches are fixtures, too! They must be comfortable, easily accessible, and there should be enough of them for busy times.

Presenting Product for Buying Appeal

Once your fixtures are in place, you need to present the merchandise in such a way so that customers will want to buy it. Here are some key points to consider when deciding how to present your product.

- There is a very fine line between too much and too little merchandise. Your shelves should never look bare nor should they look like you are trying to cram too much merchandise in too small a space. If there are not enough styles in the assortment to fully display the product in the store, then duplicate the product in the display rather than make it look empty.
- Customers visually scan at eye level. You should try to place, especially on walls, the highest profit items at eye level. Research tells us that the optimum buying height is at about 5 feet. That is the height at which most merchandise is noticed. Conversely, you should place low-margin products at waist to knee level. Products that are placed at a lower level are less visible and yet customers who are interested in bargains expect to have to "work" harder to find these lower price and lower profit items.
- Change merchandise frequently. Your product in the front and most visible area of the store, which is where you want to generate most of the excitement, should be changed almost daily. Merchandise presentations in the rest of the store should be changed according to your store marketing/promotions plan requirements. Traditionally, you have seasonal changes every four to six weeks and mid-seasonal changes every two to three weeks. In addition, you will have weekly changes to include new arrivals and to make small adjustments.

Savvy Retailer

Change makes us pay attention and notice things. Sameness makes us gloss over them. Have you ever had the experience of finding an item in a store that you regularly shop in and, when you mentioned to the cashier that you never knew that they carried that item, you were told that they have always carried it? They probably just recently moved it to a place that was different, and you saw it for the first time!

- When you shop online, you probably notice that it's sometimes easier to find the products you want. As a retailer, you must create effective, easy-to-read shelf cards—which are sometimes called shelf talkers—that describe the product in terms of its benefits to the customer and what it does for them. Stories about the product also work very well. Every product has a story that makes it unique and different. It could be where it was produced, for example, "This wine was produced in the smallest village in the entire Italian Peninsula." Or it could be a story about where the product was last featured, for example, "This coffee machine was featured in one of the last episodes of *The Sopranos.*" Customers love stories and to learn new things. Whatever you decide to include on the shelf tag, stay away from long lists of technical features that only a few customers would be interested in.

- Clean, tidy, and dramatic. If you ever shopped at Whole Foods, you probably noticed how tidy and neatly those oranges and bananas are stacked and how shimmery those apples are! Take special care in the way you present your product. A dramatic presentation contributes to a positive impression and a great experience. It also shows respect for the customer. So take the time to properly display product for maximum impact.
- Keep related products close. Place products that go well together near each other. This is called *adjacencies.* This type of placement can create a total look or total solution for the customer. It is one of your most powerful tools to sell more to the same customer, because customers can see how one product would look or function so much better with other complementary items. Think of a display of a purse and pair of shoes, a bottle of wine with a bottle opener, a printer with cartridges and photo paper, and so on.

What you sell dictates your choices when it comes to fixtures. Your goal is to make the product stand out and sell.

When selecting fixtures, always make sure that they are both good in form as well as function. Durability, flexibility, value, and appearance are all qualities that define the right choices.

Signing and Graphics

The paradox of signs is that we have to have them and that no one reads them! You can have a sale sign up in the store, and yet customers are still amazed that it is on sale when they pay for the item! The reason is because we are bombarded with so many signs everywhere we go that we often do not pay attention to them any more.

However, when we do read them, we tend to believe them. Remember the TV program called *Candid Camera* in which they used to play tricks on people and film their reactions with a hidden camera? On one show, they put a sign up on the side of a highway saying that the state ahead was closed. About 80 percent of the cars who approached this sign stopped and then turned around. The joke was that the road was not blocked in any way!

Signs help your customers find what they need and learn about your products and promotions. Of all the visual elements in a store, graphics and the use of words in particular, create a dialogue between your store and the customer. Through them, customers learn what you are about and what's unique about your store and your products.

Because signs and graphics are part of the visual elements that help create the right environment for your customer, they need to reflect their lifestyle and overall social needs.

When selecting signs and graphics for your store, it is important that you achieve a proper balance of aesthetics, functionality, and accessibility.

- **Aesthetics.** You can enhance and reinforce the brand image or the promotional message through the aesthetics of your graphic images. In order to do so, images, typography, and colors must work together for a unified, consistent, and recognizable look. It's the look that will appeal to your target customer. This is particularly important if you are using lifestyle images. For example, Abercrombie, the young clothing retail chain (www.abercrombie.com), appeals to its customer base by making large use of lifestyle signs and posters that portray young women and men engaged in activities that mirror their target customer's lifestyle. No matter how controversial their signs might be to some people, they succeed at reaching out to their customer segment and significantly help drive the company's profits.

- **Functionality.** Functionality refers to how well graphics and signs perform every time and over time. It will cost you more money to produce signs and graphics that will last you a long time. But have you thought about how much it's going to cost you to regularly replace less expensive ones to ensure you maintain a good image? Or, if you decide not to replace worn out signs, have you thought about the cost (lost sales) of having signs that scream: "cheap," "old," "no respect for the customer"? Remember, you are in retail to provide a unique experience for your customer, and details truly matter.

  Functionality also means that a sign's main purpose is to sell. That's why they are often called "silent salespeople." When no sales associates are available to help the customer, signs should give information that the customer can use. Signs must sell benefits. They should tell the customer how the item will help them, not just describe features. For example, if you saw a sign that said "Brazilian Hardwood" you would likely say "Who cares?" But if you saw a sign that said "Lasts 50 Years, The Always Perfect Hardwood Floor" you would have a very different impression of the product!

- **Accessibility.** Signs must be user-friendly. For instance, if it is a product description (shelf-talker), make sure it is not too technical for the average shopper. Make it fun, engaging, benefit oriented, and easy to read, understand, and remember. And speaking of fun, I know an artsy store that uses a fun, artsy font that makes reading the signs enjoyable. Remember, stores that work don't just sell product, they sell entertainment.

Telling a Story with Displays

Although display uses most of the techniques introduced under merchandise presentation, it is considered a function in itself. While merchandise presentation is for customers' selection, display is the more "technical" arrangement of merchandise, such as windows or formal in-store displays that showcase a product or tell a story. Effective display techniques are meant to properly show the merchandise while at the same time adding excitement.

In addition to just having all the categories in their own areas as you saw earlier, you should have a "story" or a reason why merchandise is grouped together. Always ask yourself: "What kind of a story would interest my customer?"

Typical themes or story topics for display include:

- **Commodity or item selling story.** Put merchandise that is very similar in one place, such as all your French wines, all your vintage posters, or all your Chinese silks, and so on.
- **Price story.** Group similar or identically priced merchandise together. For example you might have a display of all your gift ideas below $20, all your value wines between $8 and $18, and so on.
- **Color story.** Use your products to make a color statement. Develop color blocks by pulling together a display with a single, dominant color so that the customer sees the same groups of colors together. Make sure to stay abreast of fashion trends in colors. When fashion designers come out with their styles for a season, they always have a few key colors that they focus on. Everyone else, including cosmetic, furniture, appliance, electronics, and many other industries, then rush to feature those colors in their products. Their retailers are encouraged to create displays by these fashionable colors. For example, if white is hot this season, make sure to have lots of white stories in your store.

- **Brand story.** Create blocks of products with the same brand so that the customer sees them all in one place. Your ASICS shoes in different styles should all be in one place or window if ASICS is a hot brand that season. Once again, check for trends in the market and make sure not to miss out on them.

- **Seasonal story.** Create visual displays based on the seasons, such as fall, winter, spring, or summer.

- **Calendar story.** Create visual displays based on the calendar, such as back to school, holidays, country events, anniversary sales, Olympics, Halloween, Christmas, and so on.

- **Markdown story.** Display all your markdown products together in one section of your store. What is the best location for your markdowns? Place them at the back of the store except in January and August. You want the customer to go through your best merchandise before they get to your reduced price inventory.

I've given you just a few of the millions of stories that you can tell your customer. The stories you choose can be different, but the key thing to remember when creating your stories is that they should all be related to your customer's lifestyle and your products' unique benefits.

The Least You Need to Know

- Stage your products to create an environment that generates excitement and improves your sales.

- Present your products to create a feast for the senses that makes your customers want to stay and look.

- Use signs to get your story across, but realize that many people won't read them.

- Use your visual displays to tell a story either about your brand, a season, an event, or a special markdown or sale.

Part 5
Nuts and Bolts of Opening and Running the Store

Once you've designed your store and bought your inventory, you then need to market it, find the right people to staff it, choose the right technology to operate it, and with these tools in place, decide how you will provide customer service to go that extra mile. As a retailer, you'll need to be able to negotiate with almost everyone that you come in contact with every day—suppliers, customers, employees, your bank, and your landlord. You'll also need to be able to keep the books, so you can track how well you are doing. In this part, I review the basic skills you need to open and run a store on a day-to-day basis.

"I'm not so worried about the zoning—it's the neighbors."

Chapter 15

Market Your Store and Get Customers to Come Back

In This Chapter

- Getting the word out
- Making a plan
- Promoting your store
- Building relationships

You are in business to sell, and in order to do so, you need to have customers who want to buy from you. Through marketing, you establish a dialogue between your store and your customers. The key is how you reach out to them and give them reasons to shop with you.

In this chapter, I talk about how you can use advertising to attract customers to your store and then tools you can use to keep them coming back.

Spreading the Word

Your first year of operation, you need to spread the word about your new store. Media advertising is the best way to do it. In your ads, you need to convey your secret weapon to your target customers—how your business alone can meet both their apparent and their deeper needs.

With a successful advertising campaign, by the end of your first year of operation, you will have served thousands of customers and identified your "best" customers. As you develop this customer base, you should begin collecting information for a relationship-marketing program, which is discussed in greater detail later.

But let's first focus on your start-up year and how you can use media advertising. You can use a wide range of media to advertise your new business. In the table called, "Advertising Alternatives," I outline the reach, cost, and market for some of these.

There are four columns in the table:

- Medium lists the types of media that can be used.
- Reach refers to the number of people you are speaking to with each advertisement.
- Cost refers to the relative cost of using the type of media.
- Market refers to the extent to which you can target or focus your message.

Advertising Alternatives

Medium	Reach	Cost	Market
Catalogs	Individual	Moderate/high	Personal/mass
Coupons	Broad	Low	Personal/mass
Direct mail/ e-mail	Individual	Low	Personal
Display	Local	Low	In-store
Flyers	Local	Low	Custom
Internet	Unbelievably broad	Moderate	Mass or focused on a special interest
Local cable TV	Broad	Moderate	Mass
Local TV	Broad	High	Mass

Medium	Reach	Cost	Market
Magazines	Broad	Moderate/high	Mass
Newspapers	Broad	Moderate	Mass
Outdoor billboards	Broad	Moderate	Mass
Radio	Broad	Moderate	Mass
Signage (in-store)	Local	Low	In-store
Word of mouth	Individual	Low	Personal
Yellow Pages	Broad	Moderate	Mass

To show you how to use this table, let's consider the impact of newspaper advertising:

- The reach is broad because many people buy the paper. Depending on the newspaper, you may be able to reach potential customers anywhere in your community, city, region, or country.
- The cost of newspaper advertising is usually moderate, depending on the size of the ad you run and the rates the paper charges.
- The market for newspaper advertising is definitively mass market. You do not know who will read your ad—a multimillionaire flying on a private jet or someone using the paper to shield his eyes from the sun while sleeping on a park bench. If you have a good local paper that reaches your customer, then by all means use it. But if it is not proven to be read by your customer, then avoid it.

Selling Points

You can create an ad and negotiate with newspapers and outdoor ad companies to publish it when they don't have anything else to run that day/week/month and offer to pay 25 percent of the normal cost.

For new retailers, I recommend that you use these five alternatives—flyers, Yellow Pages, websites, direct mail, and word-of-mouth. Let's take a quick look at each.

Flyers have a local reach. You can often work with a flyer-distribution company or the post office to target a specific neighborhood or area—one, for example, where you have fewer customers than you think you should have. The cost of flyers can be low if you focus on a particular area.

The Yellow Pages can be a powerful form of media advertising for attracting new customers to your store. Many people still let their fingers do the walking. The difficulty with Yellow Pages advertising is that you need to book your space far in advance and design an ad that can last a full year. Your message in the Yellow Pages should be concise and easy to understand because potential customers literally just flip through the pages.

Websites are a crucial new tool for retail stores. More and more customers surf the web to find out where they can buy what they need well before they start looking at ads or walking around in their neighborhood or city in search of a store. A customer is looking to buy a new pair of eyeglasses, and while searching the web for the right product to buy, they also look for the right store to buy from. That is when and how the shopper finds out about your store. If you are not present on the web and your competitors are, where do you think that shopper is going to go to buy her eyeglasses? The advertising message you deliver through your website should match the look and feel of all your other advertising, and the service you deliver using Internet technology should match the high-quality service you provide in your store.

Direct mail is the most-important media alternative for any owner-operated retailer. The reach is individual—letting you shoot right at the target—the cost is low, and the market is very personal. During your first year of operation, you may want to purchase a commercial mailing list to augment the one you are building.

Word-of-mouth advertising, as you intuitively know, is the most powerful media alternative on the list. In Chapter 18, I talk about the crucial importance of providing extra-mile service so that you can create, encourage, and build on the power of word-of-mouth advertising. Its reach is individual, it doesn't cost you anything, and it works at the same personal level as direct mail.

Savvy Retailer

Word-of-mouth works particularly well with the Millennium generation (people born between 1984 and 2000). The Millennials, as they are called, don't trust any form of advertising but do trust each others' opinions. Toyota learned this very well when they launched their Scion limited edition cars. They used what's called viral marketing, or word-of-mouth advertising generated by the Millennials themselves. About 80 percent of all Scion buyers were new to the brand, and it was viral marketing that attracted them.

You may be wondering how much you should spend on each type of marketing. Successful owner-operator retailers generally follow these percentages:

Newspapers	10.0%
Direct mail (includes e-mail)	35.0%
Website	10.0%
Relationships	15.0%
Radio	10.0%
Other: includes catalogs, coupons, flyers, local cable TV, magazines, outdoor billboards, Yellow Pages	9.5%
Display	5.5%
Signage (in-store)	5.0%

Selling Points

Newspaper advertising is declining as a tool for retail stores as readership by customers is also declining. Most retailers are gradually shifting their newspaper advertising dollars to direct mail and relationship marketing.

Developing a Marketing Plan

All media advertising costs money, and to manage this expenditure, you will need to develop an advertising plan similar to the one shown the following figure.

In developing this plan, we suggest that you follow the slogan, "Fish while the fish are biting." By this, we mean that the money you spend on advertising in a given period should be directly proportional to the business you expect to do in that period. If your objective is to push sales 10 percent higher, it only makes sense to focus that 10 percent increase on a big month rather than a 10 percent increase on a small month.

For example, if December is your peak month, you should put much of your advertising money into late November and early December. We suggest starting in late November because, when you are planning promotional advertising—as opposed to clearance advertising—you should always launch the campaign ahead of the selling period.

ADVERTISING PLAN
For year two (includes relationship marketing)

	Clearance		Spring			Summer			Fall		Christmas		Total
	Jan.	Feb.	March	April	May	June	July	Aug.	Sept.	Oct.	Nov.	Dec.	
Sales last year	$35,000	$30,000	$60,000	$58,000	$65,000	$62,000	$45,000	$45,000	$62,000	$70,000	$78,000	$150,000	$760,000
Sales plan	$40,000	$32,000	$64,000	$60,000	$68,000	$64,000	$48,000	$48,000	$64,000	$72,000	$80,000	$160,000	$800,000
Catalogs													$0
Coupons													$0
Direct Mail			$1,500	$1,000	$1,000	$1,000		$1,000	$2,000	$2,000	$2,000		$11,500
Display			$200	$150	$200	$200		$250	$150	$150	$300	$150	$1,750
Flyers									$1,000		$1,000		$2,000
Internet	$300	$300	$300	$300	$300	$300	$300	$300	$300	$300	$300	$300	$3,600
Local cable TV													$0
Relationships	$400	$400	$400	$400	$400	$400	$400	$400	$400	$400	$400	$400	$4,800
Magazines													$0
Newspapers	$300		$300		$300	$300		$600		$600	$500	$500	$3,400
Outdoor													$0
Radio								$800	$900		$900	$1,000	$3,600
Signage	$250		$200		$250		$200		$250		$250		$1,400
Word of Mouth	FREE	FREE	FREE	FREE	FREE	FREE	FREE	FREE	FREE	FREE	FREE	FREE	$0
Yellow Pages	$200	$200	$200	$200	$200	$200	$200	$200	$200	$200	$200	$200	$2,400
Total	$1,450	$900	$3,100	$2,050	$2,650	$2,400	$1,100	$3,550	$5,200	$3,650	$5,850	$2,550	$34,450
% to sales plan	3.63%	2.81%	4.84%	3.42%	3.90%	3.75%	2.29%	7.40%	8.13%	5.07%	7.31%	1.59%	4.31%

Sample of a one-year advertising plan for the second year of a business.

The other thing to consider when developing an advertising plan is that you must at least cover your breakeven expenses each month regardless of the sales volume you do. So you need to plan for a certain amount of "maintenance" advertising each month to generate enough sales to cover your breakeven expenses.

When planning your advertising, split up the year into periods that you consider unique. Adjust the amount you plan to spend on each period based on the sales you expect to make. For example, in the sample plan in the previous figure, I split the year into five periods:

- Clearance—During the months of January and February, the retailer plans for clearance of leftover items after the major Christmas push. Note that the sales revenue planned during those months is the lowest during the year and very little spending is planned for advertising. Internet and relationship marketing, the retailer's two "maintenance" marketing expenses, are the same every month. But in these two months the retailer spends nothing on direct mail, display advertising, flyers, or radio. Signage is an expenditure at the beginning of each of the five periods.
- Spring—In addition to maintenance marketing, the retailer adds expenses for direct mail, display, and newspaper advertising. Note how those expenses differ month to month. For example, the big push for direct mail is in the first month of Spring—March.
- Summer—In addition to maintenance marketing, the retailer spends money on direct mail, display advertising, newspaper advertising, and radio in August. Note that the retailer is starting to build extra traffic for the last quarter—the biggest—so the retailer added radio in August.
- Fall—In addition to maintenance marketing, the retailer spends money on direct mail, display advertising, flyers, newspaper advertising, and radio. In the fall period, the retailer is also building recognition for the store for the big final push—the Christmas period.
- Christmas—The months of November and December are the retailer's biggest for the year and the amount the retailer spends on advertising shows it. Note that the biggest spending for this period is actually in November. In October, the retailer starts Christmas promotions. In December, the retailer spends nothing on direct mail, little on display advertising, continues maintenance advertising and newspaper advertising, but increases radio advertising.

The unique sales pattern of your business may be different from the one shown in the previous example. You may decide to break up the year into fewer periods or give less emphasis to the Christmas selling season. You know your customers and your market.

> **Savvy Retailer**
>
> I have no fixed rule as to how much you should budget for media advertising. The absolute high for an owner-operated retailer would be 5 percent of sales. The absolute low would be 2 percent of sales. Somewhere in between is probably right.

Developing an advertising plan will help you look at advertising the same way you look at every other expenditure—as a percentage of sales. That is why you start by entering your expected sales from your sales plan and then divide it up into months. You then work line by line through the various media alternatives, planning this much for newspaper advertising during your January clearance, that much for a website update to announce your spring season, and so on.

Avoid Black Holes—Use Promotions

You never want to face a period of inactivity in your store, which is known as a *black hole.* Plan your promotions carefully to avoid black holes by using a combination of weekly and monthly promotional events.

Weekly promotional events are effective because they help you create a sense of urgency for customers to shop now for that week's featured specials. Any occasion for gift giving represents a great opportunity to use a weekly "theme" to link your store with your customers' need to purchase a gift (for example, a Valentine's Day gift in mid-February or a Father's Day gift in mid-June).

Monthly promotional events are "umbrellas" that reinforce the overall position of your store during the most important months of the retail year—for example, Christmas or back-to-school. These events take advantage of the longer time period to reinforce the store's advertising as the best place to shop by integrating the whole look of your business, including windows, signage, special bags, and employee name badges.

Other types of promotional events that work include a new product launch, guest appearances, charity nights, or just hosting a party. You can also build awareness for your store by sponsoring local events or local charities. Also stay aware of local school events that might be a good opportunity to promote your store with a sponsorship of the event.

Understanding Relationship Marketing

While relationship marketing does not replace the one-to-many communication venues that media advertising offers, it still plays an important role for keeping your customers and generating new ones by word-of-mouth—the free advertising we all like. You should always set aside part of your total communication budget for the personal connection that I believe you should have with each of your existing, loyal customers.

To help you understand what this "personal connection" might be, here are examples of real-life relationship-marketing programs from owner-operated retailers that I know and respect. Each demonstrates a different level of connection with customers—and some great ideas for you to start with.

Relationship-Marketing—Direct Mail Plan

This level of relationship marketing is the simplest to operate and primarily involves the building and maintaining of a mailing list that is used for direct mail marketing. Tasks include:

- Providing comment cards that let customers send feedback "postage paid." This not only helps to get feedback about the store experience but also enables the retailer to build a database with customer addresses.
- Keeping your mailing list "current" by asking the post office to return undelivered mail. This does add to the cost of mailing, but it is well worth the expense.
- Offering incentives to encourage sales associates to ask customers if they want to be on the mailing list and collecting e-mail addresses. Let customers complete the actual enrollment form.
- Sending direct mail pieces to customers twice each season. Your first mailing should be a regular-price, full-color catalog and the second is an "end of season" promotional piece. This second mailing includes a motivator that says, "Please bring in this card to receive your discount." By keeping track, the store identifies which customers buy mostly at sale prices.

Relationship Marketing—VIP Club

This type of relationship marketing requires more staff time, but builds strong, long-term relationships with your customers. You will need to add incentives for your sales staff to encourage their participation.

Tasks include:

- Developing a loyalty program called the VIP Club that customers "join" automatically when they spend a certain amount of money in your store, such as $3,000 a year. You set the limit that works for your store.
- Offering VIP Club customers additional services such as free alterations, shopping by appointment, personal fashion consultations, fashion shows and seminars, advance notice of sales, and free delivery within a specified area.
- Using client books in which sales associates track purchases made by their personal customers. Sales associates also keep notes on a customer's size, color preferences, birthday, and any relevant career or family information.
- Contacting each VIP Club member at least eight times a year through telephone calls, personal e-mails, thank-you cards, and other personal touches. But place the full responsibility for building VIP Club relationships in the hands of sales associates.
- Sending a "thank you for your business" gift to the store's very best customers each Christmas.

Relationship Marketing—Using the Telephone

One retailer I know gave up direct mail completely and now uses the telephone for all his relationship marketing. This unique program includes:

- Demonstrating to his customers that he cares about them by filling the wall behind the cash register with photos of—and postcards from—his customers.
- Employing sales associates who must really enjoy their jobs because they are always smiling.
- Hiring university students to call all 5,000 customers in the database. Callers do not try to "sell" something, only to "tell" about something new in the store. Twenty percent of the customers they call come into the store.
- Developing a loyalty program called the Bonus Club that gives customers a $30 gift certificate when they reach $300 in purchases.
- Using technology to link every transaction to a customer name, address, e-mail, and telephone number. The store can identify which customers bought a given item so that staff can call those customers when a coordinating, matching, or

complementary item arrives. Fifty percent of the customers they call come into the store. I talk more about this type of technology in Chapter 19.

Relationship Marketing—Mining Your Sales Information

With the proper technology, you can use the information you collect when transacting sales to develop a powerful relationship-marketing package. One retailer I know makes great use of the technology available by:

- Providing each sales associate with a list of his or her customers who spent more than $200 in the last two weeks, including a breakdown of the items that each customer bought. The sales associates then call their customers to ask one question: "Is everything satisfactory?"
- Using database queries to target promotional e-mails to very small groups of customers. For example, if a shipment of high-end bathrobes arrives, sales associates may write personal e-mails to the 20 or 30 customers who purchased silk pajamas but not a bathrobe during the past twelve months.
- Tying new items to specific customer profiles. When considering whether to stock a line of very expensive dress slacks, for example, the manager might buy a small number and then personally phone his best dress-slack customers and ask them to try the item and give him their comments.
- Adds an additional personal touch by having sales associates write a brief note on every "form letter" they send. This little extra adds an additional 25 percent to the response rate.

Relationship marketing offers you business savings in four important areas, savings that go straight to the bottom line.

- You can reach customers much less expensively by mail than you can through advertising in the traditional media.
- E-mail has become so common and related to spam in some customers' minds that these customers may respond better to old-fashioned postal mail.
- Your sales associates spend much less time with good customers because they already know so much about them. This saves significant time determining the customer's needs.

- Good customers are more forgiving of errors, and they return less merchandise.
- You make higher margins from your good customers because they do not "nickel and dime" you every time they visit the store.

You probably won't be able to take advantage of relationship marketing in the first year of your store's operation. You'll need that time to set up a relationship-marketing program because it typically takes a year to identify your 100 or 200 best customers by dollar volume. After you get to know them, you can then design rewards or incentives so that these customers will benefit most from them.

Building Your Relationship-Marketing Database

As you begin building your relationship-marketing program, you will need to create a relationship-marketing database. Think about the key things you want to know about each of your best customers and how you will eventually use the information. I talk more about database software available for retailers in Chapter 19.

When collecting information for the database, the very minimum you'll want to be able to access is the big three: frequency, recency, and amount:

- The frequency query tells you how often each customer shops in your store. One may buy from you every second week, while another may only buy from you once or twice a season. There is a huge difference in the importance of these two customers to your business.
- The recency query tells you when each customer last shopped in your store. One may have shopped only two weeks ago and will have seen all of the latest merchandise, while another may not have shopped yet this season. You will say different things to these two customers when you call them.
- The amount query tells you how much each customer spent in your store during whatever period you choose to examine.

With a good integrated retail software package, the customer relationship management (CRM) or database function can be a powerful tool. For example, a computerized database will let you find the name, address, and phone number of every customer who used to spend at least $200 in your store once a month but who has not shopped with you for the past three months. Once you know who these people are, you can call them personally to ask why—or send them a "come back soon" letter and an incentive to do so.

To understand how powerful this information is, take a moment to recall the last time that any store you used to shop at did something similar to this for you. I don't think you can come up with many examples, if any, and that is why this is such a great way to provide extra-mile service for your customers—and stand out from the competition. And while you do that, you may even manage to get them back.

You may not build your database all at once—and you certainly won't get all of the information at once—but you should at least establish the basic structure by understanding what you are trying to achieve. You should also decide which items you "must know" in order to conduct your relationship-marketing program.

Whether you intend to store your customer database on index cards or in a computer, you will want to track at least some of the following "fields." Here is a list of key information you would ideally like to have about each of your customers:

Information	Format	Must Know	Information	Format	Must Know
Prefix (Mr., Ms., Dr.)	Text	❑	Spouse's name	Text	❑
First name	Text	❑	Spouse's work phone #	Text Number	❑
Middle initial	Text	❑	Can call spouse	Yes/No Number	❑
Last name	Text	❑	Spouse's cell phone #	Text Number	❑
Suffix (MD, Jr., Sr.)	Text	❑	First purchase date	Date	❑
Birth date	Date	❑	Last purchase date	Date	❑
Home street address	Text	❑	Last purchase date	Currency	❑
Home city	Text	❑	Spouse's birth date	Date	❑
Home state/ province	Text	❑	Spouse's favorite color	Text	❑
Home zip code	Text	❑	Spouse's size	Text	❑

continues

continued

Information	Format	Must Know	Information	Format	Must Know
E-mail address	Text	❏	Spouse's e-mail	Text	❏
Home phone #	Number	❏	Wedding anniversary	Date	❏
Calls at home?	Yes/No	❏	Number of children	Number	❏
Best time to call	Time	❏	Name of child (1)	Text	❏
Mail to home	Yes/No	❏	Birth date of child (1)	Date	❏
Mail to office	Yes/No	❏	Name of child (2)	Text	❏
Work/ business name	Text	❏	Birth date of child (2)	Date	❏
Work street address	Text	❏	Name of child (3)	Text	❏
Work city	Text	❏	Birth date of child (3)	Date	❏
Work state/ province	Text	❏	Other …		❏
Work zip code	Text	❏	Other …		❏
Work telephone	Number	❏	Notes	Memo	❏
Calls at work?	Yes/No	❏	Preferences	Memo	❏
Best time to call	Time	❏	Important information	Memo	❏

This list is more like an inventory of some of the details that you might want to gather about your customer. You may not need some of the items on this list, or you may want to add other items. But this will help you get started developing the fields for your database.

In order to build your database of customer names, addresses, and telephone numbers, you will need to get this basic information and much more from the customers themselves. The challenge is to do it without being intrusive or pushy—and without slowing your point of sale.

The ideal situation would be for each of your customers to carry a plastic card that contains a unique bar code. Each time the customer shops, you would scan first the bar code and then each of the items the person is buying that day. But how do you get your customers to carry plastic cards and present them each time they shop? This is difficult to do without an incentive.

That is why we suggest you "buy" the information from your customers by giving them several incentives that make it worth having their name in your database. You could then market these incentives as the VIP Club so that you can say something like the following:

> "We have a VIP Club that we would like you to join. Membership offers a number of benefits, including a 5 percent discount on every regular-price item you buy in the store. You also get advance notice of our semi-annual sales and a quarterly electronic newsletter that provides helpful information about the products that we carry. Beyond this, we would like to send you a card and a small gift certificate on your birthday. Would you like to join?"

If the customer says yes, you would then provide a brief application form that asks for her basic information—name, address, telephone number, e-mail, and birthday. The application should also ask if the customer wants you to call her at home or at work, and at any particular time of the day. Finally, the application should provide a reassurance that you will not sell or lend your mailing list to any other business—something no extra-mile retailer should ever do.

As part of this application form, you could have a detachable VIP Club Membership Card, one that contains the bar code that we mentioned earlier. Customers will be much more likely to carry the card if they get a 5 percent discount each time they shop in your store plus all of the other benefits of "membership." You can also have this as a simple sticker that they place on the back of their favorite credit card so it is always handy. As an alternative to asking your customers to carry cards or stickers, you could store them for the customer alphabetically in a box that you keep near the cash register.

However you deal with the cards, we believe you should design your VIP Club so that it rewards customer loyalty. The intention is not to give a discount to as many customers as possible. Rather, it is to give your best customers—more and better services, more attention, more thanks, and more reasons to shop regularly.

These people have chosen your store as the place that they want to buy certain items. This suggests that the most appropriate reward for their loyalty would be more of those same items—perhaps a $10 gift certificate for every $100 spent in your store.

These would be easy to track and easy to redeem, two things that also represent extra-mile service for your best customers.

Relationship marketing can have an unexpected benefit for your business: it can literally add value to your balance sheet. Although you may not be thinking of this now, you may someday want to sell your business as an ongoing concern.

When it comes time to sell, you can provide inventory reports and use these to negotiate a fair price for your inventory. You can also provide your balance sheet and use this to negotiate a fair price for your leasehold improvements such as your fixtures, racks, and carpet.

Selling Points

But what about goodwill? How can you demonstrate the value of the ongoing relationships that you have with your customers?

A good way to prove this asset would be to provide the name, address, and telephone number of every customer you have had in the past five years, complete with his or her purchase history by dollar volume. This could be worth literally thousands of dollars to you—and to the purchaser of your business.

You can do a great job of marketing your store, but if you don't back that up with a good sales force, your advertising money will be wasted. In the next chapter I talk about how to find the right people.

The Least You Need to Know

- Use a strategic mix of media advertising to build your customer base.
- Carefully plan your advertising expenses based on your expected sales volume each month.
- Build long-term relationships with your customers through various relationship-marketing programs.
- Design and build a powerful database with key information about your customers and their spending habits.

Chapter 16

Find the Right People

In This Chapter

- Know who you need
- Develop a job description
- Design a job application
- Identify the right people

Staffing your store can be one of your most difficult challenges. You must decide how many employees you should hire, how much you should pay them, what they will do, and what qualifications they must have. After you hire the people you need, you'll have to train and groom them to be the type of sales associates you want and need for your store.

Attracting the right people for your store, educating them, and keeping them motivated are an absolute must if you want to succeed. In this chapter, I discuss how you establish staffing requirements, attract the right people, select the best among those you have attracted, and then train and motivate them to sell and amaze your customers every day.

Hire Round Pegs, Not Square Pegs

As you get ready to start hiring sales associates, you will need to understand that not everyone can work in the retail business. There are some "square pegs" out there that simply will not fit into the "round holes" your business offers. You cannot take just anyone and mold that person into a good employee for your store.

Your choice of sales associates will be critical to the success of your business. A mistake in staffing is fundamentally different from a mistake in something like your buying. When you make a buying mistake, you just take out your red pen, record a markdown, and learn from the experience. But you cannot do something equivalent with your staffing mistakes. Labor laws in some states and provinces see to that.

Termination is an area fraught with legal landmines, and, in any case, most business owners hate firing an employee. It is much better for all concerned if you simply avoid the whole situation by hiring properly in the first place.

If you do make a mistake and hire the wrong person, you will definitely lose customers because they will not be treated appropriately. That alone could end your relationship with a customer who might have had a "lifetime value" of $50,000 or more to your business. A square peg can also destroy the team spirit of all the "round pegs" that are doing a good job for you. The square peg can aggravate both your customers and your staff.

The entire experience of hiring a square peg wastes time and money. You will have invested significant time in training the square peg and paid full wages to a less than productive person. You will then throw all of this away as you start over with someone new.

Better Not!

Although many owner-operated retailers employ family members and friends, this is not always a good idea—unless one particular person offers the exact set of skills you need. If you do decide to hire a family member, be sure you know whether you will be able to manage that person if something goes wrong.

Staffing Requirements

Before you start hiring people for your store, take the time to develop a written job description for your staff and, most important, your sales associates. The job description should define the perfect sales associate for your store. Perfect cannot be an ever-changing notion in your head. Having a printed document will give you something to refer back to, pass around, and measure applicants against.

As your business evolves, you will no doubt revise your job description for sales associates to keep it current. However, you should not use this as an excuse to avoid putting pencil to paper now, even if you just come up with a preliminary sketch.

Writing a Job Description

You may wonder how you can even get started writing a job description. In case you need some help, here is a sample job description appears later in this chapter. Now let's take a look at how you develop each section.

You should always start with a job title. People like having a job title that explains what they do. They find it much easier both in the store and when out with friends if they can tell others that they are a "something." As a job title, "sales associate" has been around for at least 100 years. When it denotes a true professional, as it always should, this is a title that people can be proud to have.

Duties and Responsibilities

The next section provides a summary of the sales associates' duties and responsibilities. This will be a thumbnail sketch that you can use when discussing the job with other people, but you will need to create the duties section of the form before you fill in the summary section.

The people who work for you must have a clear understanding of the reporting relationships in your business if you want to avoid needless he-said–she-said conflicts. You must make it clear at the outset that the sales associates report either directly to you or directly to the store manager if you employ one. In the latter case, the sales associates might report indirectly to you.

The core of the sales associates' job description is a list of their duties in the order of priority and the relative importance of each duty to the total job. This is the section of the document that you really need to get right, but it is the toughest one to think through.

For example, you should not list a duty that says sales associates must, "Be nice to customers." This is not specific enough for everyone to know what it means. You could waste time in endless debates about whether this or that behavior qualifies as "nice to customers" and the whole point of having a job description would be lost.

Instead, you need to list a duty that says sales associates must do something observable and measurable—in language specific enough for everyone to know what it means. This could be something like, "Make customers feel welcome in the store by giving them a warm and friendly smile and saying, 'Good morning' within fifteen seconds of them entering the store."

In the sample job description, I have allotted just eight lines for the sales associates' duties, but as you start to think through what you want your employees to do, you likely will realize that they will be doing hundreds of things every day. You can't list them all, so you need to prioritize their duties and then list the top 8 to 10. Setting a percentage of importance helps your employees know where to focus their efforts.

> **Selling Points**
>
> Always state each duty clearly and list what it entails. Then you will be able to just watch and listen to your sales associates and figure out if they are meeting requirements, because your expectations are both observable and measurable.

You really need to decide what you are trying to achieve in your business before you can assign a relative importance to each of the sales associates' duties. If you place a high importance on housekeeping, you will have a clean and neat store. If you place a high importance on greeting customers, you will have customers that feel welcome.

I do not doubt that you will want to have a clean and neat store, but in your mind, is that clean and neat store more or less important than welcoming your customers? Or are these two tasks more or less important than having your sales associates spend more time with customers and consistently suggesting additional items for a complete solution to the customers' needs?

Once you have established the duties, then you will be able to write the narrative summary of the sales associates' duties and responsibilities. This is the thumbnail sketch you will use when discussing the job with other people.

Job Description for Sales Associates	
1. Title	Sales Associate
2. Summary of Duties and Responsibilities	The job of a sales associate is to sell merchandise to customers in a professional and ethical manner and to function as part of a team whenever necessary. A sales associate provides top-quality customer service and complete customer satisfaction. To receive a "satisfactory" rating in his or her work, a sales associate must also meet specific sales and average-transaction goals.
3. Directly Reports to: Owner/Manager **Indirectly Reports to:** N/A	

4. Duties in Order of Priority	**Percentage of Importance to Job**
•Greet and make customers feel welcome	10
•Determine the customers' needs	15
•Provide knowledgeable presentations	15
•Suggest additional items	30
•Answer any objections	5
•Close the sale	10
•Send thank-you notes or phone customers	10
•Handle maintenance, housekeeping, other duties as assigned by store manager	5

5. Necessary characteristics	•Positive attitude •Healthy ego •Friendly •Neat in appearance •Degree of extroversion •Empathy •Goal oriented •Willing to learn
6. Necessary qualifications	•Extensive experience using store's products •Life experience appropriate to the store's target customers •Basic proficiency in math
Objectives to Be Met in First 3 Months	
7. Sales	Define your sales goal.
8. Average Transaction	Set your average transaction goals.
9. Other	Complete the store's standard new-employee training program and attain a rating of at least satisfactory on each of the eight duties listed above.
10. Objectives to Be Met (Ongoing)	New sales, average transaction, and other objectives will be established at the end of the three-month probationary period and discussed in regular performance-review meetings after that.

As you define your sales associates' duties, think about what you want them to achieve. Prioritize these duties and list them in order of importance. Here is an example of a priority list based on the nine steps of selling in my book, *Retail Selling Ain't Brain Surgery, It's Twice As Hard*:

Duties in Order of Priority	Relative Importance
Make customers feel welcome in the store by giving them a warm and friendly smile and saying "Good morning" or "Good afternoon" within 15 seconds of their arrival.	10 percent
Determine your customers' needs by asking a series of good, open-ended questions.	15 percent
Provide knowledgeable merchandise presentations using benefit statements to explain how the products you are showing meet the customers' needs.	15 percent
Suggest that customers consider the most logical of all the additional items that could complete their original purchases.	30 percent
Answer any objections that the customers may have.	5 percent
Close sales by thanking the customers, encouraging them to contact you with any questions about their purchase, and inviting them to come back.	10 percent
Within 10 days, send a thank-you note to every customer who purchased more than $50 in a single transaction and phone every customer who purchased more than $100 in a single transaction.	10 percent
Handle maintenance, stocking, visual merchandising, cashiering, and housekeeping tasks in a timely manner plus other duties that the store manager will assign from time to time.	5 percent

While the sample job description provided earlier identifies duties and responsibilities in general terms, here we dig deeper and define them in behavioral terms. This will ensure that any new hire or current hire knows exactly what duties she is responsible for and how she should perform those duties for best results.

Characteristics

After you've clearly identified the duties and their priorities, you then need to think about the characteristics you want your sales associates to have in order to do the job. In other words, you will not hire anyone who does not have the characteristics on this list.

You'll see that having a positive attitude tops the list. It is tough to measure this scientifically, but you will know one when you see it. People with a positive attitude tend to approach things with a "go for it" mentality and see life as a glass that is half full instead of a glass that is half empty. People with positive attitudes make significantly better sales associates than people who are less positive.

> **Better Not!**
>
> Be cautious about the characteristics you want, because you are on shaky legal ground. Under the law in most jurisdictions, you cannot consider age, sex, religion, ethnic background, sexual orientation, and a number of similar things when you are hiring.

You want candidates with a degree of extroversion—outgoing but not overbearing. Shy people just do not make good sales associates. The job entails meeting new people and building long-term relationships with them. Candidates who have trouble looking someone in the eye will be hopelessly lost when it comes to having the two-way conversation that is crucial to understanding a customer's needs.

Sales associates also need a healthy ego. The day-to-day life of sales associates involves a certain amount of skepticism and rejection. Customers tend to doubt what they hear and they often say no. If your sales associates feel okay about who they are and have a high level of self-confidence, they will understand that this is not directed at them personally and they will not get discouraged.

You also want to find people who have empathy. This is the ability to identify with another person's situation, feelings, and motives—to stand in another person's shoes and see things from that perspective.

Selling professionally involves asking a series of good open-ended questions, listening to the answers, and responding with an appropriate merchandise presentation that is what the customer needs and not what the sales associate feels that they should buy based on their taste or value system. A sales associate might feel that $1,200 for a barbeque grill is a huge amount of money, but if this is what the customer is willing to spend to have the perfect solution, that is what she needs to sell the customer. The customer's value system (and purchasing power) might be different from the associate's, and the latter needs to look at things from the customer's perspective. Empathy enables a sales associate to present merchandise that meets a customer's needs.

Other necessary characteristics could be things like friendly, goal oriented, neat in appearance, and willing to learn.

Qualifications

Under the heading "necessary qualifications," you should list the *qualifications* that people must have in order to do the job. In the case of qualifications, you can hire people who do not have every item on the list initially because you can always provide training to help them become qualified. As was the case with characteristics, you need to walk with caution here because you are on shaky legal ground.

def•i•ni•tion

Qualifications are skill sets that people need to do the job. For example, people cannot be lifeguards at the local pool unless they have a certain level of training and proficiency that has been tested and certified by the appropriate authority.

The retail industry does not have an "appropriate authority" that tests and certifies sales associates. The skill set that people need to work in your store could be very different from the skill set they would need to work in another retail store. This leaves you—and hundreds of thousands of other owner-operated retailers—on your own to set qualifications and standards.

If you operate a store that sells only high-performance racing bikes, it would be considered fair in most jurisdictions to require that your sales associates have a high level of experience with those specialized vehicles. A "weekend athlete" might simply not be able to answer the technical and performance questions posed by your knowledgeable customers.

It would also be fair in most jurisdictions to require that your sales associates have a life experience that is appropriate to the store's target customers. For example, an individual who has some personal experience with travel would probably be better qualified selling travel accessories than somebody with no travel experience, because he would better understand the difficulties that travelers face.

You also can require proficiency with math in most jurisdictions, because your sales associates will be dealing with cash, checks, and charge-card transactions. Have you ever shopped at a store where the sales associate got confused while recording a multi-item transaction or could not count the correct change even when the cash register indicated what that change should be? Do you really want to put your customers through that kind of torture?

Legal issues aside, you need to be careful not to set qualifications that screen out potential "superstars." Do people really need a college education to work in your store? If so, then list that as a necessary qualification—but spend a lot of time asking "why" before you do. Remember, you may find a candidate that doesn't have product knowledge and technical skills to the necessary degree and yet is just perfect for the job because of her attitude and people skills. If that's the case, hire her and then train her on your product so that she can reach the desired level of competence.

Job Objectives

When developing the objectives section of the job description, lay the foundation for much of the coaching work you will do with new sales associates during the first three months of their employment. (I discuss coaching in Chapter 17.) These objectives will be the yardsticks by which you ultimately measure your new sales associates' success or failure.

Your list of objectives should be your expectations for the first three months of employment, which includes specific objectives that new sales associates must meet during their "probationary period." In most jurisdictions, employers have a certain time during which they can dismiss new employees without legal notice, "just cause," or severance pay.

This probationary period exists because people make mistakes. No matter how careful employers are in their hiring and employees are in their job searches, things sometimes just do not work out. The probationary period lets either side walk away without penalty. After the probationary period is over, different rules govern the employment relationship. You will find it critical that you read and understand all of the employment laws that apply in your jurisdiction. If something isn't clear to you, consult your attorney to be sure you don't run into problems with the Labor Department or end up with a lawsuit.

Selling Points

If the law allows for a probationary period, I recommend strongly that you use it. In 90 days, you should know whether or not that sales associate will work out and if you should keep him as an employee.

Your sales associates' main objectives are their sales goals. You are hiring people who have the job of selling to customers. While you may want to allow for some kind of a learning curve, new sales associates must get up to speed quickly in order to become productive members of the team. You should express their sales objectives in dollars per hour, because you cannot know for certain how many hours per week people will be working three months after they start.

You also want to set average-transaction objectives. Thirty percent of their job is suggesting a complementary product for a complete solution of the customer's needs. The main product will look, feel, taste, or perform better with all the additions that sales associates (who are the experts) should always recommend.

Other objectives to be met in the first three months could be things like completing the store's standard new-employee training program, learning how to create an in-store display, and learning how to shut down the POS system at night. These are not as crucial as average transaction, but they are good things to include.

You may have noticed that I am not drawing any distinction between full-time employees and part-time employees in our job description. This is because your customers do not care whether sales associates work full time or part time, they only care about receiving professional service. All of your sales associates should have the same title, duties, characteristics, qualifications, and objectives. The number of hours they work should not enter the picture.

Selling Points

Average transaction, also called average ticket sale, is the average amount spent at your store by each customer in a day, week, month, or year. It is calculated by dividing total sales by the number of transactions. This number should always be increasing as a result of sales associates suggesting higher-price items and/or additional items to every customer.

Design a Job Application

You should develop a printed job application form so that every candidate who applies for a job will be providing the same information and answering the same questions. If a candidate has a written resumé, she can submit it with the application form, but she should still answer all of your questions.

The best way to develop a job application form is to visit some of the major retailers in your area and get copies of their application forms. These stores will undoubtedly have sought expert legal advice when designing their forms, so you should be able to find out what you can and cannot legally ask in your jurisdiction based on a close examination of what others are doing. Even after you have done this, it would be a good idea to let your lawyer review your wording.

Selling Yourself and Your Store

An employment relationship will last only when it is a true win-win relationship between the employer and the employee. The truth of today's labor market is that, while almost everybody needs a job, nobody needs a job in your store. This is why you need to sell the benefits of working in your store to prospective employees.

The competition for good sales associates is fierce. It always has been, and it always will be. You'll find it easy to attract average and below-average sales associates. But you will have to work hard if you want to get and then keep the good ones.

Consider Employee Benefits

Long before you start interviewing, you will need to think through the list of benefits that you plan to offer prospective employees. Viewed as a whole, this list must be strong enough to get the sales associates that you choose excited about the possibility of working for you.

First think about the "hard" benefits you can offer, such as pay and insurance coverage. Although money may or may not be the most important item in your employee benefits package for any particular sales associate, it certainly is the most visible. You need to pay a competitive wage. You cannot expect to pay 10 percent less than the store down the street and keep good sales associates.

Money being equal, the medical and dental insurance coverage you offer could well be the deciding factor in winning or losing the battle for a good sales associate. Providing medical and dental insurance coverage is not cheap—in fact it costs a lot of money—but this can be an important way that you identify yourself as a "real" and fair employer.

Selling Points

You should pay an hourly wage that is more than competitive with the wages paid for equivalent jobs in your area. When it comes to employees, you will get what you pay for. However, be careful not to "shoot yourself in the foot" by paying an above-average wage to an average or below-average sales associate. If you pay more than your competitors, expect more and be more selective.

People who work in other industries generally have medical and dental insurance coverage, and I believe that the people who work in the retail industry should, too. If you do not provide that kind of coverage, it is only fair that good employees—who offer both experience and productivity—move somewhere else to get the protection they need.

As an owner-operated retailer, you have many other benefits to offer prospective employees. The following list includes some of the "perks" you may want to present as the "soft" benefits of working for you.

- Employee discounts: First-hand product knowledge will really help your sales associates sell. This implies that you should encourage your sales associates to use the products they sell by giving them those products at cost. This should be up to a certain limit each month and only for their personal use. You should offer a lesser discount for items that they want to give as gifts.
- A chance to learn: As an owner-operated retailer, you can offer prospective employees a unique opportunity to learn about the retail business in general and the products you carry in particular. Someone working at the sales associate level today may very well want to be a chain-store buyer or even an owner-operated retailer in the future.
- Fun: Working in retail can be demanding, so you need to make sure that your employees have a little fun along the way. I'm not talking about late-night parties. I'm talking about team contests, achieving goals, and a few chances each season to socialize as a group.
- Status: For some people, status comes through having a job title and a business card. This alone is a valid reason for giving all of your employees the title of sales associate and for having properly printed business cards waiting when they arrive for their first day on the job or as soon as they pass the probationary period.
- Flexible hours: The extended hours of the retail business were once a liability, but now they are just right for many people. If you need a sales associate who will start at 10:30 A.M. or just work Mondays, there are probably several good people nearby who want to do exactly that.
- Opportunity for advancement: If there is an opportunity for advancement beyond the position of sales associate in your business, you should explain this clearly. If there is no opportunity for advancement, you should be sure the new hire understands that but realize that not everyone wants to "move up" in the world—and that this has nothing to do with them being "good."

One of the realities of retailing is that you will probably hire at least some students who do not intend to make your business their careers. Although these young people may be working primarily to earn tuition money—or to buy their first car—you have a lot to offer them besides money.

A job in a well-run retail store provides opportunities to take responsibility and demonstrate self-discipline. The understanding of customer service and the selling skills first learned in the retail business will be surprisingly useful in every job that person ever holds.

Determine How You Will Pay

Staffing your business will be a classic "what comes first, the chicken or the egg" situation. You cannot get good people until you pay good wages, but you cannot pay good wages until you get good people making high sales. If you want to run a profitable retail business, you must break this cycle and take a stand.

By yourself, you could at best be one-half of a mom-and-pop business, the generally accepted smallest form of retail that can survive. As such, you would need to be in the store every hour that it is open—and deal with all of the other business-related matters as well as have some sort of a personal life after that.

Even while you are building your business in the early days, you should have the help of at least a few competent and capable sales associates. If you cannot pay them an hourly wage that is at least competitive and still make a profit, you might be better off getting out of the business gracefully. The writing is on the wall.

The retail industry uses three basic methods of paying store managers and sales associates: a weekly wage or "salary," an hourly wage, and a straight percentage of sales or "commission."

A store manager typically earns a weekly wage. You agree to pay so many dollars for so many hours of work. In most cases, the employee's hours of work and earnings do not change from week to week. In other cases, store managers are paid a weekly salary plus a bonus at the end of each quarter or year based on sales results. This is the case for larger stores, where the store manager has broad management responsibilities, a sales goal to achieve, and a large staff to supervise and lead.

Part-time or full-time sales associates typically earn an hourly wage. You agree to pay so many dollars for each hour of work. In most jurisdictions, this would be up to 20 hours a week for a part-time sales associate and up to the maximum number of hours allowed (usually 40 hours) before you must pay overtime for a full-time sales associate. Employees' hours of work and earnings may be set or they may change from week to week.

A full-time sales associate in a "selling" store—a store with a strong sales focus—typically earns a straight percentage of sales. You agree to pay a certain portion of every dollar that the employee rings through the cash register. Although minimum wage laws still apply—and overtime laws cap the employee's hours of work—earnings are "open-ended" and totally dependent on sales. For some employees, this is a strong incentive to sell more effectively.

One of the advantages of paying straight commission is that you always know what your selling cost will be. For example, if you pay your sales associates 10 percent of their sales, your selling cost will always be 10 percent plus the cost of their benefits—typically 2 or 3 percent of their sales.

This system can work well for all concerned as long as your employees never earn less than the minimum hourly wage for your jurisdiction, usually calculated over a complete pay period.

Weighing against this is the fact that some perfectly good sales associates are truly afraid of working on commission. Although they could probably earn more money on commission, they prefer the stability and predictability of a set wage. There is nothing wrong with that as long as you enjoy a win-win employment relationship.

In an effort to get the best of both worlds, some stores "blend" the above methods and pay a weekly or hourly wage plus a commission. In addition to a weekly or hourly wage that at least satisfies minimum wage laws, you agree to pay a certain portion of every dollar that the employee rings through the cash register. Because you are "guaranteeing" part of the employee's total earnings, this commission rate should be lower than the one you pay to straight-commission employees.

Under a "blend" pay system, the employee's hours of work may be set or they may change from week to week, but earnings are always "open-ended." For some employees, this is a strong incentive to sell more effectively.

As long as you stay within the labor laws in your jurisdiction, there is no right or wrong pay system to use in your business. The one that feels comfortable to you and lets you get—and keep—good sales associates is the one that you should use.

Selecting the Best

After you have thought through your job description for sales associates, developed a printed job application form, built a competitive benefits package, and decided on a pay system for your store, you will be ready to start interviewing prospective sales associates.

Interviewing Basics

Interviewing is not something that comes naturally to most owner-operated retailers. If you have not done it before, you will first need to understand the process and then work hard at improving your skills. Here are some guidelines you should follow to avoid the most common mistakes that interviewers make:

- **Interview only three candidates.** From however many applications you collect for a given position in your store, you should select the three candidates that best match the characteristics and qualifications you established on the job description. These are the only candidates you should invest time in meeting.
- **Schedule enough time.** The sales associate you are hiring could bring a million dollars in business to your store over the next five years, so you should be willing to set aside at least an hour to interview each candidate properly.
- **Meet in a suitable location.** Given the importance of the decision you are making, you will need to give each discussion your full, undivided attention. This means that you will need to meet in a quiet place where there are no interruptions (including phone calls).
- **Put the candidates at ease.** For many people, interviews are a frightening experience. This could be for many reasons, not all of them bad. As the person conducting the interviews, you will need to get past the fright in order to meet the potential sales associates and for them to open up and share with you important details about their past experiences.
- **Ask productive questions.** One-hour interviews go by very quickly, so you should stick to questions that will get you the information you need to make a good decision. The whole point of holding an interview is to gain employment-related information. If you talk about anything else—the weather, for example—you are just wasting time.
- **Ask behavioral questions.** These deal with things that the candidates have actually done in real-life situations. All too often, interviewers waste time asking hypothetical questions that deal with imaginary situations—ones where the candidates can easily make up what they think are the "right" answers. For example, try answering the following hypothetical question: "How do you think the other sales associates will feel if you are ever late for work?" A behavioral question would sound like. "Tell me about a time when you had a customer who was very upset because he had to return a defective product. What happened? How did you calm him down? What did you say to him? How did he respond? How did you feel about it?"

- **Hide any personal reactions.** As an interviewer, it is all too easy to telegraph the desired responses to your questions. For example, if a candidate starts telling you about something that happened in her last job and you start to frown, the candidate will know immediately that she should switch to a different version of the story.
- **Focus mostly on listening.** The person who does most of the talking in an interview will view the conversation favorably. In other words, if you do most of the talking, you will think that you had a wonderful interview—but know very little about the candidate you were supposedly judging. You should probably talk for no more than 20 percent of the total time.
- **Promise an answer in reasonable time.** At the end of each interview, you need to establish what will happen next. Because you are meeting only three candidates for the position, you should promise each of them a telephone call within the next few days. This is simply being polite—and professional—and avoids continuous calls from them wanting to know your decision.
- **Allow time between interviews.** You will need a surprising amount of time after each interview to make notes while the discussion is fresh in your mind—and then a bit more to let your head clear and get ready for your next candidate. When conducting several interviews, it is all too easy to mix the candidates in your mind.

The best way to conduct your hiring interviews is to give them structure and always follow a set routine. You should ask the same basic questions of every candidate and hold each discussion under approximately the same circumstances. This will let you be consistent and fair, and help you make meaningful comparisons between the candidates.

Evaluating Candidates

Evaluating candidates against the necessary characteristics and qualifications on the job description will help you make meaningful comparisons and the right decision. Ignore any superficial "first impressions" you get at the start of an interview and listen to all of the candidate's answers before forming an opinion. Also ignore the "contrast effects" that will make any candidate who follows a good candidate look less attractive. And finally, stay away from your natural inclination to select someone who is similar to you. Each prospective sales associate will offer a unique set of strengths and weaknesses. Your challenge is to have a good understanding of these by the end the interview.

Asking the Right Questions

You should probably include at least some of the following standard questions in your interviews. As the candidates answer each question, you should follow up on one specific part of their answers and then move on to the next question on your list. The reason for asking everybody the same questions is that this gives you a good basis for comparing the three candidates you interview.

- To determine self-motivation and the candidate's capacity for self-supervision: What individual project have you enjoyed the most in your life? What made that enjoyable? What team project?
- To determine level of aspiration and ability to form goals: Which interests you more, doing a job well or making lots of money? Why do you say that? Tell me about a recent project at work or in school. What were the goals and did you have any contribution in setting them? What was your expected outcome and how did you achieve it? If not, how did you feel about it?
- To determine self-perception: Tell me three things that will provide a good composite picture of you and help me make my decision.
- To determine appropriateness of choices and values: What person that you actually have met do you admire the most? What did you learn from that person? What person that you have not met do you admire the most?
- To determine attitudes toward work: What aspect of this job intrigues you the most? Why do you say that? What part do you think you would like the least?
- To determine whether the person has a good attitude: Tell me about the toughest day you have ever had and what that day was like.

As soon as the candidate leaves, you need to spend some time making notes and thinking through the candidate's strengths and weaknesses for the position of sales associate. This is the time when the duties, characteristics, and qualifications you spent so much time developing earlier will pay dividends by making your decision much easier.

For each duty in the job description, you need to decide if the candidate demonstrated an ability to handle that duty or not. This should be either yes or no, although you may prefer to use a five-point scale if you are interviewing experienced sales associates. In Appendix C, I've included a sample "Job Interview Evaluation Checklist" that you can adapt to your interview style and the items that are most important to you.

Always Check References

After you have interviewed all three candidates for the job, you need to review your summaries and interview notes from all three meetings, decide on one of the candidates, and then do some reference checks. If everything seems fine, you can proceed to offer the job to the most qualified person.

Eventually, you may hire an apparently nice person who is either a low performer or who lacks integrity. You cannot eliminate this, but you can at least reduce the odds of it happening by hiring properly and checking references thoroughly.

Many owner-operated retailers do not check references, but it is not a difficult thing to do. You just pick up the telephone, call the candidate's last two or three employers, explain why you are calling, and ask if they will speak with you.

Selling Points

Make sure to include a section on previous employment in the job application. Ask the candidate to list his previous job, the company name and telephone number, as well as their direct supervisor. Even if the candidate gives you the name of another manager to contact for references, call his direct supervisor instead or in addition.

You certainly want to ask about the characteristics that I have identified as important: attitude, extroversion, ego, and empathy. You may also want to ask about things like friendliness, goal orientation, appearance, willingness to learn, punctuality, honesty, and selling ability.

Some employers are reluctant to talk about previous employees for various legal reasons. Most, however, will answer one standard question: "Would you rehire this person?" If the answer is yes, you can interpret that as a green light to go ahead and hire.

The Least You Need to Know

- Take the time to develop a job description for your sales associates before you start hiring.
- You may get hundreds of applications, but interview only the three best and be sure to spend an hour with each.

- Remember you need to sell yourself and your store during the interview process.
- Develop a good set of interview questions that you can ask each of the applicants.

Chapter 17

Training and Motivating Your Sales Associates

In This Chapter

- Train your people to sell
- Coaching techniques
- Understand motivation and use it

After you've hired your sales associates, you shouldn't just tell them to start selling and expect them to do it the way you want. You need to train them in the sales techniques you want them to use and coach them on how to succeed. You'll also need to keep them motivated with contests and other strategies. In this chapter, I discuss basic training, coaching, and motivation techniques.

Train Your Employees to Sell

I recommend you train your employees in suggestion selling techniques. Suggestion selling is one of the most important parts of providing complete customer service, yet most sales associates feel awkward with it at first.

Like any new skill, suggestion selling will take a certain amount of time and practice to master. The rewards, however, will be great—for your sales associates, your customers, and your business.

Suggestion selling, while intimidating at first, is actually quite simple. For example, if you are operating a shoe store, the sales associate may recommend a matching purse to go with the stiletto shoes the customer is buying for a complete and fashionable look. In a kitchen store, the sales associate may suggest a set of espresso cups if the customer plans to buy an espresso machine for an "authentic" Italian-style coffee experience. If the customer says no, simply stop there. If the customer says yes, suggest the second most logical of all the additional items that could complete the original purchase and keep suggesting items until the customer finally says no. In the example of the coffee machine, the sales associate could also have suggested espresso beans, coffee spoons, creamer and sugar bowl, and so on.

Use the Watch-and-Do Training Approach

As you begin to train your employees, keep in mind that adults learn best if they first "watch" and then "do." Think about good training workshops you've attended. In the best workshops, participants spend a relatively short time watching a good example and then a relatively long time doing a role-play or hands-on exercise.

Simply watching the new skill or behavior is not as effective as watching and then doing, although watching a good example does serve a purpose. The role-play or hands-on exercise is what really helps the participants learn. People need to experience firsthand the new skill or behavior that they are trying to master.

Incorporate the Apprenticeship Method

The apprenticeship method of staff training incorporates both the watching and the doing that are so crucial to helping adults learn new skills. So you should consider using this in your store.

View every new employee—or every current employee who is learning a new skill—as an apprentice. Their job is not to "do" a complete task initially. Rather, it is to watch and learn from someone who has more experience. Restaurants are particularly good at this. New servers follow experienced servers, and observe and learn from them how to tempt the guest with an appetizer, along with the entrée or the specials of the day, the matching wines that would make the whole meal unforgettable, and a dessert that the guest can't live without!

Only after watching and learning for a time will new employees get to try some of the basic components of the complete task. And only after they have mastered every one of those basic steps will they get to try the complete task. At each step of the way, they will be under the watchful eye of a "master craftsperson"—the person with more experience who can provide guidance and additional training as needed.

As the owner of a retail business, you will have no choice but to be the master craftsperson. Your sales associates will learn their tasks primarily by watching and listening to you. They will copy and model your behavior at every level. If you greet customers with a friendly "Good morning" as they enter the store, your sales associates will do the same.

If you have experienced sales associates in your store, you may be able to delegate some staff training to them by implementing a buddy system. Under this system, you pair every new employee—or every current employee who is learning a new skill—with someone who has more experience in that area. This leaves you free to concentrate on training the trainers.

If the skill you are teaching is simple, some of your sales associates will need just one cycle of watching and then doing to master it. But don't count on it. More likely you should expect sales associates will need two or three cycles. This is because different people learn at different rates. In fact, different people learn different things at different rates.

If the skill you are teaching is complex, such as suggestion selling, you should expect that all of your sales associates will need many cycles of watching and then doing to master it. Suggestion selling requires an understanding of the way that each item in your store relates to all of the other items in your store. It also requires the ability to ask good open-ended questions and fully understand a customer's needs.

Suggestion selling, however, is just one of many skills that your sales associates will need to master before they can do their jobs effectively. This means that staff training must be an ongoing part of your business—a steady stream of watching and then doing cycles.

Coaching Your Sales Associates

Under the apprenticeship method of staff training, you will need to provide your sales associates with ongoing guidance and additional training in a process known as "coaching." This starts on an employee's first day on the job and continues as long as that person works in your business.

The guidance and additional training you provide should sound something like: "Good job. I liked the way you made that last customer feel welcome in the store by giving such a warm and friendly smile. And if you now add the words 'Good morning, welcome to (name of the store)' you will find yourself in some great conversations with your customers."

Notice in this example, the coaching contained no negatives. Comments were provided in a positive way and directed the sales associate's behavior in the direction wanted.

Now let's look at the conversation using the word *but:* "Good job. I liked the way you made that last customer feel welcome in the store by giving such a warm and friendly smile, *but* next time you need to add 'Good morning, welcome to (name of the store),'" all the sales associate will hear is the fact that they forgot to say "good morning" and will interpret your comment as negative feedback.

In order to be an effective coach, you have to know the game yourself. This includes knowing, understanding, and demonstrating the specific skill or behavior that you are trying to teach. You also have to be there to watch and listen as your sales associates try first the basic steps of the task and then the complete task. All through the learning curve, your role will be the same: provide guidance and additional training.

When you provide this guidance and additional training in a positive manner, you will be "praising" the right behavior. This is an important concept in the context of staff training and motivation because praise is an important reward—and your sales associates will do whatever you reward. I often remind retailers that "what gets rewarded gets done."

You will understand this better if you take a moment to recall the many bosses and teachers you have had in your life. I bet that most of them had an uncanny ability for catching you doing something wrong. No matter how many times you did a task correctly, you always made a mistake right when they walked into the room—and they always pointed it out. The feedback you received from these people left you feeling demoralized, angry, and decidedly unmotivated to try the task again.

What happens instead when somebody tells us that we did something right? We feel good about it, and the positive feedback encourages us to continue performing to that level and in most cases to do it even better next time.

Unfortunately, catching sales associates doing something right is not a behavior that comes naturally to most people. As a business owner, you will need to develop it consciously and practice it constantly. The very success of your business will depend on your ability to become an effective coach and catch people doing something right instead of doing something wrong.

You will be a more effective coach if you follow a sequence of six distinct steps:

- **Set goals.** You need to set goals for each of your sales associates and these must be measurable, observable, and time-specific. For example, you might set a particular sales associate's goal as increasing her average transaction from today's level of $36 to $40 in the next week. After you set the goal, you will need to speak with her regularly about it so that it stays front and center.
- **Teach the skills.** The job of a retail sales associate comprises many separate skills—specific behaviors that the person needs to adopt. Suggestion selling and the customer greeting described earlier are both skills. Processing a transaction on the POS system and sending thank-you cards are skills as well. People do not know how to do these things intuitively. You need to teach them using the apprenticeship method of staff training.
- **Build relationships.** I can summarize this step in three words: "trust, trust, or bust." Trust is an amazing thing. It takes years to build but only seconds to shatter, and you never really get it back. As a coach, you need to build a professional relationship with each of your sales associates. This is not about being "friendly." Rather, it is about being honest and fair with all of your people all of the time in an effort to first earn and then keep their trust.
- **Motivate your players.** The best way to create a positive attitude in your business is to give your sales associates positive reinforcement for appropriate behaviors on their part. This is simply a matter of saying something nice when you see or hear someone doing something right. The closer you can bring the reinforcement to the behavior, the more powerful it will be. Catching people doing something right and telling them immediately is much more powerful than telling them that they did something right an hour after the fact.
- **Monitor performance.** There is little point to the first four steps if they do not result in better performance. That is why you need to set observable and measurable goals—and then use your own eyes and ears. A few days after setting the average-transaction goal in step one, you should be able to look at real-life results and see something higher than the $36 starting point. The sales associate does not need to be at the $40 goal yet, just heading there.
- **Provide guidance and ongoing training.** No matter what the sales associate's average transaction is after a few days, you will need to continue reinforcing the good behaviors in order to keep things moving forward. Remember to provide continuous feedback and guidance to your staff and to keep it positive, because that is the only way that they are going to improve. Individual coaching in an

informal, one-on-one session is the most effective, and, because adults learn better if they first watch and then do, always be ready to demonstrate the appropriate skill.

Motivating Employees

How does coaching result in motivating your employees? Let's take a closer look at what is behind motivation and then consider motivation techniques you can use.

The secret to understanding employee motivation lies partly in understanding the work of Abraham Maslow (1908–1970), an American psychologist and one of the founders of humanistic psychology. Maslow developed a triangle-shaped model of human motivation in which a higher need becomes important only after all of the lower needs have been fulfilled.

Basic human needs like food and water are critical, so these are at the base of the triangle. Safety and security needs are on the second level. Belongingness and love needs are on the third level, followed by self-esteem needs on the fourth level. Self-actualization needs are at the top of the triangle.

In the retail business, you will typically be dealing with people who are at either level three or level four of Maslow's triangle. In other words, your sales associates will typically have either "belongingness and love" needs or "self-esteem" needs. The people in these two groups are very different, so the challenge of motivating them lies in providing the right kind of motivation.

The Options

Affiliation motivation works for people whose needs center on belongingness and love. People in this group want most to be part of a team and accepted by that team. This is good, because it creates synergy through which the team becomes greater than the sum of its parts.

The best way to motivate belongingness and love people is to provide group contests. You provide just one goal for the entire team. Activities outside the store such as parties or softball teams—anything social—will work well with this group. If you employ just belongingness and love people in the store, you will have a supporting, noncompeting group.

Achievement motivation works for people whose needs center on self-esteem. People in this group have all of their belongingness and love needs fulfilled and now want most to compete and achieve because this will lead to personal growth. This is good, because it creates achievement-oriented competition in which people meet their sales targets.

The best way to motivate self-esteem people is to provide individual goals and incentives. You provide individual targets and each person will relish the personal challenge of meeting and beating them. If you employ just self-esteem people in the store, you will have a group of competing, nonsupporting individuals.

Most problems that owner-operated retailers face in the area of motivation start with goals and incentives that are inappropriate for their sales associates. For example, if you offer individual goals and incentives to people who are at the belongingness and love level of Maslow's triangle, they will not connect with the idea at all. This suggests that if you tried paying commission to a belongingness and love group in an effort to increase sales, it probably would not work.

At the same time, if you offer group goals and incentives to people who are at the self-esteem level, they will not connect with the idea at all. This suggests that if you offered a night at the movies to a self-esteem group for meeting a team goal, it probably would not work. When competition is lacking, self-esteem people tend to lose interest very quickly.

The good news is that self-esteem people will often be part of a team if they also get personal recognition. This means that you need to provide both affiliation motivation and achievement motivation in order to cover both groups. Any professional sports team will serve as a good model of how to do this.

Whether the sport is basketball, baseball, or hockey, the individual players win only when their team wins. The team's "superstar" cannot reach the podium alone and, no matter how dominant that person may be, he knows that the team must work as a unit if it is going to be successful. This is affiliation motivation.

At the same time, everyone keeps track of exactly who made the shots and who scored the goals. This is achievement motivation. The most powerful team you can build in your store is a team of "affiliative achievers." These are people at the self-esteem level of Maslow's triangle who understand that the only way they can win is by working together.

Know the Levels Your Employees Are At

Quite probably, you will have some sales associates on your team who are affiliation motivated and do not respond to individual goals at all, and some who are achievement motivated—the "superstars" trying to emerge. You can motivate this kind of team effectively if you remember that people at the affiliation level cannot participate at the achievement level.

In other words, you need to have both affiliation and achievement rewards in place, but the affiliation reward should be the dominant one. For example, "If we make our sales goal this month, everybody will get an extra $50 in their pay. The top two performers in average transaction will get an additional $50 each."

Praise is by far the most powerful motivator you can use—and it costs you absolutely nothing. Close behind praise is an in-store contest. This can last an hour, a day, a week, or even longer and the prize can be just about anything.

Some sales associates like an hour off with pay so that they can sleep in one morning or take an extended lunch break "on you." I even heard of one owner-operated retailer who went out into the parking lot to wash an employee's car—a contest prize that was both fun and inexpensive.

If you want to run a great contest, try "passing the buck." You announce this contest at the beginning of the day by holding a quick team meeting just before opening time. During the meeting, you give one of your sales associates a $20 bill. That sales associate gets to hold the $20 until someone makes the first sale of the day. Because that first sale will be the "largest sale of the day," the sales associate that makes it gets to hold the $20. This will go on all day, with the sales associate who makes each subsequent "largest sale of the day" getting to hold the $20. At closing time, the sales associate then holding the $20 gets to keep it.

The whole point of this contest is to have fun, so add as much of it to the competition as you can. For example, you might add a presentation ceremony and a mineral water "toast" to the victor at closing time.

Now that you understand basic training techniques, and have some ideas for motivating them, it's time to look more closely at how you want your customers served. In the next chapter, we'll explore customer service best practices.

The Least You Need to Know

- Suggestion selling can be a powerful tool for your sales associates to use, so teach your employees how to use it every time with every customer.
- Train your employees using the watch-and-do method.
- Understand what motivates each of your employees, and provide contests or other rewards that match their motivation needs.

Chapter 18

Serve Your Customers

In This Chapter

- Exploring the trends
- More than a vending machine
- Extra-mile service
- Assessing your customer service success

When you ask retailers about the biggest challenge facing them now and in the future, retailers of all sizes concur that it is customer service. No matter how incredible your product, how exciting your store environment, and how enticing your advertising, if the service that the customer receives in your store is bad, it's all for nothing.

Concentrate your efforts on learning how to exceed your customer's expectations for extraordinary service, and you'll greatly improve your chance of success. In this chapter, I talk about how you achieve this by going the extra mile. I also discuss the challenges and trends retailers face today and give you tools for assessing your store's customer service.

Customer Service Challenges and Trends

Owner-operated retailers face challenges today that are quite different from the ones that an old-time retailer faced. A century ago, you would have had a store on the Main Street of your city or town, held a position of trust and respect in the community, and personally known all of the customers you served in the store. You would have known their names, where they lived, how many children they had, and what they did for a living. You would also have remembered all of the items they had ever purchased in your store.

In the past, it was relatively easy to know your customers because you lived in the same community, walked on the same sidewalks each day, and attended the same church on Sundays. Today, a more likely scenario is that Main Street is empty, customers don't always trust you, and you know almost none of them by name.

To succeed today and in the future, retailers need to go back to the past and offer the level of personalized service that was so natural 100 years ago.

In other words, the business you operate in the early part of the twenty-first century should look much like the business you would have operated in the early part of the twentieth century. This is key, because three important trends have increased the competition for customers in recent years:

- Developers and retailers for many years built stores at a much faster rate than was warranted by our population increase. Something like 100 percent more stores are now trying to sell to about 15 percent more people.
- Retailers created some very successful new formats. "Category killers" and big-box retailers are now taking business away from specialty stores the way specialty stores once took business away from department stores. Many of the biggest retailers are getting even bigger while many of the smallest retailers—those that are unprepared—are falling by the wayside.
- The customer profile is changing. You no doubt know that baby boomers—people born between 1946 and 1964—are the largest demographic group in the history of North America. By virtue of sheer numbers, these people have been a significant force in the economy of both countries as they moved through the various stages of life.

Baby boomers are now moving out of their peak-purchasing years and shifting their purchasing patterns. They do not need many more homes, cars, televisions, or clothes—and most have given up competitive sports in favor of hiking. This, however, is happening at the same time as their children graduate from college and leave home—which means that, with years to go before retirement, a lot of baby boomers have a newly found disposable income to spend on luxuries and life experiences. They remember customer service the way it used to be, and they consider it important.

In contrast, the children of the baby boomers—people born between 1965 and 1984—are just reaching the stage of life during which people buy a lot of "stuff." As their parents did before them, they will buy things like homes, cars, televisions, clothes, and tennis-club memberships. But their expectations of service will be quite different. This is discussed in Chapter 3.

Most experts predict that all three of the previous trends will continue well into the future—which means that retail will not see another wonderful "binge" like the one that it enjoyed in the 1970s and 1980s because of the baby boom. Instead, things will get more and more competitive.

If you believe that most "experts" are correct in their predictions—and if you want to sell to baby boomers and their children—the direction that you must take in your retail business becomes clear. You will need to give your customers significant reasons why they should shop with you and earn every sales dollar. This is exactly what extra-mile service and relationship marketing will help you do.

Selling Points

You will exceed your customers' expectations by doing all of the little things well that most retailers don't do at all—giving more to your customers for less cost, which means keeping your expenses under control at the same time you are "wowing" them with services. Not an easy task!

Differentiating Yourself from a Vending Machine

From the perspective of a customer, shopping at one of the "big-box" retailers is similar to shopping at a vending machine. Neither asks what you want because they expect you to know that when you arrive—and both reduce the shopping experience to its simplest terms. As a customer, you walk in, put your money in the slot, push a button, and wait as a product slides down the chute.

Vending machines are both very efficient and very profitable for their owners, but they have one big drawback from a customer's perspective—they will quite happily sell "landfill." We use this term to describe any items customers buy that do not meet their needs.

Think for a moment about your own home. Somewhere in your basement, garage, closet, bathroom, or kitchen, you probably have at least one thing that you have bought but never used. It might be a tool, a can of paint, a sweater, some skin cream, or a plastic container, but I bet you have something.

You may not think of this item as landfill just yet, but deep in your heart you already know. That item will sit in your basement, garage, closet, bathroom, or kitchen until you sell it in a yard sale, give it away, or send it with the rest of the trash to a landfill site.

Now think about where you bought this item. The odds are good that you bought it from a vending machine—a retailer who invited you to walk in, put your money in the slot, push a button, and wait as a product slid down the chute.

This retailer did not care the least bit about you as a person or your "needs." They probably sold you the item at a low price—but that did not leave them with enough money to provide a professional sales associate who could answer your questions and help you understand what you needed to buy. Instead, you bought landfill.

As you develop your retail business, you should regularly ask yourself one question: "What is the difference between what I am doing and what a vending machine does?" If the answer is "nothing," you are in deep trouble. Any vending-machine retailer can simply undercut your prices and put you out of business.

To prevent this, you need to add value to every transaction. One of the best ways to do this is to provide extra-mile service and always take the time to understand your customers' needs. This is something that you can do well but a vending-machine retailer cannot do at all.

If you can figure out what it would take to make your customers' purchases complete and wonderful—and then find ways of doing that—you stand a good chance of lasting in the retail business. Not every customer will respond to this. Perhaps 20 percent of all customers shop on price alone. They are quite happy to do their shopping at a vending machine. They do not care about nice-looking stores and they are not interested in what some retailers offer as "service."

You would be making a big mistake if you tried to build your business on this group, because you will never be able to build a relationship with customers who shop on price alone. Those people will always go down the street to save a dime and around the corner to save a quarter.

> **Savvy Retailer**
>
> Remember, price will only be an issue in the absence of value. You can probably charge 20 percent more than the lowest price in the market on a given item—if you deliver at least double the difference in value. If you do not, your business will not succeed.

This does not imply that the remaining 80 percent of shoppers do not care about price. To the contrary, these people care very much about what they pay—in relation to what they receive. In other words, they care about value. They will expect you to justify your price, to explain why an item is worth the amount you are asking for it.

I know of a building-supply retailer who had to explain the concept of "value" to one of his customers—and did it very well. A customer rushed into the store one day and asked this retailer if he had any 4' x 8' sheets of "good one side" plywood. The retailer said that he did. The customer, a contractor in the middle of building a house, then asked how much the plywood cost. The retailer replied that it was so much a sheet.

The customer responded that the same plywood was two dollars less than that at a competing store down the street. The retailer then asked the rather obvious question: "Why not buy it there?" "Because they are out of stock," said the contractor. To which the retailer replied, "When we are out of stock, our price is two dollars less than even that."

He then went on to explain that his store had plywood that day because he made it a policy to stock sufficient inventory at all times. "We don't want to inconvenience you by not having the product you want, when you want it," he said. He also explained that his store employed only knowledgeable, friendly people who could answer virtually any question—and would gladly help load purchases onto the customer's truck.

"All of this costs money," the retailer explained. "And although we may sometimes be a bit more expensive on some items, we believe that the level of service we provide will more than make up the difference."

With some tongue-in-cheek humor, he explained the value that his store delivered—in this case, to a contractor who was paying carpenters much more than the price of a sheet of plywood to do nothing until some arrived. The contractor bought 24 sheets that day and has been back many times since then.

Going the Extra Mile

I often speak to retailers about the importance of "going the extra mile." By this, I mean providing "extra-mile" service—doing things that will truly amaze your customers.

Many of these things will be both simple and inexpensive, yet few of your competitors will bother to make the effort. You will find that there is very little traffic on the extra mile.

Here is a challenge. Think back over the last six months and come up with one good example of extra-mile service that you have personally experienced as a customer in a retail store. This should be something that truly amazed you—something so good that it still stands out in your mind.

A participant in one of my workshops came up with a great example. When someone broke into her car, stole the radio, and did extensive damage, she found herself getting the runaround from The Big Insurance Corporation. It would not cover this and it would not cover that so—far beyond the amount of her deductible—being the victim of a crime was going to cost her a lot of money.

Then she met an owner-operated retailer who, unlike The Big Insurance Corporation, treated her as a valued customer. The people at this store provided extra-mile service, and they did it several times.

When she dropped off her car to have a new radio installed, a staff person drove her all the way across town so she could get to work on time. The store then did the installation, called her when it was finished, and offered to come and pick her up.

The biggest surprise came when she saw the bill. The store had given her the radio, which she was paying for personally, at cost. They had also replaced the wires on her car alarm, which the thief had cut but The Big Insurance Corporation would not cover, and fixed some related damage. There was no charge on the bill for this additional work.

When she asked the owner-operated retailer why there was no charge, he replied that when his car had been broken into four years earlier, The Big Insurance Corporation also didn't want to pay for replacing the wires on his car alarm and fixing some related damage. That's why he had decided to help her and proceeded to send to The Big Insurance Corporation the supporting documentation along with an invoice for the "not covered" work that he did on her car.

My workshop participant was amazed. She told 125 people about her good experience with the store in just this one afternoon. She very likely told other people in other situations about it as well, because that is how word-of-mouth advertising works.

Two years later, I took time to visit the business she had described. I found an owner-operated retailer who was thriving.

To create this kind of "apostle" in your business, you will need to judge the extra-mile service you provide from the perspective of your customers. If 80 percent of your customers expect you to do something and you do not do it, you are not going the extra mile. If 80 percent of your customers expect you to do something and you do it, you are still not going the extra mile.

Only when 80 percent of your customers do not expect you to do something and you do it will you be going the extra mile. You will know you are succeeding when customers react to your extra-mile service with words such as, "Wow, that's amazing. I've never heard of a store doing that before."

Here are some ideas for providing extra-mile service for your customers:

- An electronic customer newsletter that contains product information but no sales pitch, sent by e-mail only to people who want to receive it.
- A phone-ahead or web page ordering system that lets the store prepare a customer's order and have it ready for fast pickup.
- Tourist maps and change for an exact-fare bus system in a downtown tourist area.
- Batteries-included pricing in a toy store.
- A toll-free telephone number in a store that has a lot of out-of-town customers.
- Staying with a customer who arrives close to closing time until that customer has completed his shopping.
- Free delivery and installation in an art store.
- Repairing or arranging for local repairs to items that a customer would otherwise have to return to the manufacturer—a process that can take many weeks.
- Phoning around to area schools to get the school-supply lists that harried parents may not have when they do their back-to-school shopping.
- Unlimited in-home technical support at no charge for computer purchasers.
- Clothing delivered to customers' homes when the free-of-charge alterations are complete.
- Links on the store's website to good sources of "neutral" information about the main products it sells and an in-store computer on which to access it.

Earning Customer Trust and Loyalty

Even when you go the extra mile, you earn customer trust and loyalty just one small step at a time. The good news is that, as you earn customer trust and loyalty—not to mention a reputation for providing excellent service—customers will expect you to go the extra mile for them. This is a wonderful position to be in, because it will push you to find even more ways to meet and exceed those expectations.

The bad news is that out of 100 customers for whom you go the extra mile, perhaps 20 will not even notice. The majority of people, perhaps 60, will notice. Some of them may say thank you. If you are lucky, they may even remember the name of your store and come back sometime in the next three months.

That leaves perhaps 20 customers who will notice, will say thank you, will remember the name of your store, will come back sometime in the next three months—and may even tell other people about your extra-mile service. You can build a very profitable retail business if you satisfy the needs of these customers.

Looking at Your Business from Your Customers' Viewpoints

Looking at your business from your customers' perspectives can be fascinating because things often look quite different from the other side of the counter. To illustrate, here are the things that customers look for when they shop. As an owner-operated retailer who cannot compete with category killers and big-box retailers on price, you will be happy to see that it ranked sixth on the list.

- **Convenience**—Given all of the stress in their fast-paced lives, customers want shopping to be fast and easy. And they will appreciate anything you do to help make it so. For example, you could offer delivery to anywhere in the world. You would not have to offer it for free; you would just have to offer it. To a customer who needs to get a birthday gift to Sydney, Australia, by this weekend, you will be providing extra-mile service that they will gladly pay for.
- **Selection**—You can have a beautiful store and a wonderful staff, but if you do not have the products that customers want, they cannot buy from you. Many "category killers" have built their businesses around having the best selection, not necessarily the lowest prices. As an owner-operated retailer, you will deal

personally with your customers day after day. If you listen carefully to what they tell you, you should be able to offer an assortment and selection of merchandise that is almost perfect for them.

- **Peace of mind**—Most customers want some reassurance that they are buying the right item—and that you will help them if they have any problems. One of the best things you can say to a customer is, "You cannot make a mistake when buying in my store." The advantage you bring to the marketplace is your understanding of lifetime value. If an item is not right, you are going to make it right instead of worrying about making or losing money on that particular sale. You know that, in the long run, you will make significant money from that customer.
- **Product knowledge**—You provide friendly and approachable sales associates who know pretty much everything there is to know about the items they sell—and how to research anything that they do not know. One thing to avoid, however, is the use of "jargon." In most product classifications, experts use certain words to talk about how an item performs or what its components are. You should never assume that anyone else knows the meaning of your specialized words. These intimidate more customers than they impress. And remember, once the customer knows more about a product than your staff, you are in big trouble. Invest in product knowledge for your staff.
- **Total service**—This phrase implies more than just having a friendly, approachable, and knowledgeable staff. Among other things, it also implies having a complete assortment of in-stock merchandise so that customers do not waste trips, displaying merchandise so that customers can find it, and providing appropriate lighting so that customers can see colors and read price tags easily. There are many great books about customer service and, as you build your retail business, you should buy an armload of them. Spend a lot of time reading about businesses that deliver it well. Then share the books with all of your sales associates. I recommend books for you to read in Appendix B.
- **Price**—Most customers are looking for a fair price—which is not the same thing as the lowest price in the market. You probably understand this intuitively from your own experience. Nobody wants to feel cheated. It is rare that we ever question the price of something that has performed above and beyond our expectations, it is often when something breaks or does not work well that we feel cheated on price.

How Refunds Provide Extra-Mile Service

Your store's refund policy is an excellent opportunity to provide extra-mile service for your customers. As an owner-operated retailer who understands the lifetime value of a customer, there is really only one refund policy you can have: "If something is wrong, we will make it right."

> **Better Not!**
> The fastest way to kill your reputation as an extra-mile retailer is to post a sign that says, "No cash refunds." That usually happens in a store where the owner feels that one too many unscrupulous customers have purchased an item, used it, and then returned it the next day for a full refund. Resist the temptation to do this, because this type of unscrupulous customer really is rare.

Don't ever take the position that you won't allow cash refunds. While you may think some people take advantage of a cash refund policy by returning an item that they used once, it does not happen often enough compared to the store's total number of transactions. Don't punish every customer for the deceit of a few. When you look at the big picture, surprisingly few customers ever even use a store's refund policy.

It is easy to follow a make-it-right policy when you are dealing with a wonderful customer who comes in all the time, pays full price, never questions your word, and almost never complains. You are happy to do whatever it takes to make it right.

The difficult time comes when you are dealing with an angry customer who comes in twice a year, never pays full price, always questions your word, and usually complains. It is tough to make it right under those circumstances. But you must, to a point.

In both cases, you should assume that the return is a "righteous return." You should assume that somehow you sold a damaged, defective, or unsatisfactory product. In other words, you made a mistake and the problem is yours.

What should you do? Walk toward the customer and apologize. This is only polite, and it may help to calm an angry customer. Next, you ask the obvious question: "What's wrong?" Listen carefully to what the customer says and ask questions to make sure that you understand the problem fully.

Then you should apologize again and validate the quality of your store: "I'm sorry. This should not have happened. We take pride in selling first-quality merchandise and offering first-quality service. How can I make it right for you?"

The customer may want a replacement item—be certain that it works—or they may want a refund. In the end, most customers want very little beyond what they have already paid for. This is when you can really provide extra-mile service. Give them what they want and preferably a little more than what they want.

If the customer wants a replacement item, this might mean giving them the next model up at no additional charge. If they want a cash refund, this might mean giving them their money back and an appropriate gift certificate. By giving them something extra, you are making up for the time and the aggravation that your mistake cost them.

Selling Points

An important part of providing extra-mile service for your customers is ensuring that each of your sales associates has the same decision-making authority that you have when it comes to making exchanges and refunds. Having a make-it-right refund policy means little if everyone has to check with you before making what should be a no-thought decision.

At the same time, we also believe that you should protect yourself from customers who will abuse your make-it-right refund policy if you let them. If a customer wants to make what you consider a "less than righteous" return, you should give the refund but make note of the incident in a "preferred customer" book that you keep by the cash register. (We prefer that they don't shop here!)

If you get three less-than-righteous returns from the same customer in a given period—six months, perhaps—you are fully justified in declining the third request.

Finishing a Sale

When a customer shops in your store, you will no doubt try to make the entire transaction as smooth and enjoyable as possible. But what will you do at the end of the sale? What kind of a message will you give that customer as she is leaving?

The following are two very different "messages" that I have taken from real-life retailers. As a customer, which one would you prefer?

> Scenario 1: On the back of the sales associate's business card: Thank you for shopping at (store name). I have enjoyed assisting you and I want you to know that I personally guarantee your satisfaction. If you have any problem or question, please call me and I will make it right. Thank you again. (Sales associate's signature)

Scenario 2: On the back of the cash register receipt in small type: At (store name), we work very hard to provide you with product knowledge on the nature and value of everything we sell. We will gladly accept a return of merchandise within 30 days with proof of purchase (our cash register receipt) for exchange or credit. Goods can be returned for reasons of defect or dissatisfaction but we exclude accidental damage and tampering. At Christmas, out of consideration to the season, we extend the facility until January 31st. At this time of year we waive proof of purchase for readily identifiable goods but will input the lowest sale price for exchange or credit purposes. No cash refunds are possible. This includes credit refunds to charge cards. This is in conformity with independent industry standards and frankly is necessary if we are to remain in business. Within the boundaries of this policy, the staff is encouraged to seek your satisfaction. Currently we charge a minimum of $7.50 for all services and repair work (silver from $12 and up) sent out of the store. Please inquire about our extensive repair services for sterling silver and fashion jewelry. Plated items do react differently with individual customers and therefore we cannot be held responsible. Please avoid applying perfume or hairspray near any jewelry. Other warranties may apply. For further inquiries, call our head office at (telephone number).

Don't you find the personal touch in Scenario 1 a much better example of extra-mile service? It's not expensive, and it does show your customers you are willing to go the extra mile. Relationship marketing, which I discuss in greater detail in Chapter 15, is another key aspect of going the extra mile.

Testing Your Store's Customer Service

You can put a lot of time into planning how you will go the extra mile, but how do you make sure your vision is always being carried out in your store? Two good ways to test that are comment cards and customer service analysis.

Use Comment Cards

So how do you know what your customers want and how can you build that extra-mile service? One great way that you can learn more about your customers is to provide "comment cards."

Two groups of customers tend to use comment cards: those you have really made angry and those you have really made happy. For that reason, this type of research will be most useful for damage control and for getting ideas from people who really like your store. So, while still valuable, it might not help you get the opinions of a cross-section of your customers.

To help you design an effective customer comment card, we suggest that you spend time in the coming weeks collecting customer comment cards from every business you visit. Do not restrict yourself just to retail stores; grab one every chance you get.

Here are some of the things that I like to see on a comment card:

- The question "How did we do today?" in big, bold letters.
- Postage-paid so that the customer can return it by mail to the store's owner instead of handing it to a sales associate.
- The chance to rate efficiency, friendliness, accuracy, knowledge, quality, value, prices, selection, cleanliness, and overall satisfaction.
- A five-point rating scale ranging from "way below average" to "way above average," with "just average" in the middle.
- Easy to read and not too crowded, with lots of well-spaced lines for the customer's written comments.
- Lines to provide a name and contact information if the customer wants to give it.
- The name and title of the person in the company who will be reading the card and a check box that lets the customer give permission for that person to contact him or her.
- The words "Thank you for your comments."

After a month or so, sit down with your comment-card collection and review each one from the perspective of a customer.

Selling Points

You may also consider giving the customer an incentive to complete the comment card in the form of a bounce-back coupon with a discount on their next purchase (dollars off, not percentages!). Customers would be asked to complete the comment card before leaving the store and given the coupon after they drop off their comments.

Customer Service Analysis

If you were to ask most specialty retailers if they gave great service, they would look at you and say, "Of course, that is what we are known for!" Yet, if asked to quantify this, in other words, prove it, they often cannot. I believe that you cannot prove something if you cannot measure it, nor can you change something if you cannot measure it. Traffic counters have been around for over 25 years and are used by many retailers to calculate conversion rate, the number of shoppers that actually buy. This is also called close rate.

def•i•ni•tion

Customer service ratio (CSR) is the desired customer-to-staff ratio—how many customers one staff member can serve divided by the number of customers in your store at a specific time. You often calculate this in 15-minute increments.

Traffic counters will not only give you the conversion rate for shoppers in the store (which is a great number to have and the formula is total traffic divided by total transactions) but it will also give you a more important number called your *customer service ratio (CSR)*. This ratio simply tells you whether you have enough staff to properly serve the customers you have in the store and if you are losing sales.

First, ask yourself this question: how many customers can one of my sales associates serve simultaneously? The obvious and "perfect" answer is one. But the real world answer is closer to two or even three. In most cases, a good sales associate can balance three customers at the same time, but this is the maximum and more than three would surely mean that the customers are not getting anywhere near good service.

So, the question becomes, how many times last Saturday did you exceed this desired customer-to-staff ratio? For example, let's assume we agree that a good staff ratio is three customers to every sales associate, which means that each staff member can adequately serve no more than three customers simultaneously (some stores set this number at two or even one). Assume you have three staff members working, and your traffic counter tells you that between 11:00 A.M. and 11:15 A.M. you had 15 customers in the store. You had a customer service ratio of 5 to 1 instead of the 3 to 1 (the desired ratio) during this fifteen-minute period.

Obviously if you had five customers for every sales associate during this time, there were likely many customers who had questions about items that could not get answers. You also probably had long lineups at the cash wrap, as well as customers who simply walked out and were never served at all.

Think about what you do if you are shopping and would like to buy something, but have a question. If you cannot get the answer to that question, many times you just put the item back on the shelf and leave. The same thing happens when we have a CSR that exceeds 3 for longer than five or ten minutes.

Yes, there are times when a group will "rush" the store and it would not make financial sense to flood the store with additional staff; it would in most cases not even be possible. In these cases, we have to balance the potential of the group that came in against the cost (and the feasibility) of staffing for that brief period.

For example, if it was a group of tourists or runners prior to an event, the likelihood that they would be purchasing running shoes or high-involvement merchandise at that moment is low. It would be much more likely that they are buying event T-shirts or socks or other last minute accessory items. In that case, I would simply make sure that I had as much self-serve merchandise available as possible in an easy to select display, and put most of my staff at the cash registers to simply ring up items.

But if I discover that there are times on Saturday and Sunday that I consistently exceed my CSR by more than 50 percent, then I need to add more staff at these times. Here is an example of how you would determine appropriate staffing using a CSR calculation:

> Traffic counts for last Saturday indicated that in five 15-minute periods I had 24 customers in the store.
>
> I had three staff working during each of these 15-minute periods.
>
> My staff-to-customer ratio was 8 to 1 versus the desired 3 to 1 during these five periods.
>
> My customer loss was the 24 that were there minus the 9 that my staff could adequately serve, which leaves 15 customers in each of the five periods who did not get served properly or at all.
>
> This totals 75 customers who were not served during the total five periods.
>
> I would likely not have been able to sell to all 75, as my normal conversion rate is 38 percent.
>
> My average transaction is $68.
>
> So my loss was 75 times $68 times 38 percent or $1,938 in potential lost sales.
>
> What would two more staff have cost for the day?

In this calculation, you know that you had a potential loss of $1,938. Suppose you pay each sales associate $10 an hour or $80 for an eight-hour day. Wouldn't it be worth adding two associates to potentially make $1,900 or more?

Obviously, if the majority of your customers shop as couples, you can decrease this number, but your conversion rate would already take this into account. And in addition, you can often sell a couple items for both of them.

Do your own math. Take your own measures, and see what potential business you are losing by not having sufficient staff when required. Think about what your real customer service level is and how many people each sales associate can assist at the level you want.

Install traffic counters and test the logic for six months. I bet that you will notice a marked increase in sales and customer satisfaction if there were times when your CSR exceeded your target and you responded by staffing properly.

You can have excellent sales associates, but if they don't have the right technology to work with you, they may not have the tools you need to go that extra mile. In the next chapter, we'll look at the technology you need.

The Least You Need to Know

- Providing exceptional customer service is the key for most owner-operated retail businesses today.
- Don't serve your customers like a vending machine. Learn the basics of extra-mile customer service and be sure your sales associates incorporate them daily in their contacts with your customers.
- Your refund policy can be a key part of going the extra mile.
- Periodically test whether you truly are giving extra-mile service using comment cards and CSR calculations.

Chapter 19

Picking the Right Technology

In This Chapter

- Know what you need
- Software for bookkeeping
- Software for point of sale
- Training you need

You don't need to be a computer expert to pick the right technology to support your business. You just need to know what specific technology you need, why you need it, and where you can find it. In this chapter, we'll explore how to find the right technology to run your business.

Do Your Homework

Your customers do not know what technology you use in your store. They do not care whether it is outdated, state-of-the art, or expensive. What they do care about is the service they receive. If they don't find it extraordinary—efficient, accurate, and complete—they will go somewhere else, and they may never come back. You won't be able to deliver the right services to your customers if you rely on outdated technology.

Think about when you shop at an independent retailer and you have to wait in line for a long time as each transaction is handled excruciatingly slowly and the credit card processing is even slower. Or think about the last time a store you were in missed a potential sale with you because they were out of stock on an item that you needed and that was popular—i.e., they shouldn't have been out of it. Or think about when you had to shop at a different store than originally planned because the first didn't have what you wanted. And finally, think of how difficult it will be for you to coach your staff toward higher levels of performance if you don't even know how much more they should be doing.

While technology isn't the only answer to all these problems, the right technology can go a long way to solving them. True, the right technology for your business can represent a considerable investment. But have you thought about its benefits over time? Even better, have you considered what it might cost you not to have it in terms of lost sales and opportunities?

As you try to figure out what technology you need, pay close attention to checkout procedures at the stores where you shop. When you see sales associates in independent retail stores able to handle customer checkout quickly and efficiently, talk with the owner about the systems she uses. You can learn a lot about which systems may be best for you by talking with other independent retailers about their successes and failures with technology.

> **Savvy Retailer**
>
> I always recommend "retail hardened" hardware from one of the top three players—IBM, Dell, or NCR. While you might find it cheaper to get an off-the-shelf personal computer, you won't get the retail support you need.

You also can learn a lot about the hardware available for retailers by visiting the websites of the big boys—IBM, Dell, and NCR. All of them have sections on point-of-sale (POS) equipment. When it comes to hardware, it is very important that you buy the right type for your business, which might not necessarily be the cheapest. Your store's success is dependent on your being able to serve your customers quickly and efficiently, and if your hardware can't handle the volume of business that you are experiencing, expect your customers to choose to shop somewhere else.

Interfaced vs. Integrated Software

In addition to hardware requirements, you need to consider software options. There are three key types of software critical to the independent retailer—back office, accounting, and point-of-service (POS) software. You'll also need to understand whether the software you're considering will be interfaced (able to translate data between your back office and POS software) or integrated (use the same data files so the information can be updated simultaneously in both programs and can be available in real time). Appendix C provides a questionnaire you can use to get the information you need from a POS supplier.

Integrated software will save you lots of time and avoid the need to enter information into three different systems. *Interfaced software* requires you to download information from one system and upload it into the other. The big disadvantage of interfaced systems is that the interface requires that you do it manually. You won't have the information in real time. You'll likely interface the programs at the end of the business day so you won't have the information you may need throughout the day.

def•i•ni•tion

Integrated software is software that uses the same data files so the information can be updated in real-time.

Interfaced software is software that enables you to translate data between your back office, accounting, and POS software, but this must be done manually.

Accounting and Financial Reporting

The two most popular accounting software packages available on the market today are QuickBooks and Peachtree Accounting. Before picking your accounting system, check with your accountant to be sure whatever you pick can easily interface with his systems. That way you will be able to download your data and he can upload it into his system when he needs to prepare your reports, review your books, or prepare your tax returns.

QuickBooks

QuickBooks (www.quickbooks.intuit.com) gives you the best of both worlds. You'll find it relatively easy to use even if you are an accounting novice, but you'll also find extensive bookkeeping and accounting features even for the experienced bookkeeper or accountant. It's the most popular accounting software package for small business owners today.

In 2005, QuickBooks got even better for the novice with its learning center. This is an interactive program that walks you through every type of key transaction and not only shows you how to do the function, but explains the basics of bookkeeping as well.

You don't have to use the tutorial, but the option pops up when you do the task for the first time. You can also go back to the learning center for review at any time.

QuickBooks also is the most versatile accounting package if you use other software packages. It can share data with over 300 popular business software applications. Sales, customer, and financial data can be shared easily, so you don't have to enter it twice.

All the accounting programs offer add-ons and features you will likely need. If you have employees and want up-to-date tax information and forms to do your payroll using your accounting software, you will need to buy an update each year. It usually costs about $200. Credit card processing online and electronic bill paying also mean additional fees. QuickBooks also has point-of-sale software that helps you integrate your sales at the cash register with your accounting software, which is another useful add-on that helps you manage your customer contacts.

Peachtree Accounting

Peachtree Accounting (www.peachtree.com) is the other big boy when it comes to bookkeeping and accounting needs, but I don't recommend it if you are a novice. You do need to be familiar with accounting jargon to use the system, and its interface is not as user friendly as QuickBooks. Although it does offer training options inside the program, it lacks the sophistication of the excellent learning center now offered by QuickBooks.

You definitely need to know your way around the general ledger and be comfortable around accounting terms like account reconciliation, accounts payable, or cash receipts journal to use this software.

POS and Inventory Management

Your most important software package will be your point-of-sale software. Whatever system you pick, the following are the basic functions you must have:

- **Fast checkout and approval of charge purchases.** Customers are time poor and generally see shopping as a task rather than a recreational activity. That's why it is paramount that you have the right POS in place to ensure you can have them in and out as fast as possible. Don't make customers wait in line or at the counter because your POS can't handle the volume of transactions that you are experiencing on that day. Trust me, avoid that and you will have that customer for life, because if shopping at your store means fast and easy, that's exactly where they will shop.

- **Transaction suspend feature.** This is a feature that allows you to place a transaction in suspense, while the customer either goes to her car to get her check or charge card or goes back into the store to get an additional item, and resume the transaction when the customer returns. This also helps speed up processing of customers in line behind this customer and reduces waiting time.
- **Production of gift receipts.** To make returns more accurate and efficient.
- **Automatic store credits.** Automatic store credits can be given on returned items, which reduces cash refunds and tracks returned items. These store credit notes are serialized and can be used just like a gift card. They can replace manual issuance of store credit notes that are time consuming and open to fraudulent use. Again, it's about accuracy and, of course, efficiency.
- **Bounce back coupons.** Some cash register receipts can be programmed to provide a "bounce back" coupon to the customer. This will give them a discount on their next purchase, thereby increasing the likelihood of a repeat purchase.
- **Inventory management.** Your system not only has to tell you what you have on hand per department, per category, per sub-category, and line, but it also needs to show what inventory you have on order. It also needs to be capable of creating purchase orders.
- **Customer profile**. Your software should also track each customer, their purchases over time, favorites, and as much information as you can get about individual preferences. This will help you build your database for your customer relationship management programs. I talk more about CRM in Chapters 15 and 26.

Here are four excellent integrated POS software packages you should check out:

- Microsoft Retail Management System (www.microsoft.com/dynamics/rms/default.mspx)
- CounterPoint (www.synchronics.com/products/cp.htm)
- CAM Commerce Solutions (www.camcommerce.com)—Cam offers a free trial version for small retailers with only one machine
- Retail Pro (www.retailpro.com)

Pay for Training

The problem with retail software and hardware today is that it is too cheap! What I mean is that the purchase price of software in particular is deceptively inexpensive. You may be thinking "Are you kidding, I just checked and it costs over $3,000 to buy the software I need!" Believe me, the price of the software is just the beginning, and that is the reason that most retailers do not have technology that works for them.

In almost every case when I hear this, I ask the retailer how much training they had on the software. Almost all will answer, "we had the person who sold it to us install it and spend a day showing us how to use it."

Buying software and not wanting to pay for additional training from the software provider is a huge problem. It is not unusual nor out of line to spend up to 10 times the cost of the software on learning how to use it. A retailer who spends $3,000 on a software package should be spending at least $10,000 on learning how to use that software in the first three months (this equates to about three weeks or 120 hours of training). This is the cost of a good trainer and does not include the hours that your staff will spend learning the software, which could easily be twice the number of hours.

> **Selling Points**
>
> Understand that there is no software that is "intuitive" and most software is not easy to learn. Software is a tool for your business, and like any tool, you have to learn how to use it properly.

Your training costs and time won't end there. Over the next year you must invest in ongoing training to make sure you are maximizing the power of the software by learning not just how to run reports, but what reports to run and most importantly, what these reports are telling you and how to change your business based on this information.

Reports alone do not change a business or make it more profitable; it is what you do with the reports that count. If you have not had any updated or ongoing training with your software, then it is no surprise that you are not benefiting from it. A good software provider will not only train you on the use of the software (what buttons to push, how to enter data, how to create a report, and so on), but it will also give you additional training on the strategic use of the software.

For example, you can maximize your vendor information by analyzing order information. This analysis will tell you which vendors are your best ones and which vendors are not worth working with.

Imagine sitting down with a vendor and showing him a report that demonstrates that last season he shipped only 50 percent on time and averaged an 80 percent fill rate with only 20 percent of his merchandise selling at full price in the first three months in the store? After showing the supplier the data, ask him, "If you were me, would you buy from you?" This negotiation strategy often opens up a real dialogue with your vendors that can lead to change in the relationship and your profitability.

If you have the right information, you can make smart decisions. The problem with most of us today is that we are drowning in data and going thirsty for information and knowledge. Learning means paying tuition, and every dollar that you invest in learning how to maximize your retail technology you will get at least $10 back in increased productivity, sales, and profitability.

The Least You Need to Know

- Analyze what types of software you need to keep your books and serve your customers efficiently.
- Use reports generated by the software to manage your sales force and negotiate with your vendors.
- Don't skimp on hardware or software or on training to use those tools.

Chapter 20

Using the Web

In This Chapter

- Why the Internet
- Website musts
- Reaching out
- Getting help

Can you afford to run a retail store and not be present on the web? No! It doesn't mean that you have to sell on the web, although it's nice if you can do that. What is absolutely necessary is that you have a website where customers can learn about you, your products, your promotions, and your events. In this chapter, I introduce you to the basics of setting up a website.

The Web—Can't Live Without It

No business today can survive without a website. There are three key reasons every retailer must have a website today:

- **Marketing**—Even if you sell a product or service that requires your customer to come to your store, a website provides an excellent way for people to find you and find out more about what you sell. Think about all the times you searched the web for something you wanted.

The web is the modern day Yellow Pages, and maintaining a website is a lot cheaper than paying for an ad each year, although doing both, if you can afford it, is the best. That way you can reach people who don't search the Internet first.

- **e-commerce**—Online sales can broaden your business outside your immediate community, as long as you sell a product or service that can be delivered by phone or mail. You can even make some extra money on the shipping and handling charges as long as you don't get too greedy and charge more than your competitors.
- **Customer support**—Many customers today look at your website for support, especially if they have a problem when the store is closed. You can offer detailed information about your products and some solutions for the most common problems a customer encounters. That will give your customers an answer quickly, even if your store is closed. They won't have to wait until the store reopens the next day.

First Thing First

The first thing you must choose is the domain name for your store. This will be your company's online identity. The domain name is your URL (Uniform Resource Locator). That's how customers will remember how to find your store on the web.

Choosing your domain name can be one of your most important decisions when putting your business online. If you pick the right domain name, it can become an asset that attracts customers to your website. It's not difficult to register a domain name, and you can easily do so for about $10 a year. You'll find hundreds of websites that can register a domain name by filling out a form online. Just type "register a website" in a Google search window, and you will find all your choices.

Selling Points

There are hundreds of websites on the Internet that offer domain reservation services. Some good ones for you to check out include: Go Daddy (www.godaddy.com), Register.com (www.register.com), and Network Solutions (www.networksolutions.com).

As you pick your domain name, the KISS principle is important—Keep It Simple Stupid. Keep the name short and simple, no more than 20 characters and less is better. Suppose your store's name was Cathy's Candles. In this case, you could check to see if the domain www.cathyscandles.com is available when you register the domain. Always have a few alternatives ready before signing up for your domain name, because you may find your first-choice name has already been taken. Also remember, people often make spelling mistakes, and if you can afford it, you should register additional sites with variations of misspellings of your original site. You can then have your web service point all the other sites to your main site.

Your Website Features

Now that you've got your domain name registered, your next step will be to decide exactly what you want to include on your website. You need to ask yourself some key questions:

- How many products do I want to display on my website? If you put too few products on the website, it could look barren. But if you put too many products on the website, it can be overwhelming to your visitors.
- What type of products will you display? This decision can greatly impact how you display your products and the quality of the pictures you use. Most products will require quite a bit of detail, as customers really want to see what they are buying.
- Do you have digital pictures of the products you sell? If you don't have them, you'll need to get them. You may be able to get useable digital pictures from your suppliers or manufacturers, or you may need to hire a local photographer to take them for you. If you do hire a photographer, be sure she understands how you plan to use them so you get them in the right format. Whatever you do, make sure to use professional-grade photos and that they convey a realistic representation of your products.

Your customers' online shopping experience should mimic their experience in your store. In a store, all their senses are stimulated to encourage them to buy—visual and tactile in particular. Online you need to recreate that feeling, and high-quality photos will do the trick.

Savvy Retailer

Design Within Reach (www.dwr.com), a retailer who sells design furniture, is one of the best examples of how a retailer can deliver an incredible online experience to the customer. Check his "detail views" and "room views" features. Why would you even need to go to the store with so much detail and such powerful visual images of what the item is going to look like in your living room or on your patio?

You should also write up a narrative description for each product, which includes key benefits about the product, any related services you offer, prices, and any discounts possible.

Your Profile

In addition to the products and services you offer, you should also include a profile about you and your store. Customers like to know whom they are buying from and that the website they're visiting is a legitimate business. There are so many scams on the web that you need to look professional and assure your online customers that you do exist and will back your products. Make sure your store address is right on the homepage along with your phone number. You will be amazed how many sites neglect this simple requirement.

Web Coupons

If you don't want to sell online, web coupons can be an excellent way to get people to come to your store. Offer Internet specials that are only available with a coupon the customer prints out. Web coupons serve two purposes—they get people to come to your store, and they give you an idea of how effective your website is as a marketing tool.

Events Calendar

You can promote any special store events on the website with an events calendar. This will help you to draw traffic to your store for the events and give your regular customers advance notice about what is planned.

Tell Us How We Are Doing

Customer feedback always helps you to improve your business. As I've said before, two types of customers will fill out feedback forms—those that were particularly pleased with your store and those who were very disappointed. In both cases, you will get critical information about how to improve your business.

Searchability Function

If you are planning more than a one-page marketing website, which you should, then you must have a function to enable your customers to search for products on your website. If you don't, customers will use an Internet search engine, and you may lose them.

Search Engine Optimization

Your website should also help you attract those customers who use a search engine to find a store that delivers in your local area. I suggest that you consider paying for clicks using key words associated with your delivery area by opening an Adwords account with Google or optimizing your website for search engines.

Financial Transactions

You need to decide whether or not you plan to sell your products through your website, or if you just want to use the website as a marketing tool. If you plan to handle transactions through your website, you need to make sure your *web host* offers secure servers for the "shopping cart" which is where customers enter their credit card information. This is called SSL encryption in technical lingo. Some web-hosting services include this as part of your package; others will charge more for it.

def•i•ni•tion

A **web host** is an online entity that provides the technical interface needed for your website to be seen on the Internet. Web hosts offer you a system for storing information, images, video, and any other content you want to put on the Internet. Web-host companies provide service space to host your website and provide the connectivity so it can be found through the Internet.

In addition to SSL encryption, you will need a private CGI-BIN directory if you plan to conduct e-commerce through your website. This directory is one to which you upload binary scripts and interactive programs for payment processing and shopping cart management.

Your shopping cart can make or break your online business, so you don't want to make a mistake in choosing one. If your customers get frustrated with the checkout process for your shopping cart, they'll leave your site and look elsewhere.

You have three choices for building a shopping cart on your site: you can buy an online shopping cart program; you can use the services of an application service provider (ASP); or you can design a shopping cart yourself. I don't recommend designing one unless you have a lot of experience doing so.

If you choose to buy a shopping cart program, expect to spend between $200 and $800. The cheaper shopping carts probably won't include all the features you need, and you'll find the add-on programs can make an affordable program unaffordable pretty quickly.

When you are just starting out, your best bet may be to build a website using an e-commerce website template. Many of these templates offered on the Internet include shopping cart systems pre-installed. That makes it much easier to set up a store on the Internet. Search for "e-commerce template" using a search engine, and you'll find lots of options. Try them out for free and find one that best matches what you want to do.

Web-Host Quality

Your store is closed on the Internet anytime your customers can't reach your website. You need to find a web-hosting company that offers at least a 99 percent uptime guarantee. This guarantee should come with some kind of compensation if the website is down, so you know the web-hosting company backs up its word. You should also ask about a web host's backup systems in case of emergencies.

Selling Points

You can check out the quality of a web-hosting company at various web-host forums on the Internet. One good forum is Web Hosting Talk (www.webhostingtalk.com).

Another thing you want to check is the customer support offered by the web host. You should only consider a company that offers customer support 24 hours a day, 7 days a week.

Look And Feel—Just Like Your Store

Remember, your website is your store online. You want your online presence to look and feel just like your online visitor would if he walked into your store. Be sure to design the website using the same or similar colors and graphics as you've chosen for your retail store.

Who Can Help You

As you can tell, there are a lot of pieces to putting your store on the web. Unless you've had a lot of experience running websites, your best bet is to work with a professional who does web designs and manages websites for other retailers.

Check with retailers in your area to get recommendations for web designers. If you don't know anyone, review websites you like for other small retailers. They don't have to be located anywhere near you. Web designers can work from anywhere. They do not have to be based in your city or town.

If you find a website that you like or that best suits what you want to do, contact that retailer and ask who designed her website and whether she was happy with the service. If she liked her web designer, get contact information and talk with the web designer about designing your website.

After you get the initial design complete and the website is up and running, you can decide whether or not you want to continue to pay your designer for updates or if you want to do them yourself. Today there are a number of good software programs that make it easy for you to do simple updates and just pay your designer for more complex ones.

Talk about ongoing maintenance issues as part of the initial contract. If you do want to maintain the website yourself, you will, at the very least, need to arrange for training on the website software the designer used.

Expect to spend between $1,000 and $4,000 for an initial website design. The price will go up depending upon what you want to do with the site and how much work is involved. Be sure you spell out carefully in writing what the web designer will do for the agreed price. It's best to set up the initial web design contract on a project basis. A contract based on an hourly wage can quickly go over budget. You can then negotiate an hourly wage for any ongoing maintenance. Also, be careful about the use of high-quality graphics or "flash" animation that may slow down your site. Many of your customers may not have high-speed access.

Keep It Current

Don't think you're done when you get your website online. You're just getting started. You'll need to keep it fresh. Plan updates at least once a week and use it to promote sales or other events. You'll also need to be found, so you'll need to optimize your web pages for search engines. Your web designer can help you do that as well, if you don't know anything about website optimization.

Once your website is up and running, you can also use it to develop and expand your e-mail marketing program. While you should be collecting e-mail addresses as part of your customer service program in the store, you can also collect e-mail addresses from people who find your store on the Internet and want to be kept informed of specials or other news. Be sure to include a method for sign-up to your store's e-mail newsletter on the front page of your website, if you have a newsletter.

Also, don't forget to make one of your associates responsible for e-mail responses. Customer service is just as important for Internet customers as it is for customers who walk into your store. Don't you just hate it when you send an e-mail to a website and then wait days for a response? Your customers will hate it, too!

You may assign one of your associates (and even all of them) the task to learn to use the Internet to send e-mail and updates to customers. Communicating with customers is part of their job and they need to do it anyway and anywhere the customer wants it, including via e-mail. After all, you expect your associates to build strong relationships with their customers, and what better way of nurturing those relationships than asking them to follow up with their customers with new products, news, promotions, or events that might excite them and get them back in the store?

You may also consider rewarding your Internet-designated associates' efforts with bonuses to be sure they provide the customer service you want your Internet customers to receive.

The Least You Need to Know

- A website can be a critical piece of your marketing plan. You can't do business today without one.
- Pick a simple domain and carefully plan out what you want to put on your site.
- If you haven't done website design before, find yourself a good web designer to help you get started.
- Once your website is up, your work is just beginning. Be sure to keep it fresh and to designate someone to take care of customers who come to you through the web.

Chapter 21

Know Your Numbers

In This Chapter

- Accounting for inventory
- Monthly reporting
- Key financial reports
- Setting up the books

You are running a business because you like it, but also because you want to make money. And counting the money that comes in (and that goes out) is something that you need to learn to do whether you have an accountant (you should!) or not. While I can't teach you accounting in one short chapter, I can show you how to use the numbers you collect and introduce you to accounting basics.

Retail Method of Inventory Accounting

Operating a retail business is different from operating any other kind of business. In both the United States and Canada, retailers may use a unique method of accounting for their inventory known as the "retail method"—also called the "dual book system." This acknowledges the fact that retailers need to use a two-column ledger in order to understand their business.

def•i•ni•tion

The **landed cost** is the cost of your goods including shipping charges.

The **retail value** of your merchandise is the dollar value at full selling price.

In the left-hand column, you keep a running record of the cost of your merchandise—the *landed cost*—and in the right-hand column, you keep a running record of the *retail value* of that merchandise.

Many accountants are not familiar with the system, and they set up retail businesses using one of the traditional cost methodologies instead. Yet the retail method offers huge advantages for a retail business of any size, including the ability to compare operating results with other retailers.

Even if you plan to learn the basics of accounting yourself, it's a good idea to hire an accountant. You should seek an accountant who either knows or will learn the retail method. Check with retailers in your area or contact your local chamber of commerce for recommendations of accountants who specialize in working with retailers.

Getting Monthly Updates

While you've probably seen an income statement and balance sheet—the two most widely used financial statements (I talk more about those later)—retailers depend most on their monthly maintained margin report. You should complete a monthly maintained margin report for each of your product classifications or categories. For more information about classifications and categories, read Chapter 12.

Here is a sample of what that report looks like for a classification:

Sample Monthly Maintained Margin Report

Line	*Cost*	*Selling*
Beginning Inventory	$25,000	$62,000
Receipts	12,000	24,000
Markups		1,000
Inventory to Be Accounted For	$37,000	$87,000
Markup on Inventory		57.5%

Calculating Maintained Margin		
Gross Sales		$21,000
Less Returns		(1,000)
Net Sales		$20,000
Inventory Reductions for the Month		
Net Sales		$20,000
Allowances		500
Regular Markdowns		2,000
Promotional Markdowns		1,500
Employee Discounts		500
Shrink (1% of Sales Is Common)		200
Total Inventory Reductions		$24,700
Cost of Goods Sold		$10,497.50
Monthly Maintained Margin		47.5%
Ending Inventory		
Inventory to Be Accounted For	$37,000.00	$87,000.00
Inventory Reductions at Cost	(10,497.50)	
Inventory Reductions at Selling Price		(24,700.00)
Total Inventory to Be Accounted For	$26,502.50	$62,300.00

Let's take a closer look at the numbers on this report and what they mean. The report starts with a beginning inventory of $25,000 value at cost and a $62,000 value at selling price. The next line accounts for the merchandise that was received during the month in this classification. The sample shows receipts of $12,000 at cost this month, and indicates that the items were ticketed to sell for $24,000.

The third line indicates any "markups." During the month, in this sample, the price was increased for certain items in the inventory that the retailer could get more money for, perhaps because his competition offered the items for more or perhaps because he had no competition on those items.

When you mark up an item in your inventory, you remove the old price ticket and put on a new price ticket that shows a higher selling price. Think about this. You are not changing the cost price of the item—you still paid whatever you paid for it—you are just increasing the selling price by whatever amount you determine you can get for it.

You then calculate one of the most basic formulas in retail—cost plus markup equals selling price.

Cost + Markup = Selling Price

$25,000 + $37,000 = $62,000

Under the retail method, the selling price of an item is always 100 percent. You can express both "cost" (the amount you pay for an item) and "markup" (the amount by which you increase the price to cover your expenses and your profit) as a percentage of the "selling price."

Cost + Markup = Selling Price

$25,000 + $37,000 = $62,000

40.3% + 59.7% = 100%

The ability to take markups is an important advantage of using the retail method in your accounting instead of a cost method. Although you can take a "markdown" and reduce the price of an item under either method, you cannot legally take a markup on existing inventory if you use the cost method.

Adding these three figures on our monthly maintained margin report, you come up with a number called "inventory to be accounted for." In our sample, this is $37,000 at cost and $87,000 at selling price. In theory, if you were to add up the price tickets on all of the items in your store's inventory in this classification, they would total this number.

Next, you want to calculate your markup on inventory for the classification. The formula for calculating your markup on inventory is a two-step process. First you calculate the profit:

Selling Price – Cost = Profit

$87,000 – $37,000 = $50,000

Then you calculate the markup on inventory:

Profit ÷ Selling Price = Markup on Inventory

$50,000 ÷ $87,000 = 57.5%

Once you know the markup on inventory, you need to determine if you maintained that markup during the month by calculating your "maintained margin." You start by listing your gross sales and subtracting any returns you have from customers to calculate net sales. In our sample, this is $21,000 in gross sales minus $1,000 in returns, leaving $20,000 in net sales. Net sales should be your largest inventory reduction.

Some retailers group the next four items into one line, but I recommend that you track them separately. Doing so will let you manage your inventory more effectively and make more-informed buying decisions.

The first line—allowance—includes items for which you reduced the price. An allowance sometimes has more descriptive names such as "scratch-and-dent" or "missing button." For example, suppose a customer comes up to your counter and says, "I want to buy this sweater but it has a missing button." In order to save the sale, you say something like, "Sorry about that. What if I take $5 off the price to compensate you for having to replace the button?"

Savvy Retailer

You need to account for allowances separately so that you can look back in your records and identify problems. For example, you might learn about the quality of a certain item, the packaging used by a certain vendor, or the selling abilities of a certain sales associate.

You can help encourage the sale of certain items in your store by decreasing the price of items that are not selling. This is called taking a "markdown." You should take two kinds of markdowns in your business: regular markdowns and promotional markdowns. I talk more about markdowns in Chapter 12.

"Employee discounts" are the price reductions you may offer to people who work in your store. Offering these discounts will let your sales associates try products themselves to gain crucial product knowledge that they can use in their selling.

Both the United States and Canada will let you reserve 1 percent of your net sales against "shrinkage." This is the difference between the book value of the inventory that should be in your store and the actual physical inventory that you have in your store. Shrinkage occurs when someone steals an item from your store, or you make a counting or paperwork error. You can reserve more than 1 percent for shrinkage if you have historical proof that shrinkage is higher than that.

On the monthly maintained margin report, you can next see the calculation for the total inventory reductions for the period. This represents the selling-price value that left the store. In the sample, the figure was $24,700 for the month.

Next, you calculate how much the merchandise sold cost you. The formula for cost as a percentage of selling price is cost equals selling price minus markup on inventory. Here is the calculation:

Selling Price – Markup on Inventory = Cost as a Percentage of Selling

100% – 57.5% = 42.5%

The "cost of goods sold" is the total inventory reductions for the period times the cost as a percentage. In the sample, this is $24,700.00 times 42.5 percent equals $10,497.50.

Total Inventory Reductions × Cost as a Percentage = Cost of Goods Sold

$24,700.00 × 42.5% = $10,497.50

To calculate your "monthly maintained margin," you use the formula net sales minus cost of goods sold equals monthly maintained margin. Here is the calculation based on our sample report:

Net Sales – Cost of Goods Sold = Monthly Maintained Margin

$20,000.00 – $10,497.50 = $9,502.50

To determine your monthly maintained margin as a percentage, use the formula monthly maintained margin divided by net sales. Here is the calculation based on our sample report:

Monthly Maintained Margin ÷ Net Sales = Monthly Maintained Margin

$9,502.50 ÷ $20,000.00 = 47.5%

def•i•ni•tion

Your **breakeven point** is the percentage of net sales that it takes to cover all the expenses of your business except the cost of merchandise. In your first year of operation, you will need to use an estimate. After that, it is a number your accountant can calculate easily.

You can see that in the sample monthly maintained margin report, an initial 57.5% markup on inventory eroded into a 47.5% maintained margin due to the allowances and discounts that were given and the markdowns that were taken. If the *breakeven point* for this business was 35 percent, however, this would show a net profit of 12.5 percent and we would be very happy retailers.

The final step on the monthly maintained margin report is to reset your inventory for the next month.

In the sample, I show the beginning inventory at $37,000.00 at cost and subtract the $10,497.50 cost of goods sold for the period. This gives you the "total inventory to be accounted for at the end of the period," which is $26,502.50 at cost.

> Opening Inventory at Cost – Cost of Goods for the Period at Cost = Total Inventory to Be Accounted for at Cost
>
> $37,000.00 – $10,497.50 = $26,502.50

Then you take the $87,000.00, which was the beginning selling price, and subtract the $24,700.00 cost of goods sold for the period at selling price. This also gives you the "total inventory to be accounted for at the end of the period," which is $62,300.00 at selling price.

> Opening Inventory – Cost of Goods Sold for the Period at Selling = Total Inventory to Be Accounted for at Selling
>
> $37,000.00 – $10,497.50 = $26,502.50

Finally, you calculate your markup on inventory using the same formula as before. You may recall that this is selling price minus cost equals profit divided by selling price. Your inventory always resets to the same markup on inventory that you had at the start of the period. If it does not, you did something wrong, because the retail method always accounts for a loss in the month in which it occurs.

The difference between your markup on inventory and your breakeven point tells you how much "room" you have to keep your inventory current by taking markdowns. If your markup on inventory is 57.5 percent and your breakeven point is 35.0 percent, you have some room to take markdowns and clear out old inventory. But if your markup on inventory is 57.5 percent and your breakeven point is 55.8 percent, you have very little room. The problem is, if you do not take markdowns and clear out old inventory, it will become "older and moldier" and worth even less.

Reporting Your Results

At the end of every accounting period, you want to have a summary of how well your business is doing. Two key financial statements help you do that—the profit and loss (income) statement and the balance sheet. Let's take a closer look of what each one includes.

Profit and Loss Statement

A profit and loss statement summarizes all the financial activity in your business during a particular accounting period. Here is a sample profit and loss statement with a brief explanation of each line item:

$800,000 Net Sales: The total amount received from customers.

– **$440,000** Cost of Goods Sold: The total amount paid to buy the merchandise that was sold, including any freight costs.

= **$360,000** Gross Profit: This is the amount of money left to pay all your bills. Anything left over will be your net profit.

– **$340,000** Expenses: In this section, all selling, general, and administrative expenses are shown. I've included the most common ones for retail businesses, but your categories may be different.

> **$104,000** Staffing Costs: The total amount paid to you and your staff as wages and benefits.
>
> **$68,000** Rent: The total amount paid for store rent.
>
> **$12,800** Utilities: The total amount paid for heating, ventilation, and air-conditioning (HVAC); water; and electricity.
>
> **$5,600** Maintenance: The total amount paid to fix and maintain items such as equipment and carpeting.
>
> **$9,600** Telephone: The total amount paid for telephone service and long distance.
>
> **$9,600** Insurance: The total amount paid to insure your business against liability, flood, and fire.
>
> **$18,400** Supplies: The total amount paid for boxes and bags for customer purchases and store supplies such as letterhead and pens.
>
> **$24,000** Advertising and Promotion: The total amount paid to advertise your business and attract customers to the store, including newspaper, radio, flyers, Yellow Pages, and your website.

$6,400 Relationship Marketing: The total amount paid for one-to-one communication or rewards for your current customers.

$21,600 Administration: The total amount paid for things like buying trips and payroll services.

$4,000 Legal: The total amount paid to your lawyer.

$16,000 Accounting and Data Processing: The total amount paid to your accountant for crunching all of the numbers, preparing an annual statement, and filing a tax return.

$16,000 Technology: The total amount paid for hardware, software, training, and supplies.

$4,000 Interest Expense and Banking: The total amount paid as service charges, transaction fees, and interest.

$16,000 Depreciation: The total amount paid for capital improvements such as fixtures and equipment that you are paying back over time or "depreciating."

$4,000 Miscellaneous: The total amount paid for the little things that you did not list anywhere else.

= $20,000 Net Profit: The total amount you are left with at the end of the year as profit.

If you are not familiar with the retail business, this net profit figure may come as a surprise. Like many people, you may have had a vague notion that retailers simply double the wholesale price of an item and pocket the difference.

In reality, as you can see in this typical profit and loss statement, a retailer today makes much less. In this sample, a retailer who took in net sales of $800,000 made a net profit of only $20,000 or 2.5 percent of sales. This doesn't mean that there's no opportunity for you to get seriously profitable. However, to get your profits higher, you will either need to sell more or reduce your expenses.

Balance Sheet

The balance sheet is a snapshot of the assets (everything owned by the business), liabilities (everything owed by the business), and equity (claims against assets by the business owners). It's like taking a picture of your company's financial condition on one particular date.

Here is a sample format for a balance sheet for ABC Retailer:

ABC Retailer

2007 Balance Sheet

As of December 31, 2007

Assets		**Liabilities**	
Current Assets		*Current Liabilities*	
Cash	$10,000	Accounts Payable	$30,000
Accounts Receivable	$50,000	Notes Payable	
Inventory	$85,000	Current	$12,000
		Taxes Payable	$50,000
Total Current Assets	*$145,000*	*Total Current Liabilities*	*$92,000*
Long-Term Assets		*Long-Term Liabilities*	
Land	$75,000	Notes Payable	$25,000
Buildings	$275,000	Mortgages Payable	$200,000
Equipment	$50,000	*Total Long-Term Liabilities*	*$225,000*
Organizational Costs	$20,000		
Total Long-Term Assets	*$420,000*	*Owner's Equity*	
		Owner's Capital	248,000
Total Assets		**Total Liabilities & Equity**	
$565.000		**$565,000**	

You'll note that the balance sheet is broken up into five sections: current assets (everything your company owns that you expect to use in your business over the next 12 months); current liabilities (everything you owe that must be paid in the next

12 months); long-term assets (everything you own that has a lifespan of more than 12 months); long-term liabilities (everything you owe for which you have more than 12 months to pay); and equity (everything you or other company owners have put into the business).

Current assets include cash, inventory, accounts receivable, and any other holding that you have that you expect to use in the next 12 months. Some companies will buy Certificates of Deposit or other marketable securities to put their extra cash into until they need it, so it can earn additional money. The balance sheet would show those holdings in the current assets section as well. Accounts receivable is the account where you track any sales you have made to customers on credit.

Current liabilities include accounts payable, notes payable, and taxes payable, as well as any other line items that represent things your company owes over the next 12 months. Accounts payable is where you track any vendors' bills that you have not yet paid. Notes payable are payments on long-term notes that will be due in the next 12 months (such as 12 months of payments on a mortgage). Taxes payable is where you track taxes that need to be paid, which can include sales taxes and payroll taxes, as well as other taxes you owe a state, local, or federal entity. Taxes for which your business is liable vary from state to state, as well as by type of business. Also, if you incorporate your business, you'll have to pay corporate taxes.

Long-term assets include anything you own that you expect you'll still have at the end of the business year. This includes any land your business sits on, the buildings you own or lease, any vehicles you own, etc. A new business also usually has an account called "organization costs." These are costs that you incurred to start up your business that you cannot write off in the first year, such as special licenses and legal fees. Check with your accountant to find out what initial expenses can be charged against the business in the first year and what expenses need to be written off over a number of years.

Long-term liabilities are loans that will be due beyond the next 12 months. The equity section shows any money put into the business by you or anyone who has invested in the business. After the first year, you'll also add an account called "retained earnings." This account is used to track any profits that you keep in the business to finance future growth plans.

Time to Set Up the Books

Now that you know what financial information is important for you to keep track of in your business, it's time to tackle the hard part—setting up your business books to track all your numbers. Yes—that's accounting. Many business people think about it as a tedious task and save it for last.

But don't do that. In fact, you have some key accounting decisions you must make before you spend or take in your first dollar. You must decide whether you want to operate your business on a cash or accrual basis. You must set up your chart of accounts (list of all active accounts) and you must decide whether or not to computerize your books. I can't imagine operating a retail store without computerized accounting.

Cash-basis accounting is based on how cash flows into and out of your business. When you use this type of accounting, you record your transactions only when cash actually changes hands. Accrual accounting is based on when the transaction actually happens, even if cash has not yet changed hands. For example, if you are selling items using a cash-basis accounting system, you would not record the sale until the customer actually pays cash for the item, even if he took it out of the store and promised to pay for it next week. Hope you wouldn't offer that option to your customers too often if you use cash-basis accounting. You'll quickly lose your shirt.

In fact, if you do plan to sell items on credit, you should definitely use an accrual accounting system. In that system, when the customer bought the item on credit and took it out of the store, you would consider that a completed transaction even though you had not yet received payment. You would record this transaction in your accounts receivable account. When the customer actually pays the bill you would then subtract the amount due from the accounts receivable account and add the money received to your cash account.

You can start your business using cash-basis accounting, which is simpler to manage than accrual accounting. But after you start selling on credit or as your business grows, you will find you have a much better handle on your business's financial transactions using accrual accounting.

Selling Points

To learn more about accounting and how to set up the books, I recommend you read *The Complete Idiot's Guide to Accounting* by Lita Epstein (Alpha Books, 2006).

While you likely will not be able to afford having an accountant on staff as you start up your business, you should definitely sit down with an accountant to set up your accounting system. Many businesses will keep an accountant on retainer and have him check the books monthly, quarterly, or yearly. Accountants provide a good, objective eye to how your business is going and what financial management changes may be needed to keep the business profitable.

Now that you know how to gather the numbers in useable reports, you'll need to know how to analyze your results. I discuss that in Chapters 23 and 24.

The Least You Need to Know

- Work with an accountant who understands the retail method of accounting and set up your books using that method.
- The monthly maintained margin report will become your most important tool for managing your store's inventory and profitability.
- Understand what goes into the two critical financial reports—the profit and loss (income) statement and the balance sheet.

Chapter 22

Negotiate Like a Pro

In This Chapter

- Finding space
- Exploring styles
- Figuring out emotions
- Getting to the deal

Negotiation is a fact of life. We negotiate with our parents when we are kids, we negotiate with our partners in our personal relationships, and of course, we negotiate every day in business. When you run a business, you negotiate with pretty much everyone: banks, landlords, manufacturers and distributors, your staff, and sometimes even customers. In this chapter, I explore how to negotiate not just for the best price, but also for the best deal and terms.

Why We Negotiate

We negotiate with others because each side in the negotiation has something the other side needs. As a negotiator, it's critical for you to understand what the other side really needs from the negotiation.

We also negotiate when what we need is truly significant. For example, you are not likely to spend a lot of time negotiating for a piece of gum, but you will take the time to get a good deal if you're trying to buy 1,000 pairs of shoes for your store. So the ultimate value of the outcome of the negotiation will impact the amount of time you spend on a negotiation.

We also need to feel comfortable negotiating for what we want. We are not likely to enter into a negotiation unless we have mastered the skills that we need to successfully do it. In this chapter, I help you develop the skills you may need.

One key thing to remember is that we are all most comfortable negotiating on our own "turf," such as our office, our store, or wherever we feel comfortable. So when you expect to negotiate terms, the best place to do it is in an environment you know you can control and will have any information you need at your fingertips.

Negotiation Space

The first step in any negotiation is determining the negotiation space. No, I'm not talking about the design of the room you're going to negotiate in. I'm talking about the amount of space between you as a buyer and your vendor as the seller or anyone else with whom you plan to negotiate. The space between the seller's cut-off point and the buyer's cut-off point is where the deal can be made.

Selling Points

As a negotiator, you should never go into a negotiation without having an idea of your best deal, called your target. You should also have an idea of the point at which you cannot do a deal. Generally speaking, negotiators who have a higher target will get a better deal.

Before going into a negotiation as a buyer, know your target price and the point at which you will cut off negotiation (the point at which you know you cannot do the deal).

Remember, the person you are negotiating with—the alter negotiator—also likely has his best deal in mind and the point at which he cannot do a deal. A deal can never take place if the offer is above the buyer's cut-off point or below the seller's cut-off point. A good negotiator spends time learning where the alter negotiator's cut-off point is and how to come as close to it as possible.

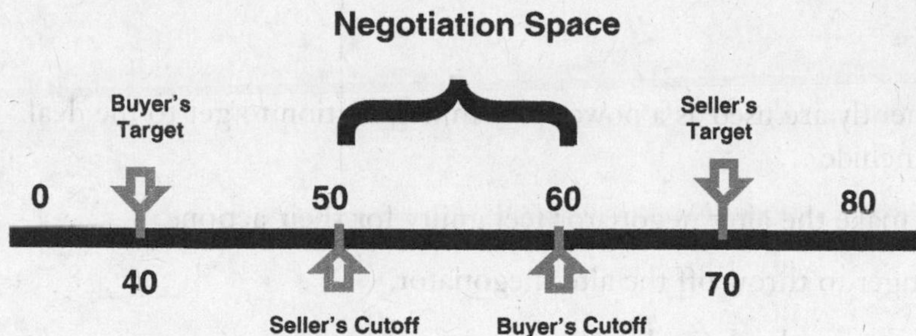

Negotiation space is the space between the seller's and the buyer's cut-off points. Somewhere in here a deal will be made.

Negotiation Styles

Negotiators can use one of four different negotiation styles based on their interest in creating and maintaining a solid relationship and/or a winning position or position of power. These styles are:

- Lose-lose style is used by a person with no interest in a relationship and no interest in power. This style is seldom seen in the business world because the person has no interest in negotiation at all. You will lose any time you deal with this kind of person.
- Lose-win style, also known as the victim style, is used by a person who has no concern for power and a high relationship need. The alter negotiator will let us win so that we will like them. To them the relationship is more important than the negotiation. This is the kind of negotiation where if the supplies, for instance, buys the retailer lunch, the retailer feels compelled to place an order. We do not see much of this style in business, because the alter negotiator wouldn't last long in the business world!
- Win-lose style is used by a person with a high concern for power and a low concern for relationship. He uses his power to win over the other person at any cost. You will find this style in business, but probably won't want to work with this type of person.
- Win-win negotiation is used by a person with a high concern for a relationship along with a high-power style. With this style, the power is directed in a positive manner—as power to do something. Any deal that meets the criteria of being above the cut-off point for the seller and below the cut-off point for the buyer is win-win.

Emotional Ploys

Emotional ploys frequently are used as a power play in negotiation to get to the deal. Emotional ploys can include …

- Guilt: Trying to make the alter negotiator feel guilty for their actions.
- Anger: Faking anger to throw off the alter negotiator.
- Lies: Telling a lie to get the desired deal.
- Aggression: Using physical or psychological aggression to intimidate the alter negotiator.
- Crying: Crying to gain the alter negotiator's sympathy.
- Unreasonable demands: Making unreasonable demands by high-balling or low-balling the offer. A high ball is when one makes what appears to be an unreasonably high initial offer. The counter to this is often a low ball, which is an unreasonably low initial offer. The most common result of this tactic is no deal.

For example, suppose you go to a vendor to buy a shoe you've been buying for the last three years, and ask for a slight variation of a high heel expecting to pay the usual $50 price. Instead the vendor says: "What a season! I had to negotiate a labor contract. My labor just jumped up by 15 percent. Have you also seen where leather has gone lately? The price of hides is up by 15 to 20 percent for good quality hides. The government has just increased my taxes. It is absolutely crazy. I am afraid that the cost of that shoe is now $58."

Your response when you realize that you've likely lost the $50 purchase price is to counter with a low ball. You could say something like: "You should be in the retail business. My sales are down 20 percent, the customers don't want to buy anymore. They are finding our shoes too expensive. I need to buy the shoe for no more than $48 if I want to be able to sell it."

What is the danger of a high/low-ball approach? No deal, because one person is going to have a lot of difficulty coming down from $58 if the other person is trying for $48. If you find yourself in this type of situation, you probably need to look for some terms other than price to make the deal, such as free shipping, return allowances, and other things that are important to the way you do business.

Negotiation Strategies

When you come up against a win-lose negotiator, know that the negotiator is someone who thinks of negotiation as a contact sport. She must win and will use any emotional ploy to get that win. As a negotiator, you have three possibilities when dealing with a win-lose negotiator …

- Walk away. In most cases, this is the strategy to use. Generally you won't win when dealing with this kind of person.
- Expose the win-lose tactic to disarm. If the deal is important to you, you can make it clear that you are aware of their emotional ploy and will not be influenced by it.
- Play the same game. You can mirror the win-lose negotiator's tactics, but likely won't be happy with the deal you get by lowering yourself to her level.

You should always look to work with people who use the win-win style of negotiation. Key things to remember when using the win-win style include …

- **Trust.** You should always work toward a relationship of trust with people with whom you do business. This can take time to develop.
- **Problem solving.** Think about negotiation as a problem-solving and opportunity-seeking situation. Don't enter a negotiation by stating your demand and encouraging the alter negotiator to counter that demand. You'll find things won't work well if you say something like, "I want to pay $45 for that shoe, can you give it to me at that price?" But things will go much better if you say "We have a real opportunity to do some great business together. We have to fit a shoe into a price-point that requires a $45 cost. Can you help me achieve that?" As a win-win negotiator always use the "How do we solve the problem together?" approach. When you seek to build an opportunity with the alter negotiator, you will more likely find a deal you both can prosper with.
- **Don't look to "split the difference."** If you try to make sure that each side gets 50 percent of what they want, nobody wins. Work to find a solution that gives each side the feeling that they've gotten 100 percent of what they want.

Savvy Retailer

You can learn more about win-win negotiation in an excellent book called, *Getting to Yes* by Robert Fisher, Bruce M. Patton, and William L. Ury (Houghton Mifflin, 1992).

Deadlines and Concessions

With every negotiator, expect to find deadlines and concessions. But you need to understand what they are and whether there is a way to work around them.

Deadlines

The deadline for a negotiation is the time at which the deal must be agreed upon. When you set a deadline for the deal, you need to know if it's real and what will happen if you miss the deadline. Both you and the alter negotiator will have deadlines, so you need to understand his deadline as well as yours.

If a deadline forces you to make a decision more quickly than you want, step back and think about the importance of that deadline. You may consider ignoring the deadline, but this could mean the risk that you will not have what you need in your store when you need it.

Concessions

Concessions are a fact of life in any negotiation—they're just part of the give and take of negotiation. Whenever you ask for something in a negotiation, don't just throw it out on the table. Explain why you are asking for what you want.

Never give up all your concessions. You must also save a crucial concession for the last moment. That way as you approach the time for sealing the deal and meeting your deadline, you have a concession conserved that helps you close the deal.

Better Not!

When you do decide to give a concession to the alter negotiator, don't do it so easily. Make it appear more costly and larger than it really is. If you give a concession freely, it is never appreciated.

You should never give a concession without getting one in return. You should always tie a concession that you make to one that the alter negotiator makes. For example, you could say, "Yes, we have no problem paying 5 percent more if you agree to the payment terms that we outlined before." This way the concession of 5 percent is not agreed to unless you get the concession of payment terms that you requested.

As you negotiate a deal, keep careful track of what you have given up and what you have gained. Every concession that you give and get has a monetary value. Know those values as you work toward a deal.

As you near the deadline you've set for the deal, you can be in your most dangerous territory. Often the tendency is to be lenient on concessions just to get a deal done. You must be very careful and do just the opposite: tighten your concessions as you near the point of sealing the deal.

Preparation

You improve your chances of getting the deal you want by going into the negotiation well prepared. Sometimes you may think a negotiation is not worth the time. For example, ask yourself: "Is it worth the time to prepare? Is this a vendor who is 12 percent of my business or 1.2 percent? Is it a landlord that is giving me a five-year lease or just a month-to-month deal?" If you decide the deal is worth it, then you must prepare by doing your homework.

The two key steps for preparing for a negotiation include …

- Research the deal. You should research the alter negotiator and any past dealings that you have had with them. Get all the facts and figures about past performance, the last deal you did, and everything else you can get your hands on.
- Write down your objectives. Know your target and cut-off points before you go into any negotiation.

Power Techniques

Power techniques include things that you can do to improve your power or leverage before you enter into a negotiation. These include …

- **Competition or BATNA (Best Alternative to a Negotiated Agreement).** Generate competition by talking with a competitor of your alter negotiator before you start a negotiation.
- **Knowledge and information.** Go in with all the facts and figures. Yes, it's true knowledge and information are power, and you should never underestimate them. For instance, if you are a buyer, you should go into a negotiation with all the sales figures from the last three seasons, the checkout rates, the markdown rates, competitors' prices for the same product, and anything else you think relevant to the deal.

- **Persistence.** Keep going back to get a deal or a part of a deal. Don't be afraid to do it over and over again. You can wear down the alter negotiator, and you might eventually be able to get a deal. But don't put yourself in a win-lose situation unless you don't care about ever working with that person again.
- **Time.** If you have no deadline and can negotiate as if you had all the time in the world, you have power. Never tell the alter negotiator what your time deadline is. For example, when the peace talks to end the Vietnam War were scheduled in Paris, the Americans went there and booked rooms at a hotel in Paris for three months. The North Vietnamese also went there but took seven-year leases on apartments. Their message was: we are here for a long time. We have no deadline. The person who has more time has more power.
- **Silence.** Silence can be a very strong power technique and is often misused. In negotiation, after an offer is on the table, the first person to talk often loses. Whenever you hear an offer made, you should not say anything. Put your head down a little, pretend like you are writing something down, and consider what you just heard. Wait for the alter negotiator to make the first statement. Often during the silence she will give you more information about the offer, rescind it, or make it better.

Focus on Terms

When you go into a negotiation, don't focus on price if you want a good deal. Focus instead on terms. There are many terms in a deal that can destroy the whole concept of price.

For example, if you pay $15 for a product and it comes "net," is that better than if you paid $18 and got free shipping? Also, which deal would be better if return privileges, markdown money, advertising money, and guaranteed sales were included as part of the higher price?

The quantity you buy may be a factor in which deal is better, too. For example, the net deal might be better if you are buying a large quantity (as long as the quantities you order match your sales forecasts to avoid being overstocked), but the higher price—provided the other terms are included—might be better when you want smaller quantities.

When considering terms, focus on the terms of the deal that are most valuable to you. When buying, often you will find the alter negotiator is constrained on price, but he may be willing and able to give up terms that his company does not value as much as you do. For example, he may have already budgeted significant co-op advertising dollars that he can include which can lower your advertising expense and give you a lower net cost.

Be creative when suggesting terms. Often the best terms are incredibly ingenious and good for both sides.

Conducting the Negotiation

There are many different ways you can conduct a negotiation. Here are some sample techniques that work:

- **Catch-22.** Dumb can be a smart way to negotiate. Ask lots of questions and don't be afraid of appearing like you don't know the answers.
- **The bogey.** When using the bogey technique, ask questions like, "I have a problem, can you help me?" or "We have an opportunity, how can we do this?" This is a great way to start a win-win negotiation.
- **The crunch.** When the deal is almost done, ask for one more item. For example, when you are a buyer and write the purchase order on agreed-upon quantities, price, and delivery and are ready to hand it over to the vendor, say "By the way, I have indicated on the order prepaid shipping." If this technique is used on you, your defense should be silence first, and then give to get: give into the concession and ask for one with higher value to you at the same time.
- **Nibbling.** After the deal is done, call up and ask for one more item. For example, call a day or two after the deal was sealed and say: "I forgot to tell you that I really need the percentage rent to be 3 percent and not 5." If this technique is used on you, your defense should be silence, then, again, give to get.
- **What if?** You start by asking a question such as, "What if I do this and you do that?" This tactic works well. You put something on the table without committing to it so you can gauge a response without a commitment.
- **Ultimatum.** Some negotiators use this tactic when they signal they are at or near their cut-off point. They essentially give the ultimatum by saying take it or leave it. Good negotiators use it to signal that they are at or near their cut-off point, long before they are even close to it. If this tactic is used on you, don't believe it. Continue to negotiate.

- **Vinegar and honey.** When you have to give bad news, give the worst news and then come back and sweeten it. That way you can make the alter negotiator feel that it is not as bad as it originally sounded. For example: You can say something like, "Remember, I told you I could not ship until July? Well, you can now have it in June." (The original order was to be supplied in May!)

Concluding the Negotiation

Once you have reached a deal, then you need to take the time to confirm it. In order to confirm a deal, you …

- Restate the terms of the agreement as you understand them.
- Define how long the deal is good for, whether it's a week, a month, a season, a year, or more.
- Don't procrastinate; send a written order or confirmation.

When you're done, you should always compliment the alter negotiator on his work. Give him the impression that you are satisfied but not ecstatic. If you appear too happy, the alter negotiator may think he gave up too much!

The Least You Need to Know

- Know your negotiation space, your target, and your cut-off point before entering a negotiation.
- Learn to recognize various negotiation tactics and know how to counteract them.
- Walk away from negotiations if you realize the negotiator uses a win-lose style unless you really need the deal.
- Remember that price is often not the most important part of the deal. Terms can be more valuable and easier to get.

Part 6

On the Right Track

Your grand opening festivities are over. Now, the day-to-day reality sets in. There are plenty of things to take care of, including looking at your business and identifying what is working and what is not working and knowing how to fix it. In this part, I review how you can analyze your finances and sales results making sure you're on the right track to make a profit and on your way to becoming a legend of retail. I also teach you how to gather your customers' data and use that information to give them what they want, when they want it, and how they want it.

"Now when we go public..."

Chapter 23

Year One Performance—What to Measure

In This Chapter

- Testing sales
- Checking inventory
- Producing records

Throughout your first year, measuring your success regularly is crucial to your survival. While there are numerous measures of success, there are nine key performance measures that will tell you if you are on the right track. In this chapter, I review the key ratios you must calculate and show you how to calculate them.

Sales Performance

The first thing you need to know is how well your products are selling. There are three key ratios that help you quickly determine that—average transaction, items per transaction, and conversion rate.

Average Transaction

The fastest and most efficient way to get a sales increase in your store is to increase your average transaction, which is the amount, on average, that you sell to each customer. This powerful measure of productivity for both individual employees and the store as a whole indicates how well you are selling the merchandise you already have to the customers you already have. Keep this figure in the minds of your sales associates by explaining what average transaction means and how they can help increase it.

> **Selling Points**
>
> Many successful stores post their average transaction number in the back room so that everyone on staff knows that it is a goal that they collectively and individually must meet in order to be successful—and one that you will reward collectively and individually when it is met.

No matter what your average transaction is in any given week, you should aim to raise it higher in the following week. Whether the number of customers in your store is large or small, the store's average transaction will keep heading in the right direction if you have a concerted selling and service effort by your full team.

The following table illustrates the importance of paying attention to average transaction:

Store	B	C
Weekly traffic	600	600
Conversion rate	28% (168 transactions)	28% (168 transactions)
Average sale	$45	$45 + $10 = $55
Total sales	$7,560	$9,240

With the same weekly traffic of 600 customers and the same conversion rate, which is the percentage of shoppers you turned into buyers of 28 percent, the addition of one $10 item to an average sale of $45 (it could be a pair of socks for a running store to go with the shoes or the sale of an item priced at $10 more than the average—a $55 sweatshirt instead of a $45 one, for instance) would lead to a 22 percent increase in your total sales.

Here is how you do the calculation:

Sales for the Week ÷ Transactions for the Week = Average Transaction

$9,240 ÷ 168 = $55

As the store owner, you should build rewards and incentives around average transaction. If your store's average transaction was $36 this week, you might offer to pay for a fun breakfast at McDonald's if the team achieves $40 next week.

I suggest McDonald's for a reason: it is probably the best suggestion seller in the country. Ask your associates to try to order just a Big Mac from any of its associates and find out what else is suggested. So while they are "celebrating" their achievement in a fun way, they also get to further understand how simple and natural suggestion selling can be and how retailers, like McDonald's, expect their staff to do it every day, with every customer.

Items Per Transaction

Closely linked with the average transaction is the number of items that you sell per transaction. While sales associates can increase their average transaction by either selling items that are more expensive or selling additional items to increase the total sale per customer, they can only increase their items per transaction through suggestion selling. I talk more about suggestion selling in Chapter 17. Track it separately at both the store and individual levels.

This powerful productivity measure also indicates how well you are selling the merchandise you already have to the customers you already have. Like your average transaction, it should increase steadily, week by week, for as long as you operate your business.

Items for the Week ÷ Transactions for the Week = Items per Transaction

252 ÷ 168 = 1.5

The average transaction and items per transaction enable you to grow your business in a concrete way. They are also key measures of how good your service is. Customers don't need products. They need solutions. When you sell customers a solution that is made up of a main item and complementary items that will make the main item perform, last, look, taste, or feel better, you are delivering exceptional service and making a real difference in your customers' lives. Their experiences with your product will be more complete and better because you sold them a solution to their needs and not just a product. Think of a purse and belt to recommend when you sell a pair of shoes. Or a printer and cartridges to go with the new computer the customer is buying. The same thing happens when you are selling the customer a product that is more expensive than he had originally asked for (also called up-selling). You are not pushing product onto the customer by up-selling him. Once again, you are delivering exceptional service by suggesting a product that is better for his needs and will make him happier. The higher price item is not always the better product for a customer. It all depends on the customer's specific need. Always up-sell when and if it will better meet the customer's need.

Conversion Rate

The conversion rate is another important measure of your productivity as a retailer. You calculate this by totaling the number of transactions you have in a day, week, month, or year and dividing it by the number of customers who enter your store during that same period. It tells you how well you are converting shoppers into buyers—an important measure of how well you are meeting your customers' needs.

One of the comments I hear from owner-operated retailers is, "We don't get enough customer traffic to make a profit in this location." The complaint typically comes from owners who believe they are paying high-traffic rents for less than high-traffic locations.

The problem with this is the implication that the responsibility for generating sales rests outside the four walls of the store, with the property owner. Having high customer traffic is important—but it is probably less important than what you do with whatever traffic you have. In other words, the responsibility for generating sales rests inside the store, with you.

For example, the conversion rate at a typical 24-hour "convenience store" is something approaching 100 percent. Customers go to the store expecting to buy bread and milk and are able to find what they want virtually every time.

However, the conversion rate at a typical "specialty store" is much lower than that—something around 25 percent. Customers go to the store expecting to buy certain items, and are able to find what they want approximately one time in four. Plus, a lot of times, customers are just there to browse or kill some time.

This huge difference between convenience stores and specialty stores suggests that owner-operated retailers can do many, many things to increase sales before they need to worry about customer traffic. Most of these relate to meeting their customers' expectations better—and thus improving their conversion rate.

The following table illustrates the importance of conversion rate:

Store	A	B
Weekly traffic	600	600
Conversion rate	25% (150 transactions)	28% (168 transactions)
Average sale	$45	$45
Total sales	$6,750	$7,560

With the same weekly traffic of 600 customers and an average sale of $45, simply increasing your conversion rate from 25 percent to 28 percent would lead to a 12 percent increase in your total sales.

Because the conversion rate is linked with both the type of store you operate and the location of that store, defining a "good" conversion rate is difficult. If you operate a gift store, your conversion rate will probably be lower than if you operate a fashion store. If your store is located in a mall, your conversion rate will probably be lower than if your store is located on a street. Both of these differences relate to the number of "browsers" as opposed to "shoppers" you will have.

You can increase your conversion rate by creating a store layout and visual displays that your customers find attractive and by always maintaining a good "in-stock" position. You can increase your conversion rate even more by having prices that your customers recognize as good value—and then adding even more value through well-trained sales associates that have incredible product knowledge and know how to sell professionally.

Better Not!

When it comes to conversion rate, don't worry too much about good, better, and best. You should just aim to increase your conversion rate steadily from whatever it is now.

Here is how you would do the calculation to find your conversion rate:

Number of Transactions ÷ Number of Customers = Conversion Rate

168 ÷ 600 = 28%

You can check how well you are doing by looking at these common conversion rates:

Performance Check:	Gift Store		Fashion Store	
	MALL	STREET	MALL	STREET
Good conversion rate	25%	35%	30%	40%
Better conversion rate	30%	40%	35%	45%
Best conversion rate	35%	45%	40%	50%

Inventory Performance

After checking your sales performance, you should next look at how well your inventory is performing. There are three key ratios to check—inventory turnover, GMROII (gross margin return on inventory investment), and stock-to-sales ratio.

Inventory Turnover

Inventory turnover refers to the number of times you are able to sell and replace your inventory in a period of time. This is a number that you should review every six months. In general, the higher the turnover, the stronger your retail business will be. If you achieve a high turnover, you will have less money invested in inventory at any given time and face a lower risk of carrying items that your customer does not want to buy. You will also get higher sales from the same amount of space, have fresher product in your store, and always be showing something new to tempt your customer. However, with some categories of product—generally very expensive items—turnover can be low and yet the business can still be profitable.

As you think through your store, you must decide which of the two basic product strategies you will follow …

- High margin, high price, and low turnover
- Low margin, low price, and high turnover

These strategies are very different. A low-turnover item must give you high margin and high price. It has to pay its rent for sitting on your shelf for so long. By contrast, a high-turnover item does not need to pay as much rent because another one like it will be along shortly to share the load.

You can mix the two product strategies a little at the total-store level—as long as one is clearly dominant. For example, you might decide to build your business around selling low-margin, low-price, and high-turnover items but choose to stock a few high-margin, high-price, and low-turnover "related items" as a service to your customers.

If you are running a toy store, this might mean that you decide to build your business around selling popular name-brand dolls and accessories, but choose to stock a few custom-made doll furniture or clothes so that customers can consider a more complete purchase. You would expect to sell mostly dolls and accessories because these are the low-margin, low-price, and high-turnover items that fit with your basic product strategy. The custom-made beds, dressers, and kitchens for the dolls are the high-margin, high-price, and low-turnover items that you stock as a service.

The trick here is to recognize that you stock the low-turnover related items only as a service to your customers—and that you need to get a higher margin and a higher price because of that.

Selling Points

The product strategy you choose has a large impact on the level of customer service in your store. By running some numbers, you will discover that you can achieve high turnover simply by being out of stock most of the time. But think this through from your customers' perspective. If they cannot find the item they want in your store, they will probably just shop elsewhere.

The cost of stocking every item in a store 100 percent of the time is more than any retailer can afford. You therefore need to decide how many times in 100 you are prepared to tell the customer that you are out of stock but will have new inventory soon. The challenge is to balance your inventory level against your service level.

Here is how you calculate turnover:

Net Sales ÷ Average Inventory at Retail Value = Turnover

\$350,000 ÷ \$75,000 = 4.67

(Average inventory is the sum of your beginning of each month inventory at retail value and the end of the last month divided by 13.)

Here are some key turnover ratios you can use to check your store's performance:

Good Turnover = 3

Better Turnover = 4

Best Turnover = 6

Gross Margin Return on Inventory Investment (GMROII)

In addition to becoming a retailer, you should think of yourself as becoming an investment broker. You are starting your business with a certain amount of money and investing it in inventory that you hope to sell at a profit.

Instead of making this investment, you could have chosen to invest in savings bonds, mutual funds, or a money market account. If you had, you would no doubt be tracking the return you are getting on your investment. "Gross margin return on inventory investment" or GMROII lets you do the same for your retail business. It tells you how much you are getting back for every dollar you have invested in inventory.

GMROII is the only financial ratio that yields a dollar value instead of a percentage—it is never expressed as a percentage. GMROII answers the question, "What is my return for every dollar that I invest in inventory?"

We believe that if you have a GMROII of anything less than $3, your business is in trouble. Why?

> **Savvy Retailer**
>
> Calculate the GMROII of each merchandise classification in your store. That way you will have the information you need to actively build your business around the classifications that give you the greatest return.

If you only get a dollar back for every dollar you invest (GMROII = $1), you are achieving nothing. If you only get two dollars back (GMROII = $2), you are in most cases not getting enough to pay your expenses. However, if you get $3 back for every dollar you invest, you will have sufficient return to pay all your bills and make a good profit.

As you gain more experience with retail math, you will become aware of a basic caution that goes hand in hand with GMROII—it does not tell the whole story.

This is because the "average inventory at cost" figure is a calculated number that is based on the physical movement of inventory. When an item arrives at your back door, the clock starts ticking and it keeps running until you sell that item.

But what about the financial movement of inventory? If you sell an item in 15 days that you bought on payment terms of 30, 60, or 90 days, GMROII will not even pick it up. This is because GMROII calculates the average inventory at cost in the usual manner from your merchandise inventory log and does not show that you had no financial investment in that item.

So to accurately evaluate your GMROII you also need to consider the payment terms on which you buy merchandise. Payment terms are discussed in Chapter 11.

You calculate GMROII by:

> Gross Profit in Dollars ÷ Average Inventory at Cost = GMROII
>
> $140,000 ÷ $37,500 = $3.73

You take the gross profit in dollars from the income statement.

Performance check:

Good GMROII = $3

Better GMROII = $5

Best GMROII = $8+

Stock-to-Sales Ratio

Your stock-to-sales ratio is a second measure of how well your inventory level matches your sales. As an illustration, if you wanted to "turn" your inventory 12 times a year, your stock-to-sales ratio would need to be 1 to 1. Each month you would stock just the amount of inventory that you were going to sell that month.

By comparison, if you wanted to turn your inventory three times a year, your stock-to-sales ratio would need to be 4 to 1. Each month you would have in stock four times the amount of inventory that you were going to sell that month. For most non-perishable product owner-operated retailers, a turnover of four times a year is good—more than enough to run a profitable business—which gives you a healthy stock-to-sales ratio of 3 to 1.

Better Not!

Once your store is open, get regular readings on your stock-to-sales ratio. Start worrying if the figure is in the 6- or 8-to-1 range and begin to panic if it is over 10 to 1. That's excessively high, indicating that you are carrying a larger inventory than is warranted by your sales.

Your stock-to-sales ratio will vary a lot during the year, but it should always be at its lowest during your busiest sales month. You calculate your stock-to-sales ratio by:

> Beginning of Month Inventory at Selling Price ÷ Total Sales Plan for Month = Stock-to-Sales Ratio
>
> $800 ÷ $200 = 4 or 4/1

You can check how well your store is performing by comparing your ratio to these:

Good Stock-to-Sales = 4/1

Better Stock-to-Sales = 3/1

Best Stock-to-Sales = 2/1

Productivity

You want to test the productivity of your store with this final group of ratios—sales per square foot, sales per employee, and shrink.

Sales Per Square Foot

An important way to measure your store's productivity and efficiency is sales per square foot. This ratio is standard throughout the retail industry, letting any retailer compare his store against all others.

Remember: space costs money, not just the money you pay in rent, but also expenses for things like heat, electricity, insurance, and cleaning. If you are in a mall, you can add "common area charges" to the list. With all of these costs, you need to ensure that every foot of selling space is paying its own way.

Your "total selling area in square feet" includes only your sales floor. It does not include your office, your display windows, your stock room, the area behind your cash wrap, or your fitting rooms—unless these have a mirror, in which case they help "sell" merchandise and you need to include them.

> **Savvy Retailer**
>
> In case you were wondering why it matters to gather so much detail and be so specific, here is a very simple explanation. Once you reach a certain size and profitability to ensure continuous growth and possible expansion, you need to know if you are in a position to sustain it. Benchmarking, which is the practice of comparing your business performance to other businesses that are performing well, allows you to determine whether you are on track or if you are behind on various performance measures. You will not be able to draw these comparisons with your performance results unless you use the same calculations. I talk more about benchmarking in Chapter 24.

If your store has sales of less than $200 per square foot, you either have far too much space or are selling far too little from the space you have. Here is how you calculate sales per square foot:

Net Annual Sales ÷ Total Selling Area in Square Feet (SF) = Sales per Square Foot

$350,000 ÷ 1,000 SF = $350 per SF

Performance check:

Good Sales per Square Foot = $250
Better Sales per Square Foot = $400
Best Sales per Square Foot = $700+

Sales Per Employee

In addition to sales per square foot, you also need to look at the productivity of your sales associates individually. You measure that productivity by expressing their selling cost as a percent of their sales.

To illustrate, I will assume that you want to achieve a selling cost of 14 percent in your business. This means that you can pay out 14 cents of every sales dollar as wages and benefits.

At this level, a full-time employee earning $30,000 a year would need to sell $215,000 a year, and a part-time employee earning $12,000 a year would need to sell $85,700 a year to be productive (assuming you offer benefits to part-timers, too).

Here is how you calculate your selling cost:

Wages ÷ Sales = Selling Cost

$30,000 ÷ $215,000 = 14%

Being productive means that employees "pay their own way" by generating a certain amount in sales each week, month, or year. There will always be good days and bad days but, on average, everybody will produce enough in sales over the period to pay for their own wages and benefits. If they do not, they are dragging down the productivity—and the profitability—of the entire business.

I believe that you should discuss productivity often with your sales associates and link the wages and benefits you pay directly to it. For example, if the full-time employee wants to earn $33,000 instead of $30,000 a year, that person must earn the difference by selling $235,700 instead of $215,000 a year. If the part-time employee wants to earn $14,000 instead of $12,000 a year, that person must earn the difference by selling $100,000 instead of $85,700 a year.

A full-time employee who is selling $235,700 a year is worth $33,000 in wages and benefits to your business. A part-time employee who is selling $100,000 a year is worth $14,000 in wages and benefits to your business. If you pay less than these amounts, your sales associates will soon move to a store that rewards productivity. If you pay more than these amounts, your business could be on the road to disaster.

Here is a chart to check your store's performance based on the type of retail store you have:

Performance Check:	Self Service	Typical	Personalized Service
Good selling = cost	10%	12%	14%
Better selling = cost	8%	10%	12%
Best selling = cost	6%	8%	10%

No matter what pay system you use in your retail business, I believe that you should post everyone's daily sales results in the back room of the store as recognition and an incentive as well as an opportunity for improving performance.

You will not need to add any gold stars, frowning faces, or even make any comments. The sales associates who rank consistently near the top will get their reward through public recognition.

The sales associates who rank near the bottom will see their position and start coming to you for guidance and advice.

> **Savvy Retailer**
>
> I believe that far too many retailers look at their people as an expense to control rather than an asset to manage productively. Be careful not to fall into that trap and start cutting, which creates a downward spiral of lost sales because there's not enough staff to help your customers.

Shrink

Shrink, the loss of inventory, within a retail store is 40 percent external (shoplifters) and 60 percent internal. Of that 60 percent internal, 40 percent is what we call paper shrink (bookkeeping errors), and 60 percent is employee theft.

Sometimes shrink involves product leaving the store by being carried out by employees. Sometimes it involves scanning a friend's purchase and not scanning two or three items that end up in a bag. Sometimes it's voids on the cash register and taking cash.

The formula for shrink is simple. Take the numbers for your book inventory and subtract them from the numbers for your physical count. Any missing inventory is called shrink.

No book inventory I've ever done has ever matched physical inventory. It's impossible. I would really question that if it ever happened.

What's a "good" shrink? When the difference between physical and book is zero that's best, but don't expect to see it. Today most retailers need to be as close to 1 percent as possible. Here is a formula to calculate your shrink percentage:

Missing Inventory ÷ Book Inventory = Shrink Percentage

$10 \div 1000 = 1\%$

If your shrink is less than 1 percent, it's pretty much a cost of doing business today. You're not likely to get it much less than 1 percent, and that's really good performance. If it's above 1 percent, that should be a red flag. If shrink goes up to 2, 3, or 4 percent, that's a really big red flag.

Now that you know the key performance numbers to look at during your first year, we'll take a look at how to test your performance for year two and beyond in the next chapter.

The Least You Need to Know

- You need to calculate how well your products are selling daily using average transaction, items per transaction, and conversion rate.
- You want to know how well your inventory is performing, using inventory turnover, GMROII, and stock-to-sales ratio.
- You can test your store's productivity with sales per square foot and sales per employee.
- Every retailer will face the issue of inventory shrinkage. Try to keep your shrink percentage to 1 percent or below.

Chapter 24

Year Two and Onward—Benchmarking

In This Chapter

- Benchmarking
- Viability
- Planning for the future

Year two finally begins. Now you have the ability to evaluate your performance against last year. You are no longer flying blind. You have history on which to base decisions and actions.

You can assess your performance against your direct competitors and identify potential growth areas. In this chapter, I'll show you how to make use of your numbers to gauge your performance against previous years, as well as your competitors.

Benchmarking Fundamentals

You should regularly review the ratios I showed you in Chapter 23. Just because you've finished your first year, it doesn't mean you should stop analyzing your results. Your performance for each of these measures must continue to increase if your business is to grow and your store is to continue being profitable.

Key Selling Ratios

Two key ratios help you determine how well you are doing in growing your sales: average transaction and items per transaction. Are they going up every month? If not, establish goals for improving the results.

Average transaction can be improved through up selling (selling more expensive products) or suggestion selling (selling more things to each customer by recommending complementary items and complete solutions until the customer says no). If you are having a hard time pinpointing the problem, you may want to measure average transaction by classification.

Suggestion selling must become part of your store's culture. You cannot claim to be a specialty store if you do not do it. Suggestion selling begins with superior product knowledge—when your sales associates are the experts and can help the customer be sure they are getting everything they need to fulfill their wishes, hopes, dreams, desires, and needs. Your sales associates should be like teachers who help your customers understand what they really need.

In addition to your average transaction ratio, improvement in the items per transaction ratio is completely dependent on suggestion selling. So if you're not seeing constant improvement in these two ratios, take the time to train your associates in suggestion selling and up-selling. I talk more about that in Chapter 17.

Benchmarking Your Results

Few retailers will share their numbers with you, but luckily there are some websites that provide benchmarking resources. One of the best is BizStats.com (www.bizstats.com). To use this website, all you need to do is select the type of business you are running and then put in your monthly or yearly total sales.

To show you how it works, I selected, "Retailing—Clothing and Clothing Accessories" and entered $800,000 as my revenue. Here are the results for profitable companies:

Retailing—Clothing and Clothing Accessory Stores

	$	%
Total Revenue (Sales)	$800,000	100%
Total Operating Expenses	$754,996	94.37%
Net Operating Income (Loss)	$45,004	5.63%
Cost of Goods Sold & Other Direct Costs	$420,144	52.52%
Salaries & Wages	$110,457	13.81%
Compensation—Corporate Officers	$12,623	1.58%
Pension & Profit Sharing Plans	$1,861	0.23%
Health Insurance & Other Employee Benefits	$7,891	0.99%
Rent Expense	$56,918	7.11%
Taxes (Excludes Federal Income Tax)	$17,228	2.15%
Interest Expense	$6,754	0.84%
Depreciation & Amortization	$23,625	2.95%
Advertising	$18,590	2.32%
Repairs	$4,682	0.59%
Bad Debts	$2,502	0.31%
Charitable Contributions	$516	0.06%
Other Expenses	$71,206	8.90%
Total Operating Expenses	$754,996	94.37%

Once you get the results for your type of retail business, you can use these results to determine ways to improve your profitability. Consider whether your expenses are more or less than the benchmark number. For example, if your cost of goods sold is considerably higher than the benchmark national average, you want to take a close look at those costs and how you can reduce them.

Selling Points

A good website for benchmark information regarding inventory turnover, profit, and other financial benchmarks by store type is the Retail Owners Institute (www.retailowner.com).

Is Your Concept Viable?

You spent a lot of time researching your market and determining whether or not your concept was viable. Now that you've got a year of actual results for your store, do you think your assumptions were correct? Be brutally honest as you do this analysis. Take a close look at the results for the nine ratios I showed you in Chapter 23. Are you seeing steady improvement? If not, what actions can you take to improve your store's future?

Take a look at your inventory ratios. Are you buying the right things in the right amounts? Look closely at your inventory turnover and your gross margin return on inventory investment (GMROII). How frequently does your inventory turn? How much money are you making on each dollar you spend on inventory?

Better Not!

If you aren't making at least $3 for every dollar you spend on inventory, then you need to review how you're doing business. You may even need to rethink the concept for your store.

Pinpoint the inventory that sells the best and is giving you the best return. Find ways to improve its displays and position in your store. But remember the inventory that did best last year may not be the inventory that does best this year. You must constantly review your ratios and find the inventory that is doing best today and showcase that inventory.

Betting on the Future

How do you plan for future growth? One thing I can guarantee you is that product is not and will not be the differentiator for you. What will be the differentiator is your customer in your stores.

How you present your product, the basics, the cleanliness of the store, the ease of shopping and identifying where things are at in the store are crucial. But even more important is how do your customers feel when they walk in? How do they feel as they browse? How do they feel when they buy?

I go into some stores and find there is no difference between that experience and going into a funeral parlor. I walk into other stores and I swear they're pumping some kind of drug into the air. Because everybody in the store is very positive, and they've all got a smile on their faces. There's just an energy that is going on in the store. Customers pick up on that. Customers have almost a sixth sense about how successful a store is and how likely they will find what they want. That's all very much built around your staff.

Too many retailers think of their staff as an expense to be controlled rather than an asset to be developed. Now just by basic definition in business, to be a smart businessperson, what are you supposed to do with expenses? Cut them, control them, and keep them down. Try to get rid of them. And the question is often asked, "What would the world of retail be like if retailers viewed their staff as an asset to be deployed as opposed to an expense to be cut?"

For example, one of the things I have always scratched my head about is that at many companies—in particular very large ones—corporate refers to people in the company as head count. I always had this picture of all of these people just being little heads. That's all they are—head count. And when sales are slow, the strategy is always the same: trim head count; control head count. The problem with this strategy is that it fails many, many times. Not only have these companies lost some of their most qualified employees, but their market share has also dropped dramatically due to the fact that they are unable to offer exceptional service.

When you view your people as an asset to be deployed as opposed to an expense to be controlled, very different things will happen. If you have an asset in your company, what do you do with it? You protect it. You try to make that asset even more valuable.

As you plan for your store's future, don't only look at the numbers, also look at your people and how you can develop them to improve your store's success. Plan for continually coaching and training them to make each sales associate the best she can be.

You may also face the reality with some staff that you do not have the career path for them: that is fine. A truly great employee may need to move on to more challenges that you cannot provide. Let her go with grace, help her find her next challenge. As with customers, if you put them ahead of yourself, you will never lose.

The Least You Need to Know

- Always calculate your key ratios and look for ideas that will help to improve them monthly.
- Benchmark your costs and expenses and compare yourself regularly to your competitor's results.
- Think of your staff as assets not as expenses and constantly look for ways to increase their value.

Chapter 25

How to Avoid Losing Customers

In This Chapter

- Losing customers
- Valuing customers
- Complaining customers
- Customers you want to lose

You can lose a customer in many different ways. The most common way is to view them as a single sale not as the aggregate of their purchases over time. In this chapter, I review why customers "quit," what customers are worth, how to deal with a complaining customer, and when you should decide a customer is just not worth keeping.

Why Customers Quit

Research tells us that 1 percent of the customers retailers lose die. Approximately 3 percent move away. They change jobs or have another reason to move; either way, you won't see them again.

Just about 5 percent of customers that retailers lose are convinced by friends to try another store, and approximately 9 percent leave because they are enticed by the competition without any help from friends.

About 14 percent of the customers lost were nice customers who didn't complain about a product they didn't like or a service they didn't receive and they simply left and did not come back. They're like most of us when we go to a restaurant, and have a mediocre meal, and the waiter or waitress says how was your dinner? We answer, "Fine." And in our head we are saying, "Ooh. It's terrible and I'm never coming back here again."

But the majority of customers, who don't return—as much as 68 percent of customers that don't come back—do so because of the "attitude" of the store. I'm not saying that stores are negative to them. But what I am saying is even worse: they're apathetic to them. There was no real connection. So very often it's the attitude of the store that keeps the customer from coming back. Reread Chapter 18 and go that extra mile with every customer to prevent this type of customer loss.

What Is a Customer Worth?

Have you ever tried to estimate what a loyal customer could be worth to you in sales over his lifetime? Take the time to think about it. One national pizza chain did, and it came up with $13,000 as the estimated average lifetime sales value of a loyal customer. That's a lot of pizza. And it figured, why not give away a pizza or two to keep that customer happy and coming back?

A similar study done by a high-end hotel operator puts its lifetime loyal customer value at over $100,000. In that chain, a staff member can spend up to $2,000 on the spot to resolve a guest problem.

Think of your customers based on their long-term sales potential and what they will be worth if they come back again and again. Talk about this concept with your sales associates and encourage them to give ideas that will help you turn casual customers into loyal repeat business.

So how can you calculate a customer's worth? Let's take a look at a car dealership. Let's assume you sell the first car to a customer at the age of 30 and expect that customer to buy a new car every three years until the age of 60. That's 10 cars over a customer's lifetime. We'll assume an average car price of $30,000. Here's the calculation …

10 cars at $30,000 = $300,000

Service—$500/year for 30 years = 15,000

Total Customer Worth = $315,000

While you probably aren't going to sell cars, you will be able do this same calculation using your average transaction per customer. You will need to estimate how often your loyal customers come into your store each year and multiply that by your average transaction. Then multiply that by the number of years you believe you can serve a loyal customer. That will depend on the type of store you have and the age of your target customers. Remember, people are living longer today, and you might be surprised by how long you can keep them coming back.

Give your sales associates these numbers. Also remind them that a loyal customer will bring in other customers. So the value of that loyal customer will be far greater than just the sales you can make directly to that customer. Isn't it worth it to go the extra mile to keep that customer loyal?

Dealing with the Complaining Customer

When a customer complains, don't think of it as a problem, but instead as a blessing in disguise. For every person that complains, you can be sure there may be hundreds who did not bother to complain, but instead are just spreading negative comments about your store.

Deal with any complaint immediately and do your best to rectify the situation and keep the customer happy. Customers may not always be right, but you have to make them think they are.

You can solve the problem by giving the customer her money back, exchanging the item, or offering to pay for a repair. To be sure the customer is completely satisfied, you should also provide some special service to say you're sorry, such as offering another product at a reduced price or possibly some service related to the product for free—something to get them to want to come back to your store again.

Sometimes you will face dishonest customers who make false claims to get a bonus. For example, suppose you are a fashion store and you suspect a customer is returning an expensive gown after using it once and then saying she wasn't satisfied with it. You may see signs that the gown was worn. If it's the first time, assume the customer is right and return her money, but if you see this happening more than once, you just say no. Losing that type of customer is better than keeping her.

Selling Points

You should quickly solve customer complaints. Turning a complaining customer into a satisfied, loyal customer can be a challenge, but when you can, you may have won that customer for life, as well as avoided the risk that customer could turn away hundreds of others.

Customers You Want to Lose

There are some customers you would rather lose. These can be up to 20 percent of the population, depending on where your store is, who have what I call a "relaxed conscience."

These are people who just try to take advantage of you and lie to you to get what they want without having to pay for it or by paying very little. It will be very difficult for you to build a future business with those customers.

As hard as it is for you as a retailer to turn a customer away, you are better off encouraging them not to shop with you anymore. You may lose less money.

The other 80 percent of the population can be great customers. Learn to recognize the customers you want to lose and be glad you got rid of them. But don't lose the other 80 percent because they didn't receive the right service and experience when they walked into your store. Make going that extra mile a habit, and you'll build a strong base of loyal customers.

The Least You Need to Know

- You lose customers when you don't provide them with the best experience when they come into your store.
- A loyal customer can be worth hundreds of thousands of dollars. Figure out what a loyal customer is worth to you and remind your sales associates of that regularly.
- Don't treat complaining customers as a problem. Treat them as an opportunity to turn someone into a loyal customer.
- Some customers you just don't want to keep. Learn to recognize them and "fire" them.

Chapter 26

Mining the Gold in Your Customer Database

In This Chapter

- Collecting data
- Garnering loyalty
- Finding lost customers

"It's all about me! *My* needs, my time, my expectations, my way!" What if this was your customer? Well, this is your customer, and she is telling you that personalized and customized is exactly what she wants. An up-close-and-personal look at your customer database is your secret to giving customers what they want, when they want it, and how they want it. It is also your opportunity to develop a competitive advantage that will guarantee your business will thrive for as long as you continue doing it. In this chapter, we explore how you can use all the data you collect in your customer database.

Why Collect Information?

Have you thought about the value of tracking your best customers' preferences so that you can reach out to them with offers and suggestions that are right for them? If you haven't, you should.

Think about your customers' lives today. Most of them are so busy that they would shop at your store over any other store, if you were able to save them the time by selecting what's right for them from the myriads of options that are out there.

So, how do you do it? Consider updating your point of service (POS) software with customer relationship management (CRM) software. I talk more about both software packages in Chapter 19. CRM software helps you better understand your existing customers. When used appropriately, you will be able to keep in contact with your customers at the right time and to provide them with things they need but may not be aware of. This, of course, will drive more business to your store.

CRM software enables you to sort your customers by highest sales volume. You can find out who your best customers are as well as their purchase history. With that history, you will know how much they have purchased and when they made their last purchase. You will also know what the occasion was for that purchase and when you last contacted them. In fact, how much you do know will depend upon what information your CRM software captures.

How to Use the Information Captured

Once you've got all that customer data in your system, don't hesitate to use it to your advantage. You can send reminders, figure out gross profit by customer, manage a loyalty program, and find lost customers.

Reminders

Staying in touch with customers and thanking them for their business is crucial to building that loyal base of customers you need. You can program your CRM software with "reminders" that enable you to pull a list of customers from the database who have made purchases in the last month.

These reminders can prompt you to follow up with customers after they have purchased over a certain dollar amount in a month or purchased a particular item that requires a follow-up call. You can then call them or send them a thank-you note.

You can also use it to remind yourself of customer birthdays or other special notations made by your sales associates for future contacts. Any time your sales associates work with a customer and get key information that would be useful for a future reminder, the sales associates can add a note to the database. When the time comes for the future contact, a reminder can automatically be generated by the software.

Tracking Gross Profit

Wouldn't you love to know which customers are helping you to make the most money? Of course! Well CRM software can help you do that because its customer database also enables you to track gross profit by customer. You can program reports that will allow you to identify your most profitable customers. After you know who these customers are and what they like to buy, you can reward them with incentives that get them to come back to your store and increase their loyalty.

Loyalty Programs

As I discussed in Chapter 15, loyalty programs are a crucial part of building customer relationships. The CRM software helps you to offer loyalty points to your customers so you can reward your best customers for shopping at your store. If you have the right POS software with CRM, you can track each purchase and assign points for the total value of each customer's purchases over time. Even better, think about assigning point value by profit. Airlines do that today. When you purchase a full-price ticket, you get more points than when you purchase a discount ticket.

Selling Points

Loyalty incentives tracked automatically by your CRM software not only build loyalty to your store, but increase the likelihood that your customer will shop in the store again. You will also find a loyalty program can increase the average transaction and number of visits.

Armed with this information, you can send incentives to your customers when they reach certain plateaus you designate in your program. For example, you can decide that each time a customer in your loyalty program spends $500, you are going to send them a coupon for $50 on their next purchase or possibly give them an item for free on their next visit to the store.

Regaining Lost Customers

One powerful tool of CRM software is the ability to use your database to find past good customers who are not coming back for some reason. We call this the "missing customer" query. For example, you can run a report that will list the names of every customer who has spent over $500 in the store in the past eighteen months, who has shopped more than five times, and who has not been in the store in the past six months.

This is a potential lost or "missing" customer—someone who has been a good customer but for whatever reason has not been in recently. A letter can automatically be sent to every customer who meets these criteria with a gift certificate to encourage them to shop again in the store.

New Product Alerts

Wouldn't it be nice to be able to alert customers who you know will be interested in new products that just arrived in the store? CRM software can help you identify the types of products your customers prefer and generate reports that will help you notify them when a new product in a specific classification they purchased before is now available.

For example, suppose you have a customer who is constantly looking for the latest style in jeans—or any other clothing item. Each time you add new styles to that clothing classification, you can generate a report of the customers who buy products in that classification regularly. You can then send a note to let them know about the new arrivals.

Savvy Retailer

Best Buy wanted to identify its best customers as well as the customers that cost them money by abusing their customer service policies. Their best customers were called "angels," and their problem customers were called "devils." The goal is to get more angels and to stop selling and serving devils.

Identifying Your Target Customers

You may have started out with certain target customers in mind when you opened your store, but do you know who your customers are today? You need to identify the segments you serve.

For example, how many younger, middle-aged, or older customers do you serve? How many price-sensitive, quality-driven, speed-oriented customers do you have? How many of each specific group in your trade area are customers in your store? And there may be more segments that you need to identify. Are most of your customers women? Do you have a large group of fashion-conscious customers?

First you need to identify the major groups of customers that now shop at your store, and then identify what these customers have in common, how they like to shop, and what products they like. When you have answered these questions, you are ready to structure your store experience for these customer segments.

For example, if you have a large segment of younger customers, you should most likely have staff that is also part of this segment: young people often will feel more comfortable being served by sales associates that are in their age group, and this is also true for mid-lifers. Have you created an assortment of products that appeals to young customers? Have you displayed and signed it so that these customers find it easy to shop and browse? Have you planned special events that young people would find fun and interesting?

For each segment you identify, you should create a specific strategy around merchandise, display, signage, staff, pricing, and special events that address the needs of each segment. This is not an easy task!

You can use your CRM software to help you build a customer-centric store. Here is a checklist that can help you:

- Have I identified distinct customer segments? (Two or three are good, but more than five is too many!)
- Do I know the special needs and wants of each segment? (Have I asked them in either informal focus groups or by observing their current purchases?)
- Do I have products and services that meet these customers' needs and wants?
- Do I have a method to quickly capture the identity of each customer at point of sale? (Have I given each customer a reason to be in the database, for example, loyalty points, special pricing, or other recognition.)
- Have I created an environment that is attractive to each segment? (Mid-lifers, for example, would welcome easier to read price tickets, chairs, and more open areas).
- How will I communicate with each segment? (Can I identify the media that each segment reads or listens to or watches?)

- Is my staff aligned with these segments? (Can my staff empathize with each segment?)
- Is my staff trained to meet the requirements of these customers? (Have I put a training program in place?)
- How will I measure success? (What specific measures will I use to ensure that the customer service program is working?)
- Is my technology sufficient to deliver the information about these customers? Can I do real CRM? Can I get real-time data when I need it?

If you have the right answers to these questions, you will be well on your way to making your store customer-centric, and enjoying the increased sales and customer satisfaction!

Using customer data as a targeting tool is arguably its single greatest benefit. As a small business owner, you can identify your most valuable customers and make a greater investment in time or money to build upon that relationship. The limits to how you can use the database are solely up to you and your imagination. Manipulate the data you collect to target the customers you want to keep coming back to your store.

The Least You Need to Know

- Use your CRM software to collect information about your customers that you can use to reward their loyalty and get them back into the store.
- You can use your CRM software to find customers who otherwise would not come back to shop with you and offer them an incentive to come back to your store.
- CRM software can be a valuable tool in identifying your target customers and building a customer-centric store based on the specific needs of these customers.

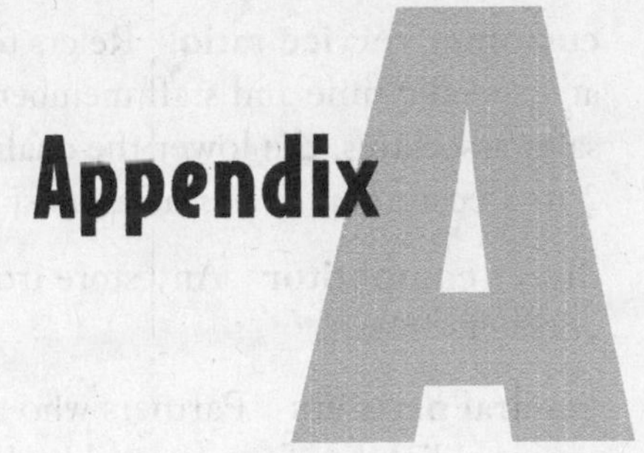

Appendix A

Glossary

anomaly In marketing terms, refers to an unmet need or a need that has not been met completely, but whose time has come to be filled.

black hole A period of inactivity in a store.

breakeven point The percentage or amount of net sales that it takes to cover all the expenses of your business except the cost of merchandise so that you are not losing money or making money.

classifications (or **categories**) A method of grouping or sorting your merchandise based on the concept that within a classification or category merchandise is deemed interchangeable by the customer.

common stock A portion of ownership in a corporation that includes the right to vote on key corporation issues and entitles the owner to share in the company's success, usually through dividends or increase in stock value.

department In retail, a grouping of merchandise that could stand alone as a "specialty store." For example, a department store can move its home furnishings department into a separate location in the mall or a drugstore could move its cosmetics department to smaller premises. In theory at least, both could succeed as separate businesses.

customer service ratio Refers to the ratio between customers waiting to be served at a specific time and staff members available. The higher the ratio of customers versus sales associates, the lower the quality of service as 1 sales associate can effectively serve 2 to 3 customers at a time at most (ratio is 1 to 2 or 1 to 3).

direct competitor Any store from which your customer can buy the same product you sell.

general partners Partners who actively run the business and are subject to the same personal liability for partnership debts and claims as sole proprietors, even if the act that caused the claim to be filed was carried out by one of the other partners. Be careful whom you partner with, especially if you plan to be the general partner with all others being limited partners.

indirect competitor Any store that serves the same customers as you but in a completely different product category. For example, a Williams-Sonoma store and a Banana Republic store both compete for the same share of the customer's wallet. The customer can decide to spend his money on a new pot from Williams-Sonoma or a new pair of jeans from Banana Republic.

integrated software Software that uses the same data files so the information can be updated in real time.

interfaced software Software that enables you to translate data between two software programs, such as your accounting and POS software, but this must be done manually.

landed cost The cost of your goods including shipping charges.

lease line A point at which the public space ends and the store begins. It is generally where the store entrance door opens.

limited partners Partners who don't take an active role in the management of the partnership. Their liability is limited to their investment in the business and any obligations they may have to make additional investments in it

markdown A reduction in the selling price of a product. Markdowns are usually applied to slow-moving or old inventory or to promote an item to increase sales.

multichannel retailing Serving a customer by whatever means the customer wants to deal with you—via telephone, mobile phone, in person at your store, through a catalog, or on your website.

needs The basic necessities of life: food, clothing, shelter, and so on. You must have these products to live.

negotiation space The space between the seller's and the buyer's cut-off points. Somewhere in this space, a deal will be made.

open to buy The amount of money you can spend in a product category or the amount of items you can buy. You calculate your open to buy by considering the amount of inventory you have on hand, the amount you have on order, and the amount you'll need at the beginning of the next month as well as your sales and markdown estimates.

preferred stock Usually has a specific dividend that must be paid prior to the dividends paid to common stock holders. This type of stock usually has no voting rights. If the company fails, these shareholders will get their share of the assets before common stock holders.

promotional markdowns When you temporarily reduce the value of items in your inventory for a special purpose, such as a weekend sale. At the end of the sale, the price will return to the original amount.

qualifications Skill sets that people need to do the job. For example, people cannot be lifeguards at the local pool unless they have a certain level of training and proficiency that has been tested and certified by the appropriate authority.

regular markdowns Permanently reducing the value of certain items in your inventory. These reductions are permanent, and the item is "red penned" to the lower price on the price ticket and will never go back to original price.

retail value The value of your merchandise is the dollar value at full selling price.

sell and buy The concept of selling your products to your customers before you have to pay for them.

suggestion selling A technique where a sales associate always suggests the most logical of all the additional items for a complete solution to customer's needs until the customer finally says "No."

wants Items that a customer desires but does not absolutely need to live. Often, as retailers, unless you are selling the basic necessities of life, you are selling to customers' wants, which are driven by emotion.

web host An online entity that provides the technical interface needed for your website to be seen on the Internet. Web hosts offer you a system for storing information, images, video, and any other content you want to put on the internet. Web-host companies provide service space to host your website and provide the connectivity so it can be found through the Internet.

wholesale The selling of goods in large quantities to retailers who then sell them directly to customers. The wholesaler is essentially the middle man between the manufacturer and the retailer.

Appendix B

Further Reading and Resources

Here are additional reading suggestions that will help you further enhance your knowledge of retail and develop your business sense. Pick the books or magazines that interest you the most and remember that good retailers never stop learning.

Print Publications

In this section, you find excellent books and magazines that can help you learn more about retailing and best business practices and keep you up-to-date on current trends.

Books

Ander, Willard N., and Neil Z. Stern. *Winning at Retail: Developing a Sustained Model for Retail Success*. John Wiley & Sons, Inc., 2004. Offers a vast array of tools retailers need to establish and implement an effective strategy for long-term growth.

Collins, James C., and Jerry I. Porras. *Built to Last*. Harper Collins, 1994. A must-read classic on quality.

Dion, James E. *Retail Selling Ain't Brain Surgery, It's Twice as Hard*. Dionco Inc., 2006. Written by me, and a great primer for sales associates.

Epstein, Lita. *The Complete Idiot's Guide to Accounting*. Alpha Books, 2006. Learn more about accounting and how to set up the books for your business.

Fisher, Robert, Bruce M. Patton, and William L. Ury. *Getting to Yes*. Houghton Mifflin, 1992. Learn more about win-win negotiation.

Friedman, Thomas. L. *The World Is Flat*. Farrar, Straus, and Giroux, 2005. A good look at the new world we are living in.

Girard, Joe. *How to Sell Anything to Anybody*. Bantam Books, 1989. A real classic on selling skills.

Johnson, Spencer, and Ken Blanchard. *The One Minute Manager.* Morrow, 1982. The best book ever written on how to manage people.

Kabachnick, Terri. *I Quit But Forgot to Tell You.* The Kabachnick Group, 2006. A great book on how to keep your staff engaged in the business.

Nierenberg, Gerard L. *The Art of Negotiation*. Random House, 1989. The seminal negotiation skills work, sometimes called the "bible on negotiation."

Rosen, Darryl. *Surviving The Middle Miles—26.2 Ways To Cross The Finish Line With Your Customers*. AuthorHouse, 2007. Provides practical and actionable ideas and recommendations for building strong and long-lasting relationships with your customers and your employees.

Silverstein, Michael J., and Neil Fiske. *Trading Up—The New American Luxury*. Penguin, 2003. One of the first examinations of the growing luxury market and how and why it is so strong.

Spector, Robert, and Patrick D. McCarthy. *The Nordstrom Way*. Wiley, 1995. A great look at a true service retailer.

Underhill, Paco. *What We Buy, The Science of Shopping*. Simon & Schuster, 1999. A groundbreaking book on consumer behavior in stores, a must read!

Magazines

You can find valuable market information in newspapers and popular magazines, such as *The New York Times*, *The Wall Street Journal*, *USA Today*, *Time*, *U.S. News & World Report*, *Newsweek*, and even *People* magazine, on occasion.

You'll find articles on market trends in business magazines such as *Fortune*, *Forbes*, *BusinessWeek*, *The Economist*, or any of the other business periodicals to which you may have access. All of these resources provide you with up-to-date and thorough information on economic, business, and market trends that can help you learn about the market and opportunities that are available.

Buy your local business weekly newspaper or magazine, if one is published in your community. One good Internet source for researching news through local business weeklies is BizJournals (www.bizjournals.com).

Online Resources

In this section, you find a list of websites that are incredible resources to help with your retail business.

Associations, Organizations, and Government Entities

National Retail Federation (www.nrf.com) is the world's largest retail trade association and represents members from all retail formats: department, specialty, discount, catalog, Internet, and independent stores, as well as chain restaurants, drugstores and grocery stores. The Federation conducts industry research, develops education and workforce development programs, and promotes retailing as a career choice. Also, if you are a member of the National Retail Federation, you receive e-mail updates and its *Stores* magazine regularly, which are incredible sources of information on trends in retail and consumer behavior. The association represents more than 1.6 million U.S. retail establishments worth more than $4.7 trillion in 2006. It also represents more than 24 million employees—about one in five American workers.

National Restaurant Association (www.restaurant.org) provides extensive information on its website, as well as industry reports you can purchase. The association represents over 300,000 restaurants.

U.S. Small Business Administration (www.sba.gov) provides excellent resources for all aspects of business, as well as loans to small businesses. For more information about its loan process, go to: www.sba.gov/services/financialassistance/index.html. The SBA has other financial programs for small businesses including disaster assistance and grants. It also has a website specifically for women business owners (www.sbaonline.sba.gov/womeninbusiness).

Score volunteers (www.score.org) provides free help to small business owners. If you've never run a business or developed a business plan before, don't try to go it alone. SCORE is America's premier source for free and confidential advice for small business owners. Since it was formed in 1964, SCORE has assisted over 7.5 million small business owners with counseling, training, and advice.

Benchmarking and Research

Few retailers will share their numbers with you, but luckily there are some websites that provide benchmarking resources. Also you can find excellent resources for researching key retail issues.

Ask.com (www.ask.com) is also a great place to look for retail-specific information.

BizStats.com (www.bizstats.com) gives you a way to determine if you are meeting the benchmarks financially. To use this website, all you need to do is select the type of business you are running and then put in your monthly or yearly total sales.

Claritas (www.claritas.com) will provide demographic reports and maps for a monthly fee or annual subscription. This marketing company gathers demographic data and target marketing information about the population, consumer behavior, consumer spending, households, and businesses within any specific geographic market area in the United States.

KnowThis.com (www.knowthis.com/studies/focus-on-market-research/reports.htm) gives you access to free market research reports on many industries.

Map info (www.mapinfo.com) has a great retail site selection component you should check out.

Allcommercialproperty.org and **LoopNet** (www.allcommercialproperty.org or www.loopnet.com) can help you find properties and companies that can help you, if you need to find a commercial Realtor.

Retail Owners Institute (www.retailowner.com) provides benchmark information regarding inventory turnover, profit, and other financial benchmarks by store type.

Retail Technology

You must have the right technology to serve your customers appropriately and track your numbers. Here are the websites for the leaders in point of service (POS) technology and accounting software.

Point of Service Technology:

- CAM Commerce Solutions (www.camcommerce.com)—Cam offers a free trial version for small retailers with only one machine
- CounterPoint (www.synchronics.com/products/cp.htm)
- Microsoft Retail Management System (www.microsoft.com/dynamics/rms/default.mspx)
- Retail Pro (www.retailpro.com)

Accounting Software:

- Peachtree Accounting (www.peachtree.com) is the other big boy when it comes to bookkeeping and accounting needs, but I don't recommended it if you are a novice. You do need to be familiar with accounting jargon just to use the system, and its interface is not as user friendly as QuickBooks. While it does offer training options inside the program, they lack the sophistication of the excellent learning center now offered by QuickBooks.
- QuickBooks (http://quickbooks.intuit.com) gives you the best of both worlds. You'll find it relatively easy to use even if you are an accounting novice, but you'll also find extensive bookkeeping and accounting features even for the experienced bookkeeper or accountant. It's the most popular accounting software package for small business owners today.

Web Hosting

There are hundreds of websites on the Internet that offer domain reservation services. Some good ones for you to check out include:

Go Daddy (www.godaddy.com)

Network Solutions (www.networksolutions.com)

Register.com (www.register.com)

You can check out the quality of a web-hosting company at various web-host forums on the Internet. One good forum is Web Hosting Talk (www.webhostingtalk.com).

Appendix C

Worksheets and Checklists

In this appendix, you will find some useful worksheets and checklists that have been discussed in the text. Following is a list of key worksheets and checklists and the chapter in which the material was discussed:

1. Analyzing Your Competitors Worksheet (Chapter 4)
2. Developing a Clear Vision Worksheet (Chapter 6)
3. Supplier Checklist to Evaluate Potential Suppliers (Chapter 11)
4. Open-to-Buy Worksheet (Chapter 11)
5. Regular Markdown Laundry List (Chapter 12)
6. Job Interview Evaluation Checklist (Chapter 16)
7. Questions for Potential POS Software Suppliers (Chapter 18)

Analyzing Your Competitors Worksheet

	Competitor: Date visited:	Competitor: Date visited:	Competitor: Date visited:
Exterior and exterior sign			
Window displays			
New experience or "same old"			
General atmosphere			
Overall visual appeal			
General organization			
Color and texture			
Mood set by lighting			
Everything visible from the front door			
Spotlights highlight merchandise			
Front-and-forward displays			
Displays with props, related merchandise			
Brand names evident			
Merchandise in departments			
Presentation tells a story			
Printed product information			
Price tickets and signs			

	Competitor: Date visited:	Competitor: Date visited:	Competitor: Date visited:
Consistency of interior signs			
Sign holders			
Number of sales associates			
Staff appearance and identification			
Level of in-store service			
Level of product knowledge			
Type of shopping experience			
Price range			
Price competitiveness			
Value			
Merchandise quality			
Merchandise "romance"			
Special sales			
Speed at checkout			
Payment methods			
Delivery service			
Returns policy			
Music			
Neat and clean			
Other			

Notes:____

____

____

Developing a Clear Vision Worksheet

Exterior and exterior sign: ______________________________

____

Window displays: ______________________________

____

New experience or "same old": ______________________________

____

General atmosphere: ______________________________

____

Overall visual appeal: ______________________________

____

General organization: ______________________________

____

Color and texture: ______________________________

____

Mood set by lighting: ______________________________

____

Everything visible from the front door: ______________________________

____

Spotlights highlight merchandise: ______________________________

____

Front-and-forward displays: ______________________________

____

Displays with props, related merchandise: ______________________________

____

Brand names evident: ______________________________

____

Merchandise in departments: ______________________________

____

Presentation tells a story: ________________________________

____

Printed product information: ______________________________

____

Price tickets and signs: __________________________________

____

Consistency of interior signs: _____________________________

____

Sign holders: ____

____

Number of sales associates: _______________________________

____

Staff appearance and identification: ________________________

____

Level of in-store service: _________________________________

____

Level of product knowledge: ______________________________

____

Type of shopping experience: ______________________________

____

Price range: ____

____

Price competitiveness: ___________________________________

____

Value: ____

____

Merchandise quality: ____

____

Special sales: ____

____

Speed of checkout: ____

____

Payment methods: ____

____

Delivery service: ____

____

Returns policy: ____

____

Type of music: ____

____

Neat and clean: ____

____

Other: ____

____

Supplier Checklist to Evaluate Potential Suppliers

List suppliers here:

PRODUCT

Demand: A wanted brand-name item, line, title

Recognition: Ease of sell-through

Packaging: Effective, environmentally friendly

Quality: High quality, long lasting, no returns

Units: Singles, six-packs, dozens

SERVICE IN TERMS OF STOCK

Delivery: On time

Barcoded: Carton, package, and product barcodes

Quantity: As ordered, all at once, no substitutes

Peak-time support: Will train staff as required

Returns: Accepted on defective/returned products

Special orders: Prompt filling

continues

Supplier Checklist to Evaluate Potential Suppliers (continued)

List suppliers here:
SERVICE IN TERMS OF SALES
Sales force: Calls regularly or as requested
Knowledge: Knows the product and about common problems
Information: Has industry, sector, and store performance figures
Review: Conducts quarterly and annual reviews
PROMOTION
Advertising: Creates shopping demand for products
Co-op advertising: Available and flexible
Promotion: Wide range of promotional items available
Support: Will help with demonstrations
FINANCES
Pricing: Consistent, good value
Discounts: Offers closeouts to present customers first

List suppliers here:
Terms: Will offer net 60 or extend payment **COMMUNICATION** **Problem solving:** Sales representative can do it all **Executive:** Can reach someone in a crisis

Open-to-Buy Worksheet

Inventory Required for Following Month

+ Sales Plan for Current Month

+ Markdowns for Current Month

= Inventory Required

– Inventory on Hand at the Beginning of the Month

= Open to Buy

Regular Markdown Laundry List

Date:______________

Class	Item	Description	Original Price	Markdown Price	Markdown Amount	Units	Total HD Dollars	Reason

Job Interview Evaluation Checklist

Name:____

Date of interview:____________________________

Demonstrated ability for duties:	**YES**	**NO**
Greet and make customers feel welcome	[]	[]
Determine customers' needs	[]	[]
Provide knowledgeable presentations	[]	[]
Suggest additional items	[]	[]
Answer any objections	[]	[]
Close sales	[]	[]
Send thank-you notes or phone	[]	[]
Handle maintenance, housekeeping, other	[]	[]

Characteristics:	**YES**	**NO**
Positive attitude	[]	[]
Degree of extroversion	[]	[]
Healthy ego	[]	[]
Empathy	[]	[]
Friendliness	[]	[]
Goal-oriented	[]	[]
Neatness of appearance	[]	[]
Willing to learn	[]	[]

Qualifications:	**YES**	**WITH TRAINING**	**NO**
Extensive experience in using store's products	[]	[]	[]
Life experience appropriate to store's target customers	[]	[]	[]

	YES	WITH TRAINING	NO
Proficiency in math	[]	[]	[]
Other:__________________________	[]	[]	[]
Other:__________________________	[]	[]	[]

Notes:

Recommendation:

UNACCEPTABLE	FAIR	GOOD	EXCELLENT	OUTSTANDING
1	2	3	4	5

Questions for Potential POS Software Suppliers

Supplier name:____________________________

Date of call:____________________________

1. How many retailers currently use your software?

2. How many stores currently use your software?

3. What are the names of 10 current users I can contact?

4. How long have you been in business? How many people do you employ?

5. How many "releases" of this software have there been?

6. How frequent and how extensive are your updates? What are the costs of these?

7. Do I have a choice in buying updates?

8. What kind of support can I get?

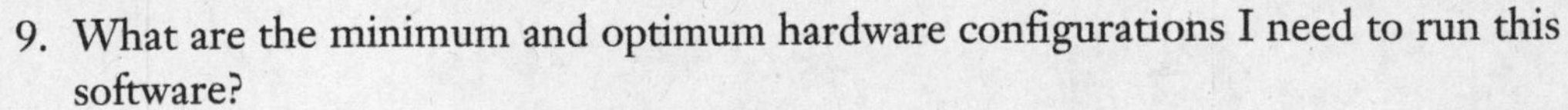

9. What are the minimum and optimum hardware configurations I need to run this software?

10. What hardware do most current users have?

11. Do I have to use specific peripherals?

12. Is this an integrated package?

13. Can I buy only part of it now?

14. Is there installation assistance?

15. What, if any, additional software do I need?

16. How will this POS software pay for itself?

Index

A

B

D

H

I

J–K

L

M

N

O

P

Q–R

S

T

U

V

W-X-Y-Z